Herrington J. Bryce

Nonprofits as Policy Solutions to the Burden of Government

Herrington J. Bryce

Nonprofits as Policy Solutions to the Burden of Government

—

DE
—
G
PRESS

ISBN 978-1-5015-1473-9
e-ISBN (PDF) 978-1-5015-0579-9
e-ISBN (EPUB) 978-1-5015-0582-9

Library of Congress Cataloging-in-Publication Data
A CIP catalog record for this book has been applied for at the Library of Congress.

Bibliographic information published by the Deutsche Nationalbibliothek
The Deutsche Nationalbibliothek lists this publication in the Deutsche Nationalbibliografie;
detailed bibliographic data are available on the Internet at http://dnb.dnb.de.

© 2017 Walter de Gruyter Inc., Boston/Berlin
Typesetting: Mary Sudul
Printing and binding: CPI book GmbH, Leck
♾ Printed on acid-free paper
Printed in Germany

www.degruyter.com

Marisa Jeanine, Herrington Simon, and Shauna Celestina
From your parents, their parents, Roy, Celestina, Emeline Yvonne
and their families
Mom Beverly J, and Dad Herrington J

Acknowledgements

Many thanks to the very distinguished professor and friend, Ronald Sims, who reviewed my proposal for this book with critical and frank eyes and with the compelling discussion to proceed and to Jeffrey Brudney, a distinguished professor of nonprofit innovations at the University of North Carolina, Wilmington for his enthusiasm over the novelty of this approach. I also extend thanks to Carol Ledoux and Kimberly Reeves of the Raymond Mason School of Business at the College of William & Mary for their gracious production assistance and rescue. To The Raymond Mason School of Business at the College of William & Mary I am deeply grateful to the Dean, students, and to Tom Marini who gave me the monitoring help of his student library assistants. Finally, I am grateful for the view of Professor Jennifer Widner, the Faculty Director of Innovations for Successful Societies at Princeton University who wrote:

> In times of political gridlock or high turbulence, non-profits have an especially important role to play in pioneering new ways of service provision and in helping citizens monitor government performance. As Tocqueville noted over 150 years ago, they also help us build—or rebuild—civic skills that we have too often allowed to lapse. This book is a wonderful guide for a new generation of leaders.

I am lucky to have been exposed to issues of government and of finance in so many direct and distinct ways as an undergraduate student, as a graduate student, as a professor, as a member of several government and finance related boards, and as one who worked closely with cities, states, and local governments across the country and internationally and across Central Eastern Europe from Russia during the point of transition to Estonia and the Republic of Georgia during the same period. For that experience, I am grateful to the National Academy for Public Administration and particularly Dr. Carole Neves, Scott Fosler and the Network of Institutes and Schools in Public Administration in Central Eastern Europe for those in-place experiences. On the domestic side, I am thankful to Ralph Widner for the opportunity to having a direct official involvement with each of the seven major government associations from the National League of Cities to the National Association of Governors and to Eddie N. Williams for working with minority elected officials throughout the country. I got a richly different perspective on nonprofits, debt, infrastructure and revenue bonds from serving as a member of the Treasury Board of Virginia where I had legal and fiduciary responsibilities to approve the terms and prospectuses of all government related bonds—general obligation or revenue—or long-term lease obligations. For that, I thank Governor Douglas Wilder.

I also wish to recognize the special contribution of Professor S.M. Miller for whom I worked as a graduate assistant and who introduced me to what it takes to do meaningful if not path-breaking work. I am grateful to my immediate family of attorneys Beverly, Marisa, Herrington Simon, and Shauna for Marisa's, "Daddy, cool down and do it. You are going to get a heart attack" as she consulted on important technical details of this issue.

Contents

Preface

The public policy issue which motivates this book exists in many countries and levels of government: the rising need for providing essential public goods ranging from public safety to major infrastructure while confronted with a strong public resistance to more government spending, increasing government debt or taxation, or increases in the size of government or involvement in their private lives. The objective of the book is to stimulating public policy consciousness of the role nonprofits may play in addressing this dilemma within the current framework of law even though many of these public needs cut across all demographics and therefore are not charitable in their motivation. The motivation is singular: to lessen the burden of government.

Current federal law stipulates that this motivation can stand alone without reference to any charitable motive. So, while one may correctly infer that by assisting the poor a nonprofit reduces the burden of government that is not the issue here. Rather it is the nonprofit being formed with the intent to lessen the burden of government (the motive) and doing this through a variety of services (not necessarily charitable). Put another way, in this context, lessening the burden of a government is not the inference but the motive for the organization's existence. This motive can be fulfilled in a variety of acceptable ways whether or not they are charitable in the traditional meaning.

We shall cite these laws, court decisions and the Internal Revenue Procedures and publications making this interpretation consistent with law. And, we shall constantly remain within the IRS's stipulated parameters throughout this book. Accordingly, we shall develop and isolate certain principles which would facilitate policy-building within this framework and through this enhance the possibilities of further creating and engaging nonprofits in the lessening of the burden of government as the motive—not the inference from an otherwise charitable cause.

Throughout we shall attest to the argument by real, readily observable examples drawn from every level of government and from across the country. But we shall do more, we shall also acknowledge that if this policy is to be successful, the nonprofit will need certain capabilities and indeed legal powers to function so that they can successfully lessen the burden of government. This acknowledgement will lead to the enumeration and discussion of specific powers and capabilities including the power to issue debt since it is almost always necessary for infrastructure planning, building, and operation. These are the very size debt for which there, in general, is public resistance but societal consequences for not undertaking.

DOI 10.1515/9781501505799-001

Because current rules allow different categories of nonprofits to exist and to operate with lessening the burden of government, this book operates within an organizing principle consistent with the law. It divides nonprofits into doers, facilitators, and those that do both. It also distinguishes between the design imperatives of internal and external networks of collaborating units. Furthermore, it shows that the doers may create their own internal facilitating structures whether it is for finance or operations and by doing so increase their contribution and sustenance in lessening the burden of government. Through embedded requirements and structures, they collaborate and magnify their ability to raise their own funds and reduce the burden on tax payers. Therefore, not only the individual nonprofit units, but the formal terms of their collaboration are described in this book.

The range of activities in which a nonprofit may be created for this purpose of lessening the burden of government and which is displayed in this book is very wide and goes beyond references to a charitable purpose, inference, or cause. It can also go from the local group of citizens that formed a 501(c)(3) to assist in the training and equipping of the sheriff's department and for financing and providing the municipal space in which the department operates to the creation of a nonprofit such as the Tennessee Valley Authority. Accordingly, this book will deal with nonprofits of all sizes and whether they are formed by citizens or by governments—highlighting their differences.

Governments as well as citizens may design nonprofits to lessen the burden of government. The range of designs that a government may employ is considerable. One of the contributions of the book is the development of a working chart that may help policymakers and rule-makers move toward the optimal: A design that allows the government to benefit, but costs it nothing including debt service or operating expenses. This design, too, will be specifically shown to exist.

Finally, this book will pull most of these thoughts together—not so much as summary but as the ingredients of a dialogue in the consideration of these thoughts whether it is within the policy-making, rule-making, or public management arena or in the advanced classroom. Can there be meaningful progress in the utility of nonprofits to lessen the burden of government as a direct policy motive?

Every policy statement begins with a purpose of the policy and every nonprofit charter begins with a purpose of the organization. When lessening the burden of the government is the purpose of the organization, it can apply to a range of policies that are not necessarily charitable in the traditional sense. In this connection, the IRS raises these investigative questions to determine if exemption is warranted:

1. Is this a burden that the government acknowledges either by its declaration or its actions such as its collaboration with the nonprofit beyond contracting with it?
2. Can the nonprofit by virtue of its purpose, organization, and operation carry out this burden and within the framework of a 501(c)(3), (4), or (6) category, an authority or as an entity that is part of the government?
3. Does it serve qualitatively and quantitatively a primordial public purpose?

See IRS. https://www.irs.gov/pub/irs-tege/eotopicl84.pdf.

The Principal Contribution of This Book

This book advances the utilization of a special class of nonprofits for lessening the burden of governments of all sizes but consistent with existing laws. See the above reference. It does so by creating a supporting theory for this strategy based on economic concepts of equity and efficiency in which users pay prices and the externalities are covered by voluntary giving—not by compulsory taxes. Further, unlike government, nonprofits that are tax-exempt and used in this way generally have to provide annual evidence of public support evidenced by how they operate or are financed or both and the public value they create but government does not. This book also furthers its case by providing the essential planks upon which nonprofits, created for lessening the burden of government, must be built, and how these nonprofits may attain self-sufficiency and therefore reduce resource dependence upon the very government they are created to relieve. It provides abundant real evidence at every step as it speaks to policy and rule makers, policy practitioners and to exploring academics interested in the theory and practice of the nonprofit as an instrument of public policy. The basic assumption: With a little bit of creative imagination, nonprofits can and are empowered to provide a range of essential services to the society well beyond the traditional charity function. Some may do this directly, others may facilitate its being done. In any event, it provides a nonprofit solution to the burden of government for big problems beyond the traditional charitable function for which it is well known.

The Experiential Origin of This Book

This book has a long personal origin beginning with a two-volume work (one of which was the consequence of surveying 1300 small municipalities on their planning practices and problems which culminated in, *Planning Smaller Cities* and four other books which dealt with city and regional planning and the limitations of government. It also relates to my books on financial and strategic management of nonprofit organizations to be in its fourth edition this year, and my *Players in the Public Policy Process: Nonprofits as Social Capital and Agents* which systematically develops a general theory of nonprofits in the full range of the public policy process. It was the 2006 Charles H. Levine Memorial Book Award for innovation in public administration.

It also has its roots in professional experiences. I have served as a member of the Treasury Board of the Commonwealth of Virginia which approves bond terms, bond indentures, and all state related and authority bonds and state depositories. For several years before I worked directly with states, cities and counties across the country and as an officer (director, vice president and President) of organizations formed precisely to assist governments (including the federal government) and to represent them in policy discussions with official departments in Washington DC and before the U.S. Congress. With respect to local economic development dealt with in this book, I was exposed directly in many cities including our nation's capital, being awarded the keys to two major U.S. cities, and serving as member of the board of the national organization of urban economic development officials throughout the country as well as a board member for organizations concerned with the built environment. I have done the same abroad including Russia, Estonia, The Republic of Georgia and other Central Eastern European countries immediately after the transition when the issues of order and reorganization were most critical and the burden of government most obvious. The burden ran along the continuum of democracy to virtual dictatorship and so too the need to lessen it. See the quotation from former Prime Minister, David Cameron, in the next chapter.

From an academic perspective, I have benefitted from my appointments as an Economic Policy Fellow at the Brookings Institution, a fellow at the Institute of Politics at Harvard University, as a faculty member at the Massachusetts Institute of Technology, the University of Maryland, Clark University, and most of all at The Raymond Mason School of Business, College of William & Mary, where using years of previous extensive training and licensure in finance I have been teaching corporate finance, cost management, and nonprofit finance and management and being an affiliate of the College's Thomas Jefferson Program in Public Policy. The Raymond Mason School of Business has singularly made this book possible.

I hold a BA from Minnesota State College and a PhD in economics from the Maxwell School at Syracuse University and a CLU and ChFC in insurance, securities and finance.

I hope this book serves its purpose.

Herrington J. Bryce

Life of Virginia Professor of Business Administration.
The Raymond Mason School of Business Administration
The College of William & Mary
Williamsburg, Virginia 23185

Chapter 1 — Purpose, Policy, Theory, Definitions and Context

Purpose

The public policy issues that motivate this book exist in many countries and levels of government: public services that are needed but are not necessarily charitable; governments strapped both in financial resources and in capacity; the unfavorable public response to increasing the size of government or its intrusion; the reluctance of the public to increase taxes or to enter into public debt to pay for these urgent public needs, the stark choice of postponing them—as in the case of infrastructure and environmental investments—or simply making them dormant in the public policy agenda or doing with inferior substitutes. Can the nonprofit offer a way out? What is the supporting theory and evidence?

This book is designed to serve policy makers and practitioners, advanced executive courses,professional seminars in public policy, public administration, government, and organization theory with a specific focus on the design and engagement of highly creative and sustainable nonprofits to advance the public interest by assuming certain burdens of government. The resulting mission of these organizations may go well beyond charitable and philanthropic purposes—and discharging this burden may require complex collaboration.

This book is intended to develop and to provide a perspective grounded in fact and in law that would assist public policy makers who design projects and programs and their delivery mechanisms, and public administrators and nonprofit managers who will have the responsibility to implement such policies through the mechanism of a nonprofit entity.

This book is therefore not a theoretical exercise and not about improving operating or financial strategies for nonprofits. Legislative and executive bodies of government craft policies and laws to meet an objective and it is up to the rule-makers who write the operating rules, the public administrators who administer them, and the nonprofit to implement them so they work for the public good and not become a failed policy.

Making these ideas become reality requires a particular organizational and managerial perspective and the purposeful embedding of specific powers to enable the organization to function with minimum, if any, dependence on government and to grow as the demand for its services grows. What these are and how they are enabled for the specific purpose of relieving the burden of government as this is defined below and, indeed, by law are the central questions of this book.

DOI 10.1515/9781501505799-002

This book proceeds with the following logic and organization: The design and engagement of highly sustainable nonprofits to relieve the burden of government requires (a) a definition and description of the specific burden and its availability for transfer and acceptance; (b) a definition and conceptualization of the appropriate nonprofit in terms of specific operating characteristics consistent with the constraints of corporate and tax laws; (c) an identification of the ability of the nonprofit to execute the mission and its capability to finance it without resource dependence on the government; (d) the organization's ability to manage assets so that they are protected against corruption and against unauthorized, uncontrolled, or uncoordinated spending (protecting the organization against the risk of failing or reversing the burden to the government); and (e) that the organization is prepared to grow to match the natural growth in the demand for that service—sustaining the utility of the transfer.

The book follows this logic and order and rests on the following concepts:

The Burden of Government

The operative foundation of this book is taken fromthe Internal Revenue Service publication "L. Instrumentalities Lessening the Burden of Government" from a series of articles published as the Exempt Organizations Continuing Professional Education (CPE) Technical Instruction Program for Fiscal Year 1984 (https://www.irs.gov/pub/irs-tege/eotopicl84.pdf) and from other IRS publications as cited throughout the book. They say:

> Lessening the burdens of government is itself charitable purpose and there is no requirement that an organization be doubly charitable in order to qualify under IRC 501(c)(3) ...

This means that lessening the burden of government is a sufficient reason for qualifying for a 501(c)(3) status. Accordingly,

> ... there are... numerous examples of situations in which an organization was held to be charitable even though it fulfilled no charitable purpose beyond relieving the burdens of government.
> This is the case where provision is made for the establishment or maintenance of parks, water supply, fire protection, public or community buildings, roads and bridges, or for various other purposes which are normally taken care of by the government...for such purposes are charitable, although they benefit the rich as well as the poor.

For example, an organization was formed to provide transportation to an isolated part of a city not served by the city bus system. The organization was given 501(c)(3) status based on the sole purpose that it relieved the burden on government without reference to or consideration of what these isolated parts of the city were, who inhabited them, or any such poverty or distressed or community development. The relevant facts quoted were:

- the project and organization were approved by the local government and local government collaborated
- the receipts were from fares, contributions, and governmental grants
- the organization was formed in conformity with a statute that defined its structure and operation

So, when we isolate and focus on "lessening the burden of government," we are employing the concept in this book as it is within the Internal Revenue Code as stated above, and also in its "Lessening the Burdens of Government," guidance by Robert Routhian and Amy Henchey (https://www.irs.gov/pub/irs-tege/eotopicb93.pdf). While it does not require adherence to the traditional concept of charity; there are constraints on acceptable projects as well as organizational design and these will shape the discussion of this book. We must not only know the rules, but what they imply or necessitate in terms of perspective, power, structure, and performance. The IRS gives the rules, but it does not define how, what structure, strategies and tools, or even when the concept may be engaged. That is for the policymaker and rule-maker, the public administrator, and non-profit management and will be described in this book.

Lessening the burden of government is an expansive concept that invites imagination as to its proper use. Lessening the burden of government covers any activity that is a planned undertaking of a government, especially if mandated by its laws, a current undertaking of a government, or an activity in which a government is a collaborator or an initiator. In so doing, the organization can and does participate with or for the government and demonstrably reduces the monetary or other resource cost of government. The activity does not have to fall within the specifically enumerated categories allowed under IRC 501(c)(3), but if the organization wishes to have that status and its benefits, it must comply with the requirements (as explained in Chapters 1 and 2) of that category whether the organization is formed by citizens or government. But, as the IRS states if that status is not available, the organization may qualify for exemption as lessening the burden of government under IRC Section 501(c)(4) or (6) or do so as an instrumentality of government all descred in this book.

Here is an example using housing to illustrate the concept of lessening the burden of government: An organization providing moderate-income housing may be denied a 501(c)(3) certification because that category of certification refers to low- rather than to moderate-income which allows some 25 of the residents to be above the poverty line. By meeting an additional requirement (that its rental prices do not disqualify poor people), it could obtain exemption either as a 501(c)(3) or (4) as an organization designed to lessen the burden of government by showing, among other things, that it was created subject to a stated government policy, has the structure to bring about an actual lessening of the use of resources by the government, and collaborates with the government for a public benefit.

Similarly, the principal reason for designing a health care organization may not be a charitable one, but one that reduces the burden of government by financing health activities for the benefit of the public. This burden may begin and end with the construction and provision for the management of a hospital owned by the public or government as described in Revenue Procedure 63–20. The implication being that the lessening of the burden of government offers an opportunity to expand the utility of the nonprofit to (a) provide a needed public service beyond the traditional charity, and (b) lessen the burden of government as a specific and traceable outcome.

But what public services? This definition provides for activities which are not necessarily traditionally charitable but where the motivation may be to (a) reduce the resource burden of government, or the size or extension of government; (b) increase the efficiency of government and lower the delivery time or cost of a project; (c) reduce or avoid the government's debt burdens—especially those that encumber current or future taxes or crowd-out other needed government-provided projects; and (d) to build a supportive infrastructure that reduces the burden of government in the variety of ways in which this may occur; for example, building and managing a structure in which the government or its agencies are the principal users and for which they pay rent even at a market rate, or to produce a project the government might otherwise need to produce itself for use of the general public and for which a user fee may be charged. The outcome must always be of meaningful benefit to the general public.

There is strong motivation for reducing the burden of government by the general public, policy makers, the government and its agencies, and the nonprofits with the capacity to deliver. To summarize, "lessening the burden of government" has a specific meaning and specific definitional hurdle in law and in its application to public policy. It must be: (a) a specific burden which the government *acknowledges* must exist and be addressed, (b) it must affect the general public, and (c) the nonprofit whether created by citizens or government must be equipped to reduce that burden in a verifiable way. It is not for the organization to claim that because it does what it does that it is reducing the burden of government. It is for the government to declare or affirm by its actions to request, initiate, or collaborate with the organization. This is the stipulation in law and in the citation of law above.

While we shall use federal, state, local, and even some foreign examples, federal law will be the ruling authority in this book. As we write, states and their localities differ (as they have a constitutional right to do) on how they perceive lessening a burden of their government. In Wexford Medical Group v. City of Cadillac, 474 Mich. At 219, 713 N.W.2d at 748, the Michigan Supreme Court ruled that what mattered is not the ability of the organization to prove that its action directly relieves a burden of government, but that its action relieves or avoids a condition that would have led to a burden on government. In Provena Covenant Medical Center, et al., v. the Department of Revenue, et al., the Illinois Supreme Court ruled otherwise. These nuances matter. Provena was denied (http://www.illinoiscourts.gov/opinions/supremecourt/2010/march/107328.pdf).

Therefore, sticking to the federal definition is more than for convenience. It is required for the organization to get exemption on the federal level which is virtually required by states to get exemption on the state and local levels; so, it has supremacy in law, policy, and in this book.

Perspective, Collaboration, Competence

A government burden may be too large, too complex, or require collaboration—even cross-collaboration (Bryson, Crosby, Stone, 2015, see endnote)—with other institutional forms. In the spirit of *Understanding Institutional Diversity* (Ostrom 2005), we see that a diversity of institutional forms can relieve the burden and pressures on government and that may, at times, be better (Ostrom 2012, see endnote). Implementing what is being described in this book will require: (a) perspective, or creativity, since this burden reduction is not traditional charity or humanitarian work; (b) a variety of forms of collaboration to bring about desired results; (c) sustained organizational competence to do it; and (d) a realization that a key Internal Revenue Service test to whether or not a nonprofit is lessening the burden of government is the extent to which it is in a collaborative arrangement with that government. It does not specify the form of collaboration so various forms of formal collaboration are discussed in this book.

Perspective

This book focuses on the details of operating rules, powers, capabilities, and the perspectives of management, government, the public and collaborators, in the assumption of a burden of government. For example, one of the experimental studies cited suggests that for some purposes, the public prefers to pay for a designated project by fees and contributions rather than by taxes. This, of course, is the principle behind user fees upon which a whole category of nonprofits depends. Perspective is important. This book is not principally using the nonprofit to solve the welfare problems of society; rather, it is about lifting a burden of the state that affects the public as allowed by current law. More policy makers may implement it if they can figure out how—and perhaps this book can contribute to that answer by presenting a structural framework and essential tools for the policy to work. It begins with perspective and creativity.

Here is Former British Prime Minister, David Cameron (https://www.gov. uk/government/speeches/pms-speech-on-big-society) speaking in 2011 about the need to involve the nonprofit sector (The Big Society) in relieving the burden of government:

> To the skeptics about The Big Society, I suggest that they go and look at what has happened in social housing over the last 20 years. Twenty years ago, housing associations were formed. They were very small; they were run by volunteers. Today, they are the dominant producers—developers of housing for those who need low-cost accommodation. There's a precedent for The Big Society too: the Housing Finance Corporation was established at the same time to provide a means to the debt carkets for these housing associations. Having established the credit, the banks now are in, and we raise at the moment £2.5 billion for housing associations at rates cheaper than the government of Japan can borrow. So, the precedents are there for this. Let me suggest one idea perhaps for the lady in the corner. Prisons are a rather specialised form of housing. Housing associations already provide housing for assisted care; they do training especially in IT skills for their residents so that they can access the web. Perhaps housing associations should take over some of the prisons.

Perspective and imagination matter: How can the nonprofit help relieve the burden of government beyond the traditional charity?

Collaboration

This book focuses on the structure and content of collaboration in a variety of forms listed below. Defining the process of collaboration is found in the seminal works of Bryson, Crosby, and Stone (2015, see endnote), and Gazely and Guo (2015, see endnote) as they note the relevance of structure. Structure matters with nonprofits for operational as well as legal and tax purposes. There are rules about how a nonprofit may collaborate and they will be discussed.

The form, complexity, and structure of collaboration matter as shown in this example where A is the government, B is a firm, C is a nonprofit, and D is another nonprofit. If A contracts with B, and B contracts with C; then C becomes a subcontractor with the primary arrangement, direction, and accountability of C flowing to B and not to A. For all intents and purposes, the contract that C has is with B—they are collaborators. On the other hand, if A contracts directly with C, the collaboration is between those two. In this sense, A has not relieved itself of the responsibility of dealing with C; that is, the burden of A is not relieved as when A collaborates with B and places all responsibilities of production, monitoring, processing, hiring, and delivery of C on B.

Although it may not intuitively be apparent, the structure is that A contracts with C, and C makes B a subcontractor. The nonprofit is the prime contractor and the firm is the subcontractor to the nonprofit. This structure of collaboration happens when the government contracts with a housing or community development corporation and it contracts with firms to do the building, remodeling, and maintenance.

The collaboration may be that A contracts with C and C subcontracts with D, or A contracts with D and C in a coordinated way so that the three are working together rather than C contracting with D making D a subcontractor to C. These collaborations are distinctly different in their implications as to the responsible party and how much of the burden is taken from the government and, therefore, what the public policy maker, public administrator, and nonprofit manager need to include in the design of the collaboration. A basic rule is that whenever one of the parties to a collaboration is a firm and a nonprofit, the rules of partnerships will apply. When a collaboration is between two or more nonprofits and the government (excluding a firm and the nonprofit), rules relating to the restricted use of assets will apply.

We discuss various types of collaborations in making specific points about rules, options, and considerations. The formal structures of inter-sector and cross-collaborations include:

1. Collaboration between the nonprofit and its subsidiaries or affiliates— independent nonprofit corporations that may have specific expertise and functions that the nonprofit calls upon but does not control (Chapter 4).
2. Collaboration with firms under various forms of arrangement but that prohibit the control of the assets of the organization by the firm (Chapter 10).
3. Collaboration of an independent nonprofit with an operating foundation (Chapter 4).
4. Collaboration with monetary rewards, rewards in-kind, and of shares of stocks (Chapter 10).
5. Collaboration with other nonprofit organization (Chapters 3–5).
6. Collaboration with manufacturers that produce royalties for the nonprofit and have no production risks (Chapter 10).
7. Collaboration as in mergers and acquisitions (Chapter 11).

8. Collaboration with government in the financing, development, and managing of infrastructure and the reduction of the burden of debt (Chapters 5 and 9).

Collaboration in the service of the public interest is more than a concept. It must take specific forms and recognize that there are both legal and practical limits to each. It must be purposeful and capable of demonstrably producing a result that benefits that public interest. The collaborators must bring something of public value to the table. What are these?

Competence: Capacity to Perform on a Sustainable Basis

Competence implies not only technical skill, which can be learned, but the power, capacity, and authority to perform; this is what policy will have to render the organization. It is more than the financial assets. The specific policy implementation problem is about authorizing the power and tools by which complex business (not charitable) transactions, such as negotiating and making loans, can occur; how complex collaboration relationships can occur without placing either the public or the government at risk; and how the acquisition and disposition of public-oriented assets may occur by the nonprofit without recourse to the government, thus relieving it of the burden of doing so and minimizing the risk of using a nonprofit.

The Prime Minister is making this statement in the context of what the policy should be and what it should accommodate or encourage. As shown in Chapter 6, it matters little that an organization may be technically competent in doing a job if it does not have a competent and functioning board—no matter its size. Why this is so has little to do with "governance" as that term is commonly used. It has to do with the fact that no counterparty (including the government) would enter into a meaningful relationship without evidence of board approval; and in many states the lack of a functioning board is sufficient cause to close down the organization (called an involuntary dissolution).

This book is less interested in board strategies than it is in the structure, functions, and tools. These are decided by policy with some room for discretion above a stated minimal level. We shall see that in its chartering of nonprofits to assume government-related activities, the U.S. Congress enumerate specific tools and structures and leave the internal strategies to the skill and imagination of the responsible management. But what are these tools, and how do they work to affect choices and strategies of management?

Why would I elect to use an example about the board to illustrate this point here? Because without a functioning board as is accepted in state law and policy and discussed in Chapter 6, the remainder of this book is moot and the organization is also headed for dissolution; that is, it is not sustainable. The lack of a functioning board may be a cause for involuntary dissolution, the attorney general of the state will close it down.

Traditional, Nontraditional, Burden

Traditional means those functions that are, in popular and legal terms, called charitable because they attend to the distressed; and if they are pure charities, they do so gratuitously and without charge (http://thelawdictionary.org/pure-charity/).

When the U.S. Treasury Department, including the IRS, refers to charities under IRC Section 501(c)(3), it includes not only the definitions above or the eight qualifying purposes listed in that section of the code, but also those unlisted activities accepted by the courts as consistent with 501(c)(3) categorization. These include activities where prices are charged and profits are made, but the target may or may not be the disadvantaged without other options. It also includes activities for the erection or maintenance of public buildings, monuments, or public works; and "the lessening of the burden on Government" (see Treasury Regulations Section 1.501(c)(3)–1(d)(1)(2), 1980).

But IRC Section 501(c)(3) also covers nonprofits that are highly profitable and can hardly be said to be motivated by charity. Ge Bail and Gerald Anderson (2016, see endnote) find that only seven of the top ten nonprofit hospitals are nonprofits. Bryce (1994, see endnotes) using various statistical approaches, finds that there is no significant difference in the rate of return on assets (a measure of profitability) between nonprofit and for-profit HMOs. These nonprofits are motivated to perform health-care for the benefit of the general public.

Another example, the Parking Facilities Corporation of New Orleans, Louisiana, a 501(c)(3), in words used to describe them:

> The corporation's primary exempt purpose is to design, finance, construct, equip, maintain, and operate, with all distribution of its funds for such purposes, a parking garage facility to be used by the traveling public at the Louis Armstrong International Airport and the employees of the New Orleans aviation board, thereby lessening the burden of government required of the New Orleans aviation board and the city of New Orleans (http://greatnonprofits.org/org/parking-facilities-corporation).

Their sole revenues are from parking fees amounting to over $9 million annually. Many such examples, a range of them, will be given throughout this book.

The Panama Canal is operated by a nonprofit to make a healthy profit that makes the canal operations sustainable and helps finance the Panamanian educational system. The Cleveland 2016 Host Committee, Inc., is an Ohio nonprofit corporation with no political affiliation. It is responsible for organizing, hosting, and funding the 2016 Republican National Convention in Cleveland. Its mission is to promote Northeast Ohio and ensure Cleveland is best represented, as well as for lessening the burden of local governments in hosting the Convention. The Committee is made up of influential businesses, civic residents, and government officials (https://www.2016cle.com/the-host-committee).

These are not traditional charities, if "charities" is the proper term, but they are created as and registered as nonprofits, are tax-exempt, and are lessening the burden of government as a stated mission. Consequently, when this book refers to *nontraditional* it refers to those organizations that could fall under 501(c)(3) in the Treasury Regulations and yet not be traditional charities to serve those unable to pay.

U.S. Treasury Regulations do not say that other nonprofits outside of Section 501(c)(3) may not act to lessen the burden of government. In fact, many of them do and the government has been able to engage them for such a purpose including self-regulation and qualification purposes where the public interest is at stake. Among these are the 501(c)(6) entities, and that is the reason for their coverage in Chapter 3 of this book. Many take on regulatory burdens that would otherwise have been the government's problem and they do so with the acquiescence of government.

When the term *nontraditional* is used in this book, it indicates those in the 501(c)(3) category, as well as those not named but the courts but the IRS find to be consistent with Section 501(c)(3) or other tax-exempt category (principally 501(c)(4), (5), and (6)), that are capable of reducing the burden of government. All of these nonprofits become candidates for engagement by public policy makers and by public administrators.

This book works within the IRS concept as to the meaning of lessening the burden of government:

1. The organization must be separate from the government and its activities and must lessen a recognized burden of government.
2. The burden must currently be undertaken by government, or would be undertaken by government, absent the organization's assumption of it. The government, by declaration or action, must acknowledge the existence of this burden as a government burden.
3. The organization must not have sovereign government powers; and if so, it has to be significantly limited to and necessary for a specific task. If not, it is a nonprofit tax-exempt organization operating as government. In this book

we examine nonprofits that are created by the government and those created by citizens to relieve the burden of government without representing
themselves as government.

4. The organization may act in collaboration with the government but more
    than by just fulfilling a contract. Collaboration does not negate that the
    nonprofit is a separate entity. Acting in collaboration with government is an
    indicator that the activity is otherwise a burden of government that is being
    relieved by the collaboration. Collaboration is a key element to the success
    and purpose of many of these nonprofits and leads to a categorization in
    this book of doers and facilitators.

5. The size of the burden is not an issue; rather, the beneficiaries of relieving
    that burden must be the general public (defined in the next chapter) and
    not private interests beyond that which is essential to bring about a greater
    public interest. Helping a firm locate profitably is acceptable if by doing so
    it helps the employment, income, and other benefits to the larger communi-
    ty even more. The public benefits have to be quantitatively and qualitatively
    a multiple of the private benefits.

6. For the organization to be entitled to the benefits of being a 501(c)(3) it must
    qualify under the tax code as a 501(c)(3). But to relieve a burden of govern-
    ment, the organization does not have to be a 501(c)(3). It may qualify for ex-
    emption as a civic organization under IRC Section 501 (c)(4) or as a busi-
    ness association under IRC Section 501 (c)(6).

7. The government through its public policy may create a variety of nonprofit
    tax-exempt organizations. These include public authorities and 501(c)(3)s.
    The government may also collaborate by written agreement with any
    501(c)(3)s, (4)s, and (6)s created by citizens with an objective to lessen a
    specific burden of government. It is a matter of crafting a linkage between
    the type of nonprofit and the type of burden relief and, therefore, the con-
    cept of organizational design.

8. The government may create nonprofit entities that are quasi-governmental
    with various degrees of independence in their relationship to the govern-
    ment to relieve the burden on the core structure of the government; but its
    exemption is as a government unit.

All of the above will be explored and illustrated in this book.

Organizational Design

A nonprofit that is formed to lessen the burden of government must have a specific format. The concept of organizational design is used precisely and techni-

cally. It refers to the fact that whether created by government or by citizens, the organization must choose among certain specific designs. It may be unincorporated as a trust, or it may be incorporated as a corporation. To qualify for exemption, the organization must be a corporation or at least have the essential characteristics of a corporation. As an exempt organization, it can performa mission or financeothers to perform a mission, or one that both, perform and finance a mission mostly its own. It can be a membership or a non-membership organization. It can be a principal organization, or an auxiliary to one or more, or a subsidiary to one or more. In collaboration with others it can be a managing partner or a partner. It can have some level of dependence on government or free control of its activities. In all cases, it must have some required form and format of accountability not only to the population, but to the legislature, the executive, or some executive agency. These are formal legal terms, and they matter, so they are specifically discussed in this book. It is not that one form is superior to another; rather, it is about the capacity and authority to lessen a specific burden of government, given its characteristic and the rules that attend each form.

Prices, Profits and Nonprofit Motives

As we shall see, a common characteristic of nonprofits that are designed to lessen the burden of government is that they have a clear motive and reason to consistently have annual revenues well exceed expenditures. See the examples above. Many of those nonprofits displayed in this book operate to earn and to report sizeable net revenues. Why? Because most of them relieve the government by being able to generate net revenues to sustain themselves, including accumulating a reserve for future capital expenditures, and sufficient to transfer annual amounts to the government for specific purposes and also to other nonprofits with functions related to the one being lessened. They do so through (1) the charging customers and clients for what they do, (2) borrowing, (3) prudent investment, (4) receiving transfers from supporting organizations, (5) by receiving tax-exempt gifts and contributions from the public, corporations, and foundations, and (6) utilizing volunteers. So, they relieve the burden of government financially and by providing a meaningful public good that would have otherwise fallen on the government, be it federal, state or local or any combination of these.

In this regard, the public good may be a hard asset such as infrastructure, available to the public at large (not just the needy) and for which a fee to fully cover the cost, plus a margin for profits may be charged, and for which participation may be excluded for those who cannot pay. This is not traditional charity; but it is what these nonprofits do. And, if they are to be successful in doing this, they must be able to self-finance in the ways described in the preceding paragraph. Hence those ways also become subjects of this book. How does the nonprofit exploit them for the benefit of reducing the burden of government?

The Context

This book is about the necessary architecture of the organization (the design and choice for engagement) and the transactions to make nonprofits as an option to lessening the burden of government. It focuses on the legal structure, tools and toolboxes, and the performance necessary for the success of the policy in this nontraditional function. Thus, the orientation of this book is not the welfare state, human services, welfare services, philanthropy, or the like. All of these are offered in highly respected publications including my own. Put another way, public policy stipulates an objective, its architecture, and its rules; it does not try to tell managers how best to operate. It does not micromanage or prescribe the strategy of delivering the nonprofit's charge—relieving the burden of government. This broadens the applicability of the book even as it focuses on the United States, where the problem is recognized and part of the public policy discussion. The book is written with a U.S. context at all levels of government and across the country, with few exceptions, and policy categories using a number of well-known and not-so-well-known specific examples.

What is the size of the problem?

Dimension of the Problem in the United States

One way of measuring the dimension of the burden of government is by the size of its debt and its distribution over the population. The size of the U.S. National Debt at the time of this writing was $19,739,283,120 with $60,784 per citizen and $165,304 per taxpayer. The Federal Financing Bank (FFB) coordinates the borrowing and the purchase of federal debt securities to reduce the cost of such borrowing to the government and the disruption to capital markets. The FFB is a nonprofit tax-exempt corporation along the continuum of nonprofits created by government to reduce the burden of government. One would find it hard to conclude that what it does is traditional charity or philanthropy. Rather, it is part of the organizational mechanism for implementing an important public policy—the debt policy as determined by the U.S. Congress and the President.

Aside from this federal debt, there is also the debt of each state and municipality. The state figures as of this writing are given in Table 1.1.

Table 1.1: Debt, Debt Per Capita and Per Taxpayer by State as of October 24, 2016

States	Debt	Debt to GDP Ratio	Debt per Citizen
Alabama	$30,719,256,860	14.57%	$6,321
Alaska	$8,800,000000	17.28%	$11,922
Arizona	$54,821,965,589	18.30%	$8,009
Arkansas	$19,577,081,735	15.55%	$6,570
California	$471,673,834,577	18.32%	$12,031
Colorado	$59,279,025,300	18.42%	$10,921
Connecticut	$47,077,090,932	17.67%	13,115
Delaware	$7,106,424,520	10.07%	$7,521
Florida	$135,718,448,500	14.69%	$6,653
Georgia	$57,922,076,692	11.20%	$5,660
Hawaii	$15,332,127,225	18.53%	$10,695
Idaho	$5,912,851,225	8.804%	$3,568
Illinois	$163,395,587,867	20.30%	$12,711
Indiana	$42,612,852,628	12.24%	$6,434
Iowa	$16,306,426,343	9.150%	$5,217
Kansas	$26,244,985,784	17.47%	$9,011
Kentucky	$41,357,839,026	20.60%	$9,342
Louisiana	$41,332,134,172	16.89%	$8,844
Maine	$9,019,281,280	15.48%	$6,788
Maryland	$51,170,699,223	13.58%	$8,513
Massachusetts	$91,447,836,567	18.46%	$13,447
Michigan	$85,099,260,192	17.57%	$8,576
Minnesota	$64,054,304,982	18.54%	$11,658
Mississippi	$14,212,858,972	12.95%	$4,884
Missouri	$44,764,452,395	14.76%	$7,355

States	Debt	Debt to GDP Ratio	Debt per Citizen
Montana	$4,812,890,709	10.18%	$4,656
Nebraska	$16,538,672,824	14.09%	$8,712
Nevada	$25,951,564,625	17.58%	$8,953
New Hampshire	$9,706,447,727	12.97%	$7,295
New Jersey	$109,893,435,531	18.65%	$12,240
New Mexico	$14,612,895,956	15.90%	$7,008
New York	$359,009.290,336	24.05%	$18,129
North Carolina	$44,532,241,095	8.537%	$4,427
North Dakota	$5,219,346,140	9.706%	$6,879
Ohio	$87,267,670,912	13.91%	$7,512
Oklahoma	$17,019,347,427	9.589%	$4,346
Oregon	$38,890,289,672	17.22%	$9,631
Pennsylvania	$136,351,525,287	19.27%	$10,650
Rhode Island	$11,919,348,018	20.24%	$11,285
South Carolina	$45,390,294,482	21.95%	$9,249
South Dakota	$5,206,449,720	10.88%	$6,063
Tennessee	$34,345,148,816	10.51%	$5,197
Texas	$284,619,141,541	17.83%	$10,330
Utah	$21,458,050,438	14.02%	$7,144
Vermont	$4,506,450,143	14.45%	$7,198
Virginia	$64,364,502,532	12.97%	$7,671
Washington	$83,015,829,429	17.96%	$11,549
West Virginia	$13,545,153,621	18.24%	$7,348
Wisconsin	$41,138,704,081	12.97%	$7,126
Wyoming	$1,706,450,850	4.502%	$2,910

Source: Compiled from http://www.usdebtclock.org/index.html

Clearly, there is wide variation; but the one constant is that even though governors may claim they run balanced operating budgets, they too have debt in their capital budgets. These debts finance infrastructure of all types. The state variations in debt are partly associated with their constitutional debt limit but also to the extent to which they use independent, nonprofit, tax-exempt entities to plan, finance, and operate major capital projects without (as allowed) the guarantee of state payments, and the extent to which they obtain federal help in financing the projects. One way of reducing state government debt is exactly like that of the federal government and the subjects of this book: the creation of nonprofits with the intent of lessening the burden of government beyond the traditional objectives of charity and philanthropy. Some of these objectives are: infrastructure, recreation, the environment, conservation, and community development—big projects with large capital needs where the nonprofit entity may have access to the capital markets and can provide self funding. That is why we pay tolls and are assessed user fees—self-financing of projects.

These nonprofits may be created by government or by citizens; they serve not only the poor or needy, but the population at-large. Their principal purpose is to relieve the burden of government, which we all share as residents and as taxpayers, since all government debt must have a public purpose. Crafting these nonprofits, whether by citizens or government consistent with the law and with the reality of their operations, is another matter and the topic of this book. What powers must be embedded in them? What are the roles of policy, the policymaker, the public administrator and the management of the nonprofit in this particular purpose?

Why the Nonprofit Option

This book sticks to the concept of lessening the burden of government as it is used consistently in the IRS Revenue Procedures, letters, and in court decisions. In that vein, it focuses on the actual and measurable reduction of a burden the government recognizes as the motive, not the consequence of the nonprofit creation or purpose. It also sticks to the concept that this does not require a charitable act or motive. But to the analysts or theorists there is more here. Specifically, the nonprofit option may be a more equitable and efficient solution for the following reasons:

1. It is financed voluntarily—not by compulsory taxation that is disconnected to even the consciousness of its existence.
2. It is financed by investors using their own assessment of the economic worthiness of the project—not by the unwilling taxpayer.
3. It will be financed mostly, if not exclusively, by user fees; thus, those who get the direct benefits pay directly.

4. Those who benefit indirectly (spillovers) pay indirectly; e.g., the truck that pays the toll incorporates the toll in what it charges and the retailer incorporates that margin in the price it charges its customers.
5. It creates an organization focused on a core mission for the same reasons that a large firm does a spin-off and subsequently an elevation of the value created by each part.

With these thoughts, and with full consciousness that some situations may not benefit from or lend to these considerations, the next chapter begins with what is an essential first step: The organization has to be created and specifically empowered to lessen the burden of government. What does that mean and how is it done?

Toward a Supporting Theory

I have constructed the following theory to support the policy decision of the choice of the nonprofit to lessen the burden of government. It goes as follows: Because it is based on fees for services—earned business income, rather than upon compulsory payment of taxes imposed by government, people can choose to purchase as much as they want of the service being performed by the nonprofit to lessen the burden of government. Others (mostly nonusers) may voluntarily choose to donate as much as they wish based on their ability to give and on their private estimates of the utility of the organization and what it provides in services not just to them, but to the community at large. Thus, both the market value and the externalities (gifts reflecting the value to the community including nonusers) are reflected.

Furthermore, because the donor, as well as the user, are operating within a fixed bucket of income and therefore must make choices as to what deserves their spending, the choice of the nonprofit lessening the burden of government reflects a comparative value choice and therefore approximates an expression of preferences; and, consequently, is more efficient. When the government does it by compulsion, this efficient choice is not available.

The IRS is an arbiter between the supply (the nonprofit) and demand (the user) and the donor. It monitors the nonprofit's performance. It requires and publicly reports annually on the organization and requires the organization to do the same. This information increases transparency, but it also reduces risks of loss or inaction due to asymmetry of information. The choice is informed.

Moreover, the IRS sets an efficiency threshold for its own decision of support in the form of tax exemption. The exemption is in reality a reservation price as much as a reward, but it is also an imprimatur; e.g., the government does not look at disfavor on the nonprofit lessening its burden in providing this service. Further, it sets a measurable minimum of public support that must be demonstrated in order to obtain this exemption, and the nonprofit has to verify it annually in its Form 990. To receive tax exemption, the nonprofit (unlike government) must demonstrate a minimum of public support as discussed in this book.

This is the logic in which this book is contained. Now, to accomplish this efficiency and all of its benefits, the nonprofit has to have both the power and the capacity to act. This book shows what these are.

Bibliography

Bail, Ge and Gerald Anderson, "A More Detailed Understanding of Factors Associated with Hospital Profitability," *Health Affairs*, Vol. 35, #5, May 2016, pp. 889–897.

Bryce, Herrington, "Profitability of HMOs: Does Nonprofit Status Make a Difference?" *Health Policy*, 1994, vol. 28, pp. 197–210.

Bryce, Herrington, Players in the Public Policy Process: Nonprofits as Social Capital and Agents (Palgrave-Macmillan, 2005 & 2012).

Bryce, Herrington, *Financial and Strategic Management for Nonprofit Organizations*, Englewood Cliffs, NJ, Prentice Hall (1986 and 1992) and Jossey-Bass (2000).

Bryce, Herrington J. "Unanticipated Budgetary Consequences of Devolution: Capacity Enhancing Potentials with the Current Russian Constitutional Framework in *Enhancing the Capacities to Govern: Challenges Facing the Central and Eastern European Countries,* Bryanne Michael, Rainer Kattel, Wolfgang Drechsler (eds.),(Slovenia:NISPACee, 2004).

Bryce, Herrington J. "Polycentric Governance, Capital Markets, and NGOs as Regulatory Bodies: Expanding the Scope of Ostrom's Understanding Institutional Diversity," *Politics & Policy*, Vol. 40, Issue 3, June 2012, pp. 519–535.

Bryson, John M., Barbara Crosby and Melissa Middleton Stone, "Designing and Implementing Cross-Sector Collaborations: Needed *and* Challenging," *Public Administration Review*, Vol. 75, issue 5, October 2015, pp. 657–663.

Gazley, Beth and Chao Guo, "What Do We Know about Nonprofit Collaboration? A Comprehensive Systematic Review of the Literature," *Academy of Management Proceedings*, Vol. 2015 2015:1 15409; doi:10.5465/AMBPP.2015.303 Internal Revenue Service (2010).

Ostrom, Elinor, *Understanding Institutional Diversity*. Princeton, NJ: Princeton University Press (2005).

Ostrom, Elinor, "Coevolving Relationship between Political Science and Economics," https://www.uni-bielefeld.de/ZIF/Publikationen/Mitteilungen/Aufsaetze/2012-1-Ostrom.pdf, 2012.

Chapter 2 – Designing, Empowering and Engaging the Nonprofit to Lessen the Burden of Government

This chapter is about the concepts, structures, and tools necessary to design and operate a nonprofit organization to lessen the burden of government. Many are detectable in the following example and will be drawn out for discussion along with other examples in this book.

The National Trust for Historic Preservation

According to its 2015 Form 990, The National Trust for Historic Preservation is a 501 (c)(3) chartered by the United States Congress and domiciled in the District of Columbia. It receives no government money for its operations Its mission, is historic preservation and conservation of objects of national scope and significance. This includes providing information, financing, technical assistance, the creation of partnerships with individuals, governments, firms, and nonprofits to meet these ends throughout the country. Its educational services include a journal and magazine. Its total expenses in 2015 was a bit over $53 million, of which $40 million was directly spent on its programs. Its principal sources of funding are membership fees, gifts, and contributions. It has business income divided between related and unrelated to the mission with the latter reported as a loss. While it has expenditures on lobbying, it has none on politicking. It has a large board of directors divided into various committees. Because it depends so heavily on contributions and membership fees, it is designated a publicly supported organization. Within the context of this book, it is also designated a "doer."

The National Trust partners with firms and other entities. It partners with the National Park Service in designating historic sites. It is the sole owner of the National Trust Community Investment Corporation, a for-profit subsidiary that raises money from private equity investors to finance historic property through the sale of tax credits. These investors include banks, brokerages, and other institutional investors.

Prepared by the author from the Form 990 of
the organization and its website.

Crafting the Intent to Lessen the Burden of Government

The final arbiter in recognizing that a nonprofit lessens the burden of government is the government itself. Rev. Rul. 85-1, 1985-1 C.B. 177 holds that lessening a burden of government occurs only if the government objectively manifests that it considers the activity to be a burden.

DOI 10.1515/9781501505799-003

How may it manifest that it considers an activity a burden? It may do so according to the Rev. Rul. 85-1, 1985-1 C.B. 177 and a series of subsequent rulings by the IRS and the courts by the preponderance of evidence given the facts and circumstances of each case. These include inferences drawn from the following:

1. There is a law or statute creating or authorizing the specific organization—its structure and purpose—for conducting an activity regularly conducted or to be conducted by that government over a significant period of time, thereby freeing up that government's use of resources for such activities.

2. That government's control over the organization's activities as reflected in such evidence as a majority of the board performing in their capacities as government officials, not as private citizens, and the amount of that government's input into the activities of the organization.

3. The interrelationship between the governmental unit and the organization, such as an agreement to work collaboratively and responsively.

4. The organization's payment of the local government's general or specific expenses or debt.

5. The government's funding of the organization through regular grants rather than as a fee for a specific performance, for example, through a contract, or through a revenue rather than a general obligation bond for the revenue bond does not commit the government as the general obligation does in requiring the pledge to back it with the full faith and credit of the jurisdiction.

6. That the activity is one that could legally be performed by the government; if it couldn't, then no burden could exist because of it. However, the case where the government formed a nonprofit entity to raise private funds to purchase narcotics in a sting operation was accepted because it furthered the government's anti-drug policy.

7. Direct attestation to the existence of this governmental burden; for example, an official government letter attached to the application attesting and acknowledging the burden as its own.

Once the burden has been established, there is a second step. That step is to prove that the organization claiming to be lessening the burden of the government could, by its capacity and structure, actually do so. It would not pass this test if the activity is merely duplicative of government, firms, or other organizations; if the government has to pay a fee for it; and if there is no evidence of reasonable and meaningful impact on reducing the actual or probable cost to government and its use of resources. The reduction has to be material and not modest, and, of course, the burden has to exist.

Finally, there is the omnipresent condition: The activity has to be for the benefit of the general public. Any private benefits must be qualitatively and quantitatively incidental to achieving the public benefit. This means that even though the nonprofit may hire or collaborate with a firm to do what it promises to lessen the burden of government, or that there are profits to be made, the amount of the profits or other private benefits should be less than the public benefit both in amount and in quality. This simple statement is more consequential than it appears. Local economic development corporations which are generally 501 (c)(3)s may use their exemptions and resources to attract businesses by using various strategies to increase business profitability. By rule, then, the public benefit e.g., employment, must be greater both in amount and quality than the private profits.

In short, crafting the intent to lessening the burden of government is more than a declaration or post facto declaration or the inferring of a consequence of the performance of the nonprofit. It begins with a declaration of intent that requires: (a) that a specific burden is acknowledged by the government either by its actions or attestations, (b) that the nonprofit is designed so that it can actually lessen the burden meaningfully, and (c) that there is a superior public benefit even if some collaborators make profits; and thus allowing collaboration and involvement of firms under the aegis of the nonprofit.

Federal and State Designation of an Eligible Burden

While some states and localities may differ with respect to their tax structures, the rulings of the U.S. Treasury reign. According to the Treasury Department "...a mission to relieve the burden of government is sufficiently meritorious to be in and of itself worthy of tax exemption whether or not that mission directly serves the poor or the underprivileged." The organization could be classified as a 501(c)(3), (c)(4), or (c)(6)—meaning that it could be purely a charity or not, a social welfare organization, or a professional or business group, and the burden to be lessened consistent with the tax exempt purposes of each category as it accepts to do so. It could be charitable in the broadest sense of a 501(c)(3), it could be for civic purposes which means it falls outside of the charity motive, or it could be for business and professional purposes but in all cases must be for a manifest benefit of the public at large—the public the government serves.

What is the public policy and attestation of burden? How, for example, may it be revealed as in the National Trust for Historic Preservation? It begins with a statement of policy in the National Historic Preservation Act, Section 16 (U.S.C. 470). Here are the last two listings of purpose and policy.

...the increased knowledge of our historic resources, the establishment of better means of identifying and administering them, and the encouragement of their preservation will improve the planning and execution of federal and federally assisted projects and will assist economic growth and development; andalthough the major burdens of historic preservation have been borne and major efforts initiated by private agencies and individuals, and both should continue to play a vital role, it is nevertheless necessary and appropriate for the Federal Government to accelerate its historic preservation programs and activities, to give maximum encouragement to agencies and individuals undertaking preservation by private means, and to assist State and local governments and the National Trust for Historic Preservation in the United States to expand and accelerate their historic preservation programs and activities.

Thus, the policy is the preservation and conservation of properties of historic interest for public benefit and the National Trust for Historic Preservation is a vehicle for the realization of that policy burden joining with private individuals and agencies to do so.

The upshot of the discussion to this point is this: Lessening or relieving a burden of government may stand alone as a motive for the creation of a nonprofit tax-exempt organization. That burden derives from a public policy traceable to at least one statute or its amendments. The role of the organization in lessening the burden of government, whether the organization is created by citizens or by government, therefore, is the implementation of a public policy for the public's benefit.

The academic reader may find indirect theoretical extensions (not discussions) by seeing Bryson, Cosby, Stone (2015) and their discussion of cross-sector collaboration, Ostrom's (2005) paradigm of alternative institutional forms for delivering public policy, Young's (1998) paradigm of the relationship between government and nonprofit and (Bryce 2005 and 2012) paradigm on the role of nonprofits in the width and breadth of the public policy process.

Classification of Nonprofits as Doers and Facilitators

The nonprofits lessening the burden of government are placed into two large categories reflecting their principal roles and how they are designed. This categorization is introduced as a way of understanding that organizations, to lessen the burden of government, may cut across tax exempt classes—501(c)(3)s charities and near charities, 501(c)(4) civic organizations not needing the façade of charity, and 501(c)(6) organizations with the principal purposes of advancing professional and business interests.

The two categories to be introduced are the *doers* and the *facilitators*. Examples of these are introduced below. I have purposefully chosen one foreign

entity, one state or multi-state entity, and one entity that is local although created by the state. As far as the Federal government is concerned, the National
Trust for Historic Preservation is a *doer* and the National Park Foundation (used
to illustrate the points for the remainder of this chapter) is a *facilitator*. The
doers do and the facilitators facilitate them as these doers carry out the work
that constitutes the burden.

Example 1

This first example is used to illustrate that while the exact laws and circumstances do vary, the basic idea of using nonprofits works even with big projects
in developing countries to serve the public and to reduce the burden of government. The United States, as a result of the treaty to revert properties acquired to
build and to operate the Panama Canal, gave back to Panama several properties
at the end of 1999. One of them was a pristine, favorably located army base with
complete infrastructure including buildings, roads, television stations, labora-
tories for testing equipment under tropical conditions and so on. Maintaining
this property would have been a burden to the Panamanian government. Instead of selling or leasing the property or using it for public housing, the Panamanian government formed a tax-exempt nonprofit, called the City of
Knowledge, and turned it over to them to run as a city of knowledge to attract
foreign technology, students, scientists, and international organizations (especially those with a wildlife, environmental or technology focus), and to raise its
own funds through a variety of fees from foreign and domestic entities including universities and corporations as well as to raise private contributions to
maintain and to operate the site. This has almost nothing to do with serving the
needy through charity, but everything to do with preserving a national asset
and shifting both its use, operation, and renovation costs to a nonprofit with the
power to set fees and receive private contributions, thereby lessening the burden to government. In the context of this book, the City of Knowledge is a doer
(Bryce 2009).

Example 2

The West Coast Infrastructure Exchange (www.westcoastx.org) is a 501(c)(3)
created by British Columbia, Oregon, Washington, and California. Its mission is
to provide assistance and information in public-private partnerships, specifically in the adoption of *Performance Based Infrastructure*. This is a method through

which private investors form a consortium to do the design, planning, operating, and maintenance of a major piece of infrastructure such as a highway. They put up, and therefore primarily risk, their own capital and the government is spared the cost of capital and other resources in this endeavor but it still owns the infrastructure. The arrangement provides an incentive for lower costs and timely completion because during that period, the risk falls upon the consortium. The government pays the consortium over time from the revenues of the project, through tax assessment, or from earmarking part of its tax revenues. In the context of this book, this nonprofit is called a *facilitator*.

Example 3

A local economic development corporation may be primarily a facilitator. Let's begin with a generic example based on the rules and examples of the IRS to demonstrate and then reveal the underlying reasoning and factors in supporting an argument for exemption of a nonprofit formed by the government, to relieve a burden of government. A local government has an area that is blighted, underserved, and with high vacancy and unemployment. It has been this way for some time and the local government's operating costs are increased by the need for police and fire protection, deteriorating infrastructure both from the lack of use, vandalism, and differed maintenance. The revenue base of the community has deteriorated and contributes substantially less to the municipal budget than it takes. The legislative body passes a law creating a nonprofit community development corporation that qualifies as an independent 501(c)(3) with the mission of raising private funds from foundations, corporations, and the community. The nonprofit involves the local community as volunteers. It also uses its income for improving the situation of area residents through education and training, and attracting industry and business to the area to improve chances for , and the improvement of employment. The legislation designates the organization's board to be made up of community residents, elected and appointed officers of the government, and designates an official body to which scheduled or periodic reports are sent.

Such a construct generally describes a local economic development corporation that qualifies for 501(c)(3) status. Acoordingly, the Hudson Valley Agribusiness Development Corporation, a 501(c)(3) membership organization in New York State, is classified as a facilitator. A local economic development corporation may qualify for the exemption as lessening the burdens of government based on a preponderance of facts, such as:

- There is a state statute specifically authorizing government funding of an economic development corporation to operate by assisting fledgling businesses within the state as a means to help alleviate severe unemployment.
- The economic development corporation was established to specifically qualify under the statute and was funded under the statute.
- The state statute provides that the funding is more than a mere grant (or revenue bond since such bond requires no commitment from the state as general obligation bonds require the full faith and credit of the state) and the jurisdiction has regular approval authority over projects to be financed by the corporation.
- The economic development corporation operates in conjunction with a state university.
- The specific government that will be the corporation's primary beneficiary provides officials who sit on the corporation's board of directors in their official capacity.
- The commissioner of the state's Department of Economic Development utilizes the corporation as an extension to carry out services formerly conducted by the Department. The Department was unable to continue such services because of budgetary constraints and is not otherwise prohibited from such services.
- The corporation is required to provide annual reports of its activities and finances to the state government.

Summary of Examples

In all of the above examples, the three critical IRS criteria are present for exemption within the meaning of "lessening the burden of government."
1. A burden is recognized by statute and by the government's own actions in carrying on this function or has public policy responsibility for doing so.
2. The creation of a nonprofit lessens this burden.
3. The public is the beneficiary even though there are private benefits that may accrue to the businesses that locate in the area; those benefits are incidental compared to the larger benefits received by the general public.

On what does the organization have to be built to fulfill this mandate? What does it take? Is there evidence of this in nonprofits ranging from those dealing with monuments to infrastructure, parks, and environments to ports and other functions having a common set of planks to guide policy and organizational designers? We begin with the essential organizational concepts in designing the organization.

The Planks on Which to Design a Nonprofit to Reduce the Burden of Government

The IRS establishes above that for a nonprofit to lessen the burden of government, there has to be a burden that the government admits by its actions or affirmation. There also has to be an organization to carry out that burden for the benefit of the public. The law only stipulates that the organization has to have a management structure, the required power to carry out that function, and that it has to be for the benefit of the public and not for personal gains or benefits by the management, the creators, the donors, the members (except in the specific case of unions), or the immediate family or business associates. But what does this mean?

It is possible to reasonably deduce what essential planks are necessary for citizens or the legislature to design a nonprofit to undertake a task under varying circumstances. Why are these planks necessary? Because without them the organization has no defined and enforceable burden or mission to perform and, if it does, it has no means to perform them. These essentials cannot be left to chance and must be, however stated, in the charter. Moreover, they are more than necessary for an ordinary nonprofit as discussed in Bryce (2007). After detailing them below, I shall demonstrate each using the National Park Foundation, an independent 501(c)(3) created by Congress to help reduce the government's burden of financing the National Park Service and in the latter's meeting of its objectives. If this book is used as a text, the instructor may wish to assign students the challenge of finding these planks in the charters of other organizations with the mission of lessening the burden of government.

The planks are never as enumerated and clearly stated as below but they are always there because they are essential to the functioning of the organization:

1. **Money:** How it may be raised and used.
2. **Marketing:** The license to persuade others to support and to participate on the merits of promise and performance. These others may be clients, beneficiaries, donors, collaborators, or participants.
3. **Membership or Public:** An identity and affinity among persons and entities with a common interest—a public to which the organization caters or serves, with or without charge or formal enrollment, and which has access to that benefit. The identity may be geographic, a specifically defined area,

or jurisdictional—the boundaries of responsibility of the government whose burden is being relieved and often referred to as the "general public."

4. **Management:** Its duties in fulfilling and in advancing the organization and its mission with a designated board of trustees at the head of the hierarchy and direction of the board's structure, terms, committees, and function.

5. **Mission:** An overarching, permanent yet dynamic, and verifiable contractual promise to always do specifically as promised in the charter and in the certificate of tax exemption for the benefit of the designated general public and without personal inurement (the legal term for benefit). In this case, that which is promised must be identifiable as a burden of government (as defined above).

6. **Collaboration and Cooperation:**Relieving a burden of government implies, almost by definition, some collaboration or cooperation, whether specifically with an agency of that government or with others. The nature of the collaboration whether with government or with others may vary.

7. **Tax Exemption:** A provision may be made for tax exemption from Federal, state, and local taxes. This provision is either by stipulation and/or by design if the organization is created by government and by design if it is created by citizens. The issues here are not simply exemption, but under what theory and under what section of the Internal Revenue Code (IRC) the exemption would be allowed. Most important, what is the value of a tax exemption when a nonprofit lessens the burden of government?

8. **Powers to Transact:** The organization must have specific powers to undertake transactions that are essential to the organization's ability to perform and to be held accountable for such transations.

9. **Accountability:** The organization must be accountable. Accountability may be in the form of scheduled regular meetings, special meetings, reports to the state and to the Federal government, and to a specific executive agency or to a legislative body as well as any required public hearings.

10. **Legitimacy:** To lessen a burden of government, an identification of that burden, the jurisdiction (state, local, or national), the location of the organization in that jurisdiction in which the burden exists, and the representation on the board of directors of residents of that jurisdiction are required. Moreover, a state seal of licensure and permission to operate is embossed on the charter.

Each of these planks will be illustrated in more detail below using the charer of The National Park Foundation, an independent corporation formed to partially relieve the burden of financing the National Park Service.

Plank 1: Money

Without money, missions are empty promises. To maximally relieve a burden of government, the nonprofit would relieve the financial burden and not itself become a financial burden on the government. In the entire charter of the National Park Foundation, there is no mention or promise of fiscal assistance from the government except that it gives the Foundation the right to call upon the National Park Service for certain in-kind services; for example, police, space, and other services at events held by the Foundation—mandating a level of collaboration. Section 6 states:

> The Foundation may utilize the services and facilities of the Department of the Interior and the Department of Justice, and such services and facilities may be made available on request to the extent practicable without reimbursement therefor.

The money flows one way from the Foundation to the National Park Service, reducing the burden on the latter and, therefore, on the United States government and the taxpayer. For this to happen, the charter has to empower the nonprofit to allow it specific ways to make money. Section 3 reads:

> The Foundation is authorized to accept, receive, solicit, hold, administer, and use any gifts, devises, or bequests, either absolutely or in trust of real or personal property or any income therefrom or other interest therein for the benefit of or in connection with, the National Park Service, its activities, or its services...

Section 4 states:

> Except as otherwise required by the instrument of transfer, the Foundation may sell, lease, invest, reinvest, retain, or otherwise dispose of or deal with any property or income thereof as the Board may from time to time determine. The Foundation shall not engage in any business, nor shall the Foundation make any investment that may not lawfully be made by a trust company in the District of Columbia, except that the Foundation may make any investment authorized by the instrument of transfer, and may retain any property accepted by the Foundation.

The organization is given a wide scope in how to raise the money from private sources. What does that mean? Who is included in private sources, why not just rely on contributions rather than including selling, investing, or leasing? A principal reason for the latter is that many nonprofits that reduce the burden of government can charge fees to users, exist to provide a service for them, and fees become the most efficient and equitable way for paying for those services. A second reason is that contributions are rarely enough even for traditional charities. We provide the historical evidence below.

Table 2.1 shows that a little over half of the expenses of smaller nonprofits are covered by contributions, gifts, and various grants from foundations or government. For the very largest nonprofits, it is less than 20 percent. Hence, a good portion of the bills have to be paid from other sources. Table 1.1 also shows that contributions were a similar percentage of total revenues; for the smaller nonprofits about 50 percent and for the largest less than 20 percent.

Table 2.1. Charitable Contributions as Percentage of Percentage of Total Revenues and Total Expenses by Asset Size Class, 2009–2012

Year	Under $100,000	$100,000 under $500,000	$500,000 under $1,000,000	$1,000,000 under $10,000,000	$10,000,000 under $50,000,000	$50,000,000 or More
2009						
Contributions as Percentage of Total Expense	1.0	0.4	0.5	0.8	0.6	0.9
Contributions as Percentage of Total Revenue	0.2	0.8	0.8	1.5	0.5	0.5
2010						
Contributions as Percentage of Total Expense	52.3	59.8	42.8	47.3	34.7	15.4
Contributions as Percentage of Total Revenue	46.1	58.2	40.4	46.2	32.9	14.3
2011						
Contributions as Percentage of Total Expense	43.3	57.6	45.9	47.2	35.4	15.5
Contributions as Percentage of Total Revenue	42.5	55.7	44.9	46.6	33.9	14.5

Year	Under $100,000	$100,000 under $500,000	$500,000 under $1,000,000	$1,000,000 under $10,000,000	$10,000,000 under $50,000,000	$50,000,000 or More
2012						
Contributions as Percentage of Total Expense	52.4	53.5	56.4	48.4	34.4	15.5
Contributions as Percentage of Total Revenue	52.6	52.5	54.4	46.7	33.0	14.4

Calculated by author from Table 1 Form 990 Returns of 501(c)(3) Organizations: Balance Sheet and Income Statement items, by Asset Size, Tax Year 2009–2012
Source: IRS, Statistics of Income Division, Exempt Organizations (Except Private Foundations), July 2015

Table 2.2 shows that most of the difference is made up by program service revenues. These are revenues the nonprofit earns from charging a fee for one or more activities or services it performs as part of its mission. Less than 5 percent of all 501(c)(3)s report gross business income unrelated to their missions. While program-related income may not be for all nonprofits (especially those dealing with the poor), it is an essential and fruitful potential source of income for most organizations that lessen the burden of government.

Table 2.2. Program Service Revenue as Percentage of Total Revenues by Asset Size Class, 2009–2012

Year	Under $100,000	$100,000 under $500,000	$500,000 under $1,000,000	$1,000,000 under $10,000,000	$10,000,000 under $50,000,000	$50,000,000 or More
2009	0.5	0.6	1.4	2.5	5.0	14.2
2010	50.1	35.8	52.4	49.8	62.0	78.8
2011	53.3	39.2	47.8	50.0	61.5	79.2
2012	42.8	42.0	58.1	49.2	61.2	78.0

Calculated by author from Table 1 Form 990 Returns of 501(c)(3) Organizations: Balance Sheet and Income Statement items, by Asset Size, Tax Year 2006–2012
Source: IRS, Statistics of Income Division, Exempt Organizations (Except Private Foundations), July 2015

Table 2.2 shows that the smaller nonprofits earn just over 40 percent of their revenues from program service, but the largest of nonprofits earn from 60–80 percent from that source. In general, there is a a secular rise in program revenues beyond any temporary make up for cyclical declines in contributions or grants. (See Kerlin and Pollack, 2011)

The net results of examining these tables is that they demonstrate a growing dependence on entrepreneurial or business-related income by the nonprofit sector—even the smaller ones—and, therefore, a greater need to develop business-related skills (not necessarily aggressiveness or objectives) in the nonprofit sector without violating their missions. These skills involve cost management that do not necessarily imply cutting of program-related functions or personnel, proper pricing and marketing where applicable, and even efficiency in the way goods and services are acquired, stored and delivered.

Table 2.3 shows that managers of associations such as 501(c)(4)s, (5)s, and (6)s are likely to face the same situation with heavy dependence on program revenues exceeding 70 percent. For the 501(c)(4) social welfare organizations it is well over 80 percent.

Table 2.3. Program Revenue as Percentage of Tota lRevenue by Groups, 2010–2012

Year	501(c)(3)	501(c)(4)	501(c)(5)	501(c)(6)
2010	72.0	90.1	72.7	71.9
2011	72.6	89.0	75.5	75.2
2012	72.2	85.8	76.8	74.6

Calculated by author from Table 1 Form 990 Returns of 501(c)(3) Organizations: Balance Sheet and Income Items, by Asset Size, Tax Year 2010–2012
Source: IRS, Statistics of Income Division, Exempt Organizations (Except Private Foundations), July 2015

These findings imply that for all these managers across the spectrum, many of whom are not 501(c)(3)s, they cannot accept charitable contributions and are not eligible for foundations grants, and they have to be prepared to take one or a combination of the following steps: increase diversification of funding by seeking funds from other sources including earning them through various mission-related activities called program revenues, lower expenses either by cutting activities or gaining substantially more efficiencies if they can. This book pays particular attention to the ways and the means of earned revenues that are not inconsistent with the mission of the organization, methods of cost control applicable to nonprofits of all types and to new ideas on fundraising—this latter specifically for 501(c)(3)s.

Here is the message for those nonprofits created to lessen the burden of government: (a) contributions may be necessary for survival but are not sufficient; (b) this is true in general even for those nonprofits, the 501(c)(3)s for which the government through its tax deduction and exemption policies have made contributions attractive; and (c) for an entire class of nonprofits such as the 501(c)(6)s for which a tax deduction for contributions is not available, cash must be earned and principally through program income—from the product and services they sell. They are discussed in this book.

Plank 2: Marketing and Persuading

In carrying out a burden, governments can compel: They can write laws and enforce them.They can adjudicate and incarcerate. They can penalize and seize properties. They can compel payments through taxes but to a politically tolerable limit. These are sovereign powers.

The tools of the nonprofit are those of effective marketing (the organization, the mission, the service) and in persuading. An effective tool the National Park Foundation, as it is for other nonprofits, is to persuade citizens to give voluntarily. Therefore, the preamble of its charter uses the word "encourages":

> Be it enacted by the Senate and House of Representatives of the United States of America in Congress assembled, That in order to encourage private gifts of real and personal property or any income therefrom or other interest therein for the benefit of, or in connection with, the National Park Service, its activities, or its services...

In relieving the burden of government, the nonprofit does not acquire the enforceable or compelling powers of government, but it substitutes the powers of marketing and persuading others to give, to participate, and to act voluntarily in certain ways. Of course, the nonprofit also has the power to deny or to exclude those who do not comply; e.g., pay the entrance fee.

Plank 3: Membership and Public

The beneficiary of government service is the public it represents and serves. Therefore, the "public" in lessening the burden of government almost always has a geographical, or jurisdictional limit; it may be undefined or be indistinguishable within that jurisdictional limit and therefore known as "general".

The National Park Foundation is like an affiliate of the National Park Service which serves the general public. Accordingly, the Organic Act of 1916 creating the National Park Service states:...the service thus established shall promote and regulate the use of the Federal areas known as national parks, monuments, and reservations hereinafter specified by such means and measures as conform to the fundamental purposes of the said parks, monuments, and reservations, which purpose is to conserve the scenery and the natural and historic objects and the wild life therein and to provide for the enjoyment of the same in such manner and by such means as will leave them unimpaired for the enjoyment of future generations..

Again, a public must be defined. For the National Park Foundation, it is reaching this future generation of Americans (the general public in this case) through the National Park Service and any of its 400 parks. A nonprofit must have a general public target which it reaches directly or through an intermediary. This is more important than may meet the eye, because it means that most nonprofits formed to lessen the burden of a state or local government are constrained geographically—meaning there is little cross-border incentive or service unless by special agreement. Local is local, and regional may be comprised of many locals in an agreement. Their markets are prescribed.

The concept of membership when the nonprofit is lessening the burden of government is also different. The members can be exclusively agencies of government and these will be discussed in this book. Specifically, the nonprofit could be formed by a government to coordinate a mission in which the primary players are government agencies. Boards of regents are examples. Others will be shown throughout the next several chapters.

Plank 4: Management

Management includes a system for effective decision-making covering what the organization will do, how, with what resources, with whom, for what purposes, and how it will operate. The board of trustees is at the top of the management hierarchy and represents the public interest and those of the stakeholders in directing and overseeing the operation toward fulfillment of the specific burden to be relieved. Consequently, nonprofits created by government as well as those created by citizens to relieve a burden of government tend to be very specific in the required makeup of the board and the terms of service. Some may even specify who holds what position. Accordingly, Sec 2 of the National Park Foundation charter says:

The National Park Foundation shall consist of a Board having as members the Secretary of the Interior, the Director of the National Park Service, ex officio, and no less than six private citizens of the United States appointed by the Secretary of the Interior whose initial terms shall be staggered to assure continuity of administration. Thereafter, the term shall be six years, unless a successor is chosen to fill a vacancy occurring prior to the expiration of the term for which his predecessor was chosen, in which event the successor shall be chosen only for the remainder of that term. The Secretary of the Interior shall be the Chairman of the Board and the Director of the National Park Service shall be the Secretary of the Board. Membership on the Board shall not be deemed to be an office within the meaning of the statutes of the United States. A majority of the members of the Board serving at any one time shall constitute a quorum for the transaction of business...

Commonly, representatives from the agency or ministry being relieved of a burden would be a significant but non-controlling percentage of the board. The National Park Service has a designated number of membrs and role assignments on the board including who will chair it. Nonprofits formed by citizens would often do the same, including and reflecting the government agency to be relieved. Why is this so? Because the design of these boards is intended to infuse them with people who are technically and operationally involved and who represent the government's responsibility of the burden being transferred. In this case, the government and its agency are stakeholders. The logic is simple: If A is to relieve the burden of B, then A must reflect the interest of B, and the efficiency of A is enhanced by the participation of B. Thus, with some citizen-created nonprofits, the board may consist exclusively by affected but credentialed parties; for example, a board to regulate the activities of accountants is comprised exclusively of persons credentialed in accounting, but from different sectors within the accounting profession. In short, the boards of nonprofits to relieve the burden of government reflect two concepts: (a) the interested or affected parties, and (b) the intimacy of information critical to the burden.

The stewardship responsibility over assets of trustees for organizations relieving the burden of government can be over inherited public assets that are of national significance. In the case above, it is by indirectly helping to preserve the National Parks, as Section 2 of the charter states:

> The Foundation shall succeed to all right, title, and interest of the National Park Trust Fund Board established in any property or funds, including the National Park Trust Fund, subject to the terms and conditions thereof...

The stewardship involves holding current assets on behalf of the public—the government Section 8 of the charter states:

> Contributions, gifts, and other transfers made to or for the use of the Foundation shall be regarded as contributions, gifts, or transfers to or for the use of the United States.

The focus of the management plank is the empowerment of trustees who are representatives of parties of interest and leaving the trustees to name managers as they deem necessary to oversee the inherited and acquired assets of the organizationso as to most efficiently relieve the designated burden as circumstances warrant. Section 7 illustrates the concept:

> In carrying out the provisions of this Act, the Board may adopt bylaws, rules, and regulations necessary for the administration of its functions and contract for any necessary services.

Plank 5: The Mission

Public Law 90-209, December 18, 1967, of the 90th Congress, S. 814, is the charter of the National Park Foundation .

It establishes the National Park Foundation as an independent entity that is tax exempt. The first paragraph of the Act gives the mission and purpose of the organization. It is the mission statement of the foundation. The U.S. Congress directs and the organization promises by its acceptance to do the following:

> Be it enacted by the Senate and House of Representatives of the United States of America in Congress assembled, That in order to encourage private gifts of real and personal property or any income therefrom or other interest therein for the benefit of, or in connection with, the National Park Service, its activities, or its services, and thereby to further the conservation of natural, scenic, historic, scientific, educational, inspirational, or recreational resources for future generations of Americans, there is hereby established a charitable and nonprofit corporation to be known as the National Park Foundation to accept and administer such gifts.

What, in general, is a mission and what are its characteristics?

A mission is much more than a statement of altruism which hardly applies to some nonprofits outside of the charitable form; rather, a mission is a contractual promise to do as stated and as may be reasonably implied or warranted to do consistent with that direction and promise. The dynamics of an otherwise static statement come from exploratory questions such as: What is the limit to what we are directed and promised to do? Because mission statements such as the one above are broad, they give management discretion that is reasonable within the boundaries of the mission statement. In general, a mission statement or promise has the following characteristics (Bryce, 1986, 1992, 2000):

1. *Social Contract*: The mission is a promise to perform a specific function for the benefit of the public and made in exchange for support of all kinds including tax exemption and the granting of a charter. In the above example,

the promises is to raise funds for the National Park Service and to assist it in meeting its service to the public.

2. *Permanence*: A mission is permanent unless it is amended subject to approval of members, trustees, the public represented by the State, and the parties to the contract. Amendments to all charters of the U.S. Congress must meet their approval. Creativity and imagination occur over time to extend the boundaries and inclusiveness of what the organization can do within reason, and must do because of the necessity of keeping the promise. Note this mission statement has no terminal date. It is presumed permanent unless otherwise specified.

3. *Clarity*: The mission statement is clear about what the organization is expected to do to relieve a specific burden of government and how it is to do it. In this case, the Foundation is to raise private funds and resources to finance projects that enable the National Park Service (a government agency) to fulfill its promise and purpose to preserve and to make available the jewels of the National Parks to the present and future generations of Americans. It is to do this on behalf of or in collaboration with the National Park Service. There is no equivocation.

4. *Approval*: The mission must be approved by the trustees (in some states, the founder may be the sole trustee), signed and accepted by the state in which the nonprofit is allowed to claim a legitimate purpose. The approval signals that there is an agreement between the state as representative of the people or membership, and the nonprofit about the mission. Note that the mission statement above is approved by the U.S. Congress as it would be by state and local legislatures with the signature of the executive for nonprofits created by these other levels of government. Approval especially relates to amendments to the mission or to the way of doing things. With nonprofits crafted to lessen the burden of government, but especially those created by government, such approval usually requires board affirmation and the affirmation of the legislature and executive of the government that created the organization or collaborates with its core activity.

5. *Proof*: There is an annual proof of continued existence, performance, accomplishment of the mission as promised, and use of revenues, expenses and other resources to do so. This annual proof is required by state and Federal governments. Action is expected and metrics of performance are required. In the above example, these metrics are how much money is raised, spent, and for what purposes related to the mission. This is part of the required annual filing of IRS Form 990 and applies to nonprofits whether created by government or citizens. Congress and other governments also re-

quire periodic performance and status reports to them or to some designated agencies if they created the nonprofit or collaborate with it.

Plank 6: Collaboration and Cooperation

Lessening a burden of government implies some level of collaboration or cooperation to make it work. The level, depth, and process of cooperation may evolve over time, but a minimum structure is stated. The preamble of the charter of the National Park Foundation uses such words as "in connection with" or "on behalf of." The point being made is that a condition for creating this nonprofit is collaboration or cooperation with others. We shall see in this book that some charters may stipulate the power to create for-profit or nonprofit subsidiaries or enter into partnerships as forms of collaboration.

Plank 7: Tax Exemption

In designing a nonprofit to relieve the burden of government, consideration must be given to the separate consideration of tax exemption. If an organization is an agency of government, it would be automatically exempt from tax on any income derived from doing that mission. However, being an independent nonprofit, whether created by government or citizens, does not automatically entitle an organization to exemption. For citizen-created nonprofits to qualify they have to meet the criteria set in law and embedded in how the organization is designed. Furthermore, if the government-created nonprofit wants the full benefits (beyond tax exemption) of being a 501 (c)(3), it has to have a similar design as the citizen-created one.

This is precisely the case with the National Park Foundation which is a registered 501(c)(3) in the same category as a citizen-created nonprofit in that category. We shall discuss these later in the book, but first note that in the preamble to the Foundations' charter, the Congress provides for this qualification by defining the mission in terms of those permitted in Section 501 (c)(3).

> ...for the benefit of, or in connection with, the National Park Service, its activities, or its services, and thereby to further the conservation of natural, scenic, historic, scientific, educational, inspirational, or recreational resources for future generations of Americans..,

These recite the activities which qualify for tax exemption under Section 501(c)(3) of the code. Section 8 further states:

> The Foundation and any income or property received or owned by it, and all transactions relating to such income or property, shall be exempt from all Federal, State, and local taxation with respect thereto. The Foundation may, however, in the discretion of its directors, contribute toward the costs of local government in amounts not in excess of those which it would be obligated to pay such government if it were not exempt from taxation by virtue of the foregoing or by virtue of its being a charitable and nonprofit corporation and may agree so to contribute with respect to property transferred to it and the income derived therefrom if such agreement is a condition of the transfer.

So why would the Congress exempt the Foundation by stipulation and also qualify it for a 501(c)(3) status making it able to qualify on its own? Because the latter not only makes the organization an independent entity but gives it the additional power to persuade donors. Donors are not attracted to making donations to government, but they are interested in donating to private organizations doing the type of work that is appealing. Together, these provisions allow the nonprofit to attract donations and volunteers to which the government may have little or no access.

Plank 8: Powers to Act

To relieve a burden of government, the organization needs specific transactional powers, that is, the powers to carry out ordinary and extraordinary transactions. In addition to Sections 3 and 4 above, Sections 6 says:

> The Foundation shall have the power to enter into contracts, to execute instruments, and generally to do any and all lawful acts necessary or appropriate to its purposes.

The embedding of these powers is in the fact of being a corporation which by relieving a burden of government, permits the following in Section 9.

> The United States shall not be liable for any debts, defaults, acts, or omissions of the Foundation.

The organization is on its own! That is what assuming a burden of government is about. What will it take in terms of tools and structures to carry out all that is quoted above? That is the purpose of the remainder of this book, beginning with the essential design of the nonprofit so that the powers and independence to act are embedded; and into what organizational form and design? This is the matter of the next chapter.

Plank 9: Accountability

The concept of accountability refers to who must say what to whom, when, and why (Alnoor 2003) and may follow a variety of formats such as Kearns (1994, 1996) and Candler and Dumont (2010). The nonprofit lessening the burden of government is required to make regular financial and performance reports to the public and to a legislative and executive body. Accountability is not a voluntary option.

Accordingly, Section 10 of the Foundation's charter reads:

> The Foundation shall, as soon as practicable after the end of each fiscal year, transmit to Congress an annual report of its proceedings and activities, including a full and complete statement of its receipts, expenditures, and investments.

Note that in addition to the above stipulation, this organization is not exempt from filing a Form 990 annually.It is formally filed to the IRS as are those of other nonprofit tax-exempt organizations.

Plank 10: Legitimacy

An essential signal of legitimacy is the board—that is:who is on it, what do they represent, where they are from. On the Fairfax County Library Foundation, to be used in the next chapter, board members must all be residents of the County, and typically in local economic development corporations they are residents, business persons and/or government officials of the locality (as far as that extends). In a national situation it is different, especially if the organization is created by government. Section 2 of the Foundation's charter says:

> The National Park Foundation shall consist of a Board having as members the Secretary of the Interior, the Director of the National Park Service, ex officio, and no less than six private citizens of the United States appointed by the Secretary of the Interior whose initial terms shall be staggered to assure continuity of administration. Thereafter, the term shall be six years, unless a successor is chosen to fill a vacancy occurring prior to the expiration of the term for which his predecessor was chosen, in which event the successor shall be chosen only for the remainder of that term. The Secretary of the Interior shall be the Chairman of the Board and the Director of the National Park Service shall be the Secretary of the Board. Membership on the Board shall not be deemed to be an office within the meaning of the statutes of the United States. A majority of the members of the Board serving at any one time shall constitute a quorum for the transaction of business, and the Foundation shall have an official seal, which shall be judicially noticed.

In all cases, legitimacy is established at the very top of the hierarchy—the board of trustees. The legitimacy of the nonprofit is also established by the imprimatur of the government. This is done in a number of ways including: open collaboration, references by the government of citizens to the organization for information and service, allowing the organization to use a government reference in its communications, government certificates, and so on.

Summary and Preview

The creation either by citizens or by governments for the specific purpose of lessening the burden of government is by definition a different reason than for conducting traditional charitable or philanthropic purposes and such purposes need not justify the awarding of a 501(c)(3) tax favored status—one in which revenues related to the organization and not taxed and donations to them for such purposes are tax deductible. for as we shall see later in this book.

The purpose of this chapter was to identify and discuss the organizational essentials for making an organization eligible as one that is lessening the burden of government. These essentials must be embedded in the organizational design at the very outset. In the next chapter, we turn to the essentials for making the organization competent so that it may be able to actually lessen the burden of government.

Bibliography

Bryce, Herrington J., *Players in the Public Policy Process: Nonprofits as Social Capital and Agents* (New York: Palgrave-Macmillan, 2005 and 2012), especially chapters 2–5.

Bryce, Herrington J.,. "Nonprofits as Social Capital and Agents in the Public Policy Process: Toward a New Paradigm," *Nonprofit and Voluntary Sector Quarterly*, Vol. 35, No. 2, pp. 311–318 (2009).

Bryce, Herrington J. "NGOs as Alternatives to Nationalization, Leasing, and Other Forms of Utilization of Public Assets in Developing Countries: A Case and Commentary," in *POLITICS AND POLICY*, Vol. 37, No.5, pp. 1083–1091 (2009).

Bryson, John M., Barbara Crosby and Melissa Middleton Stone, "Designing and Implementing Cross-Sector Collaborations: Needed and Challenging," *Public Administration Review*, October, 2015, Vol. 75, issue 5, pp. 657–663.

Bryson, John, Michael Gibbons, and Gary Shaye. "Enterprise schemes for non-profit survival, growth, and effectiveness. *Nonprofit Management and Leadership* 11 (3) spring: 271–288 (2001).

Candler, George and Georgette Dumont, "A Non-profit Accountability Framework," *Canadian Public Administration*, June, Vol. 53, Is. 2, pp. 259–279 (2010).

Ebrahim, Alnoor. "Making sense of accountability: Conceptual perspectives for northern and southern non-profits. *Nonprofit Management and Leadership* 14 (2) winter: 191–212 (2003).

Gazley, Beth and Chao Guo, "What do We Know about Nonprofit Collaboration? A Comprehensive Systematic Review of the Literature," *Academy of Management Proceedings*, Vol. 2015 2015:1 15409; doi:10.5465/AMBPP.2015.303.

Internal Revenue Service http://www.taxanalysts.com/www/freefiles.nsf/Files/EO%204.pdf/$file/EO%204.pdf

Kearns, Kevin, "The strategic management of accountability in non-profit organizations: An analytical framework." *Public Administration Review* 54 (2) March/April: 185–92 (1994).

Kearns, Kevin, *Managing for Accountability*. San Francisco: Jossey-Bass Publishers (1996).

Kerlin, Janelle and Tom H. Pollak, Nonprofit Commercial Revenue: A Replacement for Declining Government Grants and Private Contribution? *The American Review of Public Administration*, November 2011; vol. 41, 6: pp. 686–704.

National Trust Community Investment Corporation (http://ntcicfunds.com/tax-credit-basics/state-basics/)

Oster, Sharon M. *Strategic Management for Nonprofit Organizations*, (New York: Oxford University Press), p. 12 (1995).

Ostrom, Elinor. *Understanding Institutional Diversity*. Princeton, NJ: Princeton University Press (2005).

Young, Dennis, "Complementary, Supplementary, or Adversarial? A Theoretical and Historical Examination of Nonprofit-Government Relations in the United States" in Elizabeth T. Boris and C. Eugene Steuerle, *Nonprofits & Government* (Washington, D.C.: The Urban Institute), pp. 31–67 (1998).

Chapter 3 – Empowering the Nonprofit to Lessen the Burden of Government

For an organization to be designed to lessen the burden of government, it has to say so in some form in its charter, such as the wording of the purpose and description found in Section 6(b) of the charter of the Fairfax Library Foundation. It defines the existing ordinary burden, how the Foundation would help lessen it, and where—the government or jurisdiction:

> Fairfax Library Foundation is a 501(c)(3) nonprofit charitable and educational organization committed to providing supplementary support to the Fairfax County Public Library, a unit of the government of the County and City of Fairfax, Virginia. The Foundation, while reinforcing the need for continued and increased public support for the Library, serves as a catalyst for attracting private funding from individuals, businesses, and organizations to enhance library services for our community (http://fairfaxlibraryfoundation.org/aboutus/).

Given its mission and intent, the organization must have the commensurate legitimacy, authority, and power to perform as promised and as stated for it cannot be argued to a third party after it has taken action that it did not have that power. This is the legal principle of *ultra vires*—barring the organization from walking away from the liability and responsibility of an act it took that it had no authority to have taken. The authority to perform specific acts, including collaboration or the acts that such a collaboration may require, is first given upon the creation of the organization and is found in its charter. The power of the management to act accordingly is given in the *bylaws* and by an official act of the board called a *resolution*. All these are specific powers. But power does not float. It has to be invested in an organization designed to receive and to use it. This chapter is about specific powers and the characteristics of the organization that exercise them. It will help explain Planks 5 (mission), 8 (powers), 7 (exemption), why designing the nonprofit specifically as a corporation matters, and the specificity of the concept "reducing the burden of government" as defined by governments which will be the ultimate determinant of its acceptability for exempt purposes in specific jurisdictions. Finally, because a nonprofit formed to relieve a government burden may interact and collaborate with it, knowing when this interaction may cross into lobbying or politicking is important because such interactions are limited, if permitted at all. Commonly, a nonprofit created by government is prohibited from lobbying and politicking.

DOI 10.1515/9781501505799-004

The Creation of the Corporation

Even in the most obvious of cases, incorporation is necessary (a) to obtain and exercise most necessary powers; (b) for tax exemption at the Federal, state, or local levels; and (c) specifically to be exempt and be recognized as separate from government. This separation issue is huge and will be a theme in Chapter 5. Thus, the following from the State of Minnesota:

> Volunteer fire departments may qualify for exempt status if they qualify as a charitable organization and are a separate organization from the city. To be considered separate from the city, they must have either their own constitution or articles of incorporation.

Incorporation occurs on the state level. States differ in the way they express lessening of the burden of government as a motive for incorporating a nonprofit corporation. In most states it is a separate election of motives from a list consistent with the federal government and specifically with making them eligible for 501(c)(3) status and with the additional clause, "...and whatever is consistent with Federal and state law."

Utah requires that such a provision with the express wording "lessening the burdens of governments" be made in any nonprofit chartered in that state. Accordingly, Article III of the certificate of incorporation (U.C.A. Section 16-6a-202) lists several reasons. Among these are fire protection, ambulance service, and any other consistent with IRC Section 501(c)(3) status and state law. Then it requires the following specific statement as quoted:

> (a) To act and operate exclusively as a nonprofit corporation pursuant to the laws of the State of Utah, and to act and operate as a charitable organization in lessening the burdens of government, providing relief of the poor and distressed or under-privileged, and promoting social welfare by reducing unemployment through economic development

The State of New York not-for-profit law also expressly includes a motive for specific functions of interest—in this case, economic development corporation—to qualify as a 501(c)(3) corporation. It states that such:

> ...Corporations may be incorporated or reincorporated under this section as not-for-profit local development corporations operated for the exclusively charitable or public purposes of relieving and reducing unemployment, promoting and providing for additional and maximum employment, bettering and maintaining job opportunities, instructing or training individuals to improve or develop their capabilities for such jobs, carrying on scientific research for the purpose of aiding a community or geographical area by attracting new industry to the community or area or by encouraging the development of, or retention of, an industry in the community or area, and lessening the burdens of government and acting in the public interest, and any one or more counties, cities, towns or villages of the

state, or any combination thereof, or the New York job development authority in exercising its power under the public authorities law to encourage the organization of local development corporations, may cause such corporations to be incorporated by public officers or private individuals or reincorporated upon compliance with the requirements of this section, and it is hereby found, determined and declared that in carrying out said purposes and in exercising the powers conferred by paragraph (b) such corporations will be performing an essential governmental function.

The point is that a variety of ways are available to citizens and to jurisdictions to lessen the burden of government across the United States through the proper design and engagement of the nonprofit organization.

Incorporation: Process, Purpose, Powers

With few exceptions for trusts and unincorporated nonprofits, these organizations are formed as corporations. Incorporation of a nonprofit can be done by citizens, other entities, or by government by completing a state-provided form that says as in the State of Maryland:

1. That the applicant is at least 18 years of age (in the case of citizens or those signing on behalf of the government).
2. That the applicant vouches that the corporation is organized exclusively for charitable, religious, educational, and scientific purposes, including, for such purposes, the making of distributions to organizations that qualify as exempt organizations under Section 501(c)(3) of the Internal Revenue Code, or the corresponding section of the Federal tax code. That the organization has no authority to issue capital stock. The number of directors is specified, which may increase or decrease according to the bylaws and state law.
3. That no part of the net earnings of the corporation shall inure to the benefit of, or be distributable to its members, trustees, officers, or other private persons, except that the corporation shall be authorized and empowered to pay reasonable compensation for services rendered and to make payments and distributions in furtherance of the purposes set forth above.
4. That no substantial part of the activities of the corporation shall be the carrying on of propaganda, or otherwise attempting to influence legislation, and the corporation shall not participate in, or intervene in (including the publishing or distribution of statements) any political campaign on behalf of or in opposition to any candidate for public office.
5. That notwithstanding any other provision of these articles, the corporation shall not carry on any other activities not permitted to be carried on (a) by a corporation exempt from federal income tax under Section 501(c)(3) of the

Internal Revenue Code or the corresponding section of any future Federal tax code, or (b) by a corporation, contributions to which are deductible under Section 170(c)(2) of the Internal Revenue Code, or the corresponding section of any future Federal tax code.

6. That upon the dissolution of the corporation, assets shall be distributed for one or more exempt purposes within the meaning of Section 501(c)(3) of the Internal Revenue Code, or the corresponding section of any future Federal tax code, or shall be distributed to the Federal government, or to a state or local government, for a public purpose. Any such assets not so disposed of shall be disposed of by a Court of Competent Jurisdiction of the county in which the principal office of the corporation is then located, exclusively for such purposes or to such organization or organizations, as said Court shall determine, which are organized and operated exclusively for such purposes.

The end result of this is the creation of a nonprofit corporation whether by citizens or by governments except that the first point is obviously with governments since it is the legislature that is doing the creating—all assumed to be 18 years of age or more. The result is an organization with the following relevant properties automatically embedded:

1. **Motive:** A nonprofit corporation has the principal motive of advancing a public interest. Profits can only be incidental to and for advancing public welfare—it cannot be a principal motive. Hence, advancing the general public is the primary motive for transferring a burden of government to a nonprofit corporation.

2. **Liability:** Corporations have limited liability—meaning that liabilities do not normally transcend beyond the corporation. As in Chapter 1, the government is free (as would be citizens) from the liabilities of the nonprofit that it created. It reinforces this legal protection by its statement in Sections 5 and 9 of the charter as referred to in the previous chapter for the National Park Foundation:

Sec. 5. The Foundation shall have perpetual succession, with all the usual powers and obligations of a corporation acting as a trustee, including the power to sue and to be sued in its own name, but the members of the Board shall not be personally liable, except for malfeasance.
Sec. 9. The United States shall not be liable for any debts, defaults, acts, or omissions of the Foundation.

3. **Transfer of ownership:** The assets of a nonprofit can only be transferred to a nonprofit with a similar mission since it is presumed that those assets

were acquired to do that mission, preserving the use of the asset for which it was acquired no matter how or when it was acquired. This preserves the assets for relieving the burden for which they were acquired—a protection against diversion whether well intended or not. The "succession" referred to above and below has to maintain the previous mission promise of relieving the government of that specific burden. The concept here is a legal one: when a gift is made or an asset acquired from that gift, the original intent must be preserved unless released by the donor or by the courts in what is called a *cy pres* decision.

4. **Permanent Life**: Unless specifically stated otherwise, a corporation has perpetual, permanent, life and it and its mission to relieve the burden continues until it is dissolved in a way stipulated by state corporate and federal tax laws including any legal transformation (succession). Section 5:

   The Foundation shall have perpetual succession, with all the usual powers and obligations of a corporation acting as a trustee

5. **Centralized management**: A corporation can centralize management in a third party freeing the trustees to hire and design management and set procedures best suited to the burden that is being assumed. Therefore, understanding the concept of a functioning board of trustees is a chapter in, as are other features below, in this book.

6. **The issuing of capital stock**: A nonprofit cannot issue capital stock, so other ways of raising funds must be designed and the authority to do so given the trustees as the gifts, bequests, properties, and devises. But the nonprofit corporation needs money and tools by which to acquire it.

7. **Payment of dividends**: A dividend is technically either a return of capital or a return to capital—a return of part of an investment or income on that investment. It is a payment from the corporation to its owners. Nonprofit corporations do not have private owners, nonprofits do not have capital stock. Therefore, nonprofits cannot pay dividends so that, except in the case of cooperatives or a mutual, dividends are automatically prohibited and no provisions for them need be made, except as they may describe transfer of profits to the government or another nonprofit as the sole member.

8. **Bankruptcy**: The bankruptcy of a nonprofit corporation cannot be involuntary—meaning that the bankruptcy must be initiated by the nonprofit itself rather than the creditors, although in some instances the creditors can petition the Attorney General of the state to declare the nonprofit bankrupt. Further, with nonprofits there may be limitations on which assets may be liquidated to

satisfy the creditors. This is so because some of the assets of a nonprofit were acquired by mission promises of the nonprofit. When the burden is in a nonprofit corporation, therefore, some bankruptcy protection is available.

9. **Dissolution:** The right to dissolve is equivalent to the right to die and to completely terminate or to be reborn in another form through *conversion or succession*. A nonprofit is required to write its will at the time of incorporation and it becomes part of the terms upon which its charter and tax exemption are given. Moreover, a dissolution plan for a nonprofit is very simple in its requirements: The assets must go first to satisfy creditors, then to and only to another organization, 501(c)(3) with a similar mission so as to honor its restricted use. An alternative is to the State for its distribution to an organization with a similar mission; in this case, the relieving of government of that cited burden.

The above is the legal essence of a nonprofit corporation—the organizational form into which the burden of government is transferred. It brings with it specific limitations, privileges, utilities, and protections. In this case, the motive is not charitable, but public welfare; charity being one form in which the public welfare can be served. Note its characteristics, one of which is to outlive its founders and managers and to have a separate and sustainable life. They go, it stays. Also note that it cannot pay dividends, even though it may make a profit, which means that more can be retained for sustaining and fulfilling the burden of government the organization assumed and there is no private inurement. Note too that it is separate from its founders and managers, which means it is not beholden to them and may separate from them and they from it as it continues focusing on the burden it has assumed with that burden being its purpose for existing.

Now what are the organization's powers to act? Without specific transactional powers the organization cannot fulfill its purpose or promise; that is, relieve a government of a specific burden because it could not conduct basic transactions that that would require.

The Powers of the Nonprofit Corporation

A common assumption, which is incorrect, is that the specific powers of a nonprofit corporation are automatic and universal. In fact, they may differ by state and by the specific charter used to create the organization. There are standard powers and those special powers placed in the organizational design to enable the organization to tackle a specific burden.

For the normal nonprofit, part of the organizational design is choosing the right state in which to incorporate but when the mission is to tackle a specific localized burden, that choice is restricted. An organization intending to assume a burden of the government should have at least these powers enumerated by the District of Columbia, Section 29.505 where the Federal government charters its nonprofits, in order to function; to reduce its dependence on the government, and thereby truly relieve its burden; and, further, to reduce the risk to which the government would place itself by having an organization which it does not control but which could otherwise be free to act on its own. Accordingly, the standard powers are:

1. To sue and be sued
2. To purchase, take, receive, lease, take by gifts, devise or bequest, or otherwise acquire, own, hold, improve, use, and otherwise deal in and with, real or personal property, or any interest therein, wherever the situation
3. To sell, convey, mortgage, pledge, lease, exchange, transfer, and otherwise dispose of all or any part of its property and assets
4. To purchase, take, receive, subscribe for, or otherwise acquire, own, hold, vote, use, employ, sell, mortgage, loan, pledge, or otherwise dispose of, and otherwise use and deal in and with, shares or other interests in, or obligations of, other domestic or foreign corporations, whether for profit or not for profit, associations, partnerships, or individuals, or direct or indirect obligations of the United States, or of any other government, state, territory, governmental district, or municipality or of any instrumentality thereof
5. To make contracts and incur liabilities, borrow money at such rates of interest as the corporation may determine, issue its notes, bonds, and other obligations, and secure any of its obligations by mortgage or pledge of all or any of its property, franchises and income
6. To lend money for its corporate purposes, invest and reinvest its funds, and take and hold real and personal property as security for the payment of funds so loaned or invested
7. To conduct its affairs, carry on its operations, hold property, and have offices and exercise the powers granted by this chapter in any part of the world
8. To elect and appoint officers and agents of the corporation, and define their duties and fix their compensation
9. To make and alter bylaws not inconsistent with its articles of incorporation or with the laws of the District of Columbia, for the administration and regulation of the affairs of the corporation
10. Unless otherwise provided in the articles of incorporation, to make donations for the public welfare or for religious, charitable, scientific research, or educational purposes, or for other purposes for which the corporation is organized

11. To indemnify any director or officer or former director or officer of the corporation, or any person who may have served at its request as a director or officer of another corporation, whether for profit or not for profit, against expenses actually and necessarily incurred by him or her in connection with the defense of any action, suit, or proceeding in which he or she is made a party by reason of being or having been such director or officer, except in relation to matters as to which he or she shall be adjudged in such action, suit, or proceeding to be liable for negligence or misconduct in the performance of a duty
12. To determine the voting powers of members and procedures for voting by proxy
13. To determine the manner of providing notice about meetings
14. To determine what constitutes a quorum
15. To dissolve

Note that these powers give the nonprofit a wide range of financing and operating authority, including the making of loans, issuing of bonds, and selling of goods and services, tangible and intangible, and finally the right to die—to dissolve. In some cases, especially with developers, a limited power of eminent domain may also be given; and sometimes a limited policing power will be given so that the nonprofit may protect the property, users and area under its responsibility. The nonprofit may also be given powers to set prices and user fees using the most sophisticated and applicable methods. Powers may include setting user conditions, penalties and rewards, and assessment. In short, the above is a listing of basic powers, but the purpose of the organization may expand and particularize the powers of the organization even to include some sovereign powers (powers only a government is authorized to use) but restricted to the accomplishment of the mission assigned the nonprofit. Powers are part of the specific design to accomplish the objective of the nonprofit in a specific project, that is why they are enumerated by the U.S. Congress in the National Park Foundation's charter in the previous chapter and these powers are different to the ones given to a local economic development corporation or to the Virginia International Terminals which manages a port and the surrounding area.

Prohibitions

In addition to granting certain powers, state law also places specific prohibitions on nonprofits domesticated in or operating in their jurisdictions even if they were founded (domesticated) elsewhere. These prohibitions include what name may not be used. In New York State, some 24 names may not be used. In Utah, a name that does not relate to the mission of the organization cannot be used. In other states, certain words must be used such as incorporated, or corporation in Maryland.

A common set of prohibitions are;

1. A provision prohibiting the issuing of capital stock; that is, common stock for raising funds
2. A provision prohibiting the use of the assets of the organization for personal benefits (called personal inurement)
3. A provision prohibiting profit-making as a principal purpose
4. A provision prohibiting the use of the organization's assets for political purposes—except where the mission of the organization is political (Chapter 5)
5. A provision prohibiting the use of certain names or the abbreviation Inc.
6. A provision against making loans to trustees
7. A provision against inactivity especially by the board but also by the organization
8. A provision against self-dealing and conflicts of interest
9. A provision against misrepresentation and false statements in annual and other reports
10. A provision requiring annual registration

States also have prohibition on foreign (meaning chartered in another state in the U.S.) and alien (meaning chartered outside of the U.S.) corporations.

Prohibition on Nonprofit Foreign Corporations

Every state requires foreign (as defined above) nonprofit corporations to obtain authority to operate in it. A nonprofit formed to assume a burden in one state is not automatically permitted to do the same in another without its permission. But this permission is not necessary for certain types of transactions. Utah 7–135–101 describes the usual exceptions:

1. For settling disputes in its own behalf
2. For holding meetings of its board and for conducting internal corporate affairs
3. Maintaining a bank account
4. Maintaining offices or agencies for the transfer of securities or registration of membership or depositories
5. Selling through independent contractors

6. Soliciting and obtaining orders—if the orders are accepted outside of the state
7. Obtaining security interest (as lender or borrower) in real or personal property
8. Collecting debt in its own behalf
9. Owning real or personal property
10. Conducting isolated transactions and within days
11. Conducting affairs in interstate commerce
12. Grant-making
13. Distributing information to members

Of course, a foreign corporation may always apply for domestication. This is like a naturalization process in which the organization changes its charter (citizenship) from one state (country) to another. Changes in domestication are unlikely if the organization is dealing with a problem that is location-specific.

Sometimes conflicts between different state rules can be minimized or avoided by setting up independent (each having a different state of domestication) but related organizations. There is not a problem for most routine transactions, but surely every major exposure of the organization, every innovation, deserves the question: Is this consistent with our charter (the license to perform a promised mission) and is it consistent with that state's laws about how any nonprofit may perform in that specific state?

Prohibition in the By-laws and Charter

The charter is a state-granted license to operate as promised above and the state statutes and constitution address how nonprofits in general and those with specific missions must operate within that state. Commonly, a nonprofit domesticated in one state can operate directly or through chapters, branches, or affiliates in other states. These states set their own specific rules that may apply to their domestic organizations and *foreign or alien* organizations operating within their borders. Charters give the right to operate with certain powers to enable that operation; specific state codes on nonprofits specify how that right may be discharged within its borders.

The *bylaws* sometimes called the *organizing document* dictates how the organization intends to organize itself (how many officers) and conduct itself (how many meetings) within the parameters set by its charter, the rules of its state of domestication, the rules of other states where it intends to operate, and the rules of tax exemption (to be discussed next). Bylaws provide for a large range of discretion in the details of how the nonprofit may be governed and operated and still remain within the parameters set by law. Bylaws are not necessary for incorporation or to get a charter, but may be necessary to get a bank account, to attract some large donors, and to get or maintain tax exemption. They are the blueprints of the operational design of the organization and often are necessary to obtain tax exemption.

Financial Advantages and Disadvantages of Exemption

Why tax exemption? Why would the nonprofit seek it and especially to relieve the burden of a government? Note that a government does not need to seek tax exemption for a nonprofit it forms to handle its burdens as long as it keeps that nonprofit as an agency because government agencies are automatically tax exempt as such. This will be explored in future chapters. But the government and citizens may seek a separate and independent nonprofit organization and seek a 501(c)(3) exemption status. Why?

A principal advantage of a tax-exempt nonprofit is financial. It is the tax savings that can be used to help finance the mission. This is so because income and other revenues of the nonprofit are not taxed and because property and purchases (sales) are also not taxed. Exemption therefore increases the cash available to the nonprofit to do its mission. Firms have no such exemption—but they have other tax benefits such as depreciation, deductions, credits, and special tax rates on certain types of income that reduce their otherwise tax liability. Here is an itemization of the advantages of tax exemption (Tables 3.1 and 3.2).

Table 3.1. Financial Benefits of a Nonprofit Organization

1.	Exemption from certain taxes: In general income that is related to their mission and certain passive income are exempt.
2.	Lower prices: Anti-trust laws allow vendor to sell items to a charity at lower price, as long as the item purchased is for use of charity.
3.	Lower postage rates: Nonprofits pay lower postage rates provided that the envelope does not advertise a for-profit firm.
4.	Lower labor costs. Nonprofits have lower labor costs because of volunteers.
5.	Lower fees: Federal, state, and local governments may reduce or exempt nonprofits from certain fees charged firms in the same line of activity pay.
6.	No quid pro quo: Donations or fees should not require the rendering of a service or product of at least equivalent value.

7. Building and equipment: These may be obtained by donation or, in some cases, from government surplus.

8. Limited liability: The liability exposure may be limited or partial (as compared to the liability of a firm).

9. Tax-exempt borrowing: The cost of borrowing is lowered by the amount of tax exemption of interest earned by the lender and the exemption from registration.

10. Contract bids: Some government contracts either set aside or give special considerations to nonprofits.

Note: All of these benefits apply to all exempt organizations. The donor in items 6 and 7 gets a tax deduction for the donation only if the recipient organization qualifies. Of the organizations in this book only the 501(c)(3) qualifies.

Table 3.2. Financial Disadvantages of a Nonprofit Organization

1. Limited access to capital markets: Nonprofits cannot raise capital through the sale of stocks.

2. Limitation on personal inurement: Nonprofits, except certain cooperatives and associations, cannot attract capital by promising or distributing the assets of the organization to individuals as if they were owners or investors, but they can borrow in capital markets.

3. Limited profits: While there is no dollar limit on profits, profits cannot be the principal or overriding aim of a nonprofit organization.

4. Limited capacity to self-finance: Many nonprofits cannot charge enough to cover costs by virtue of the income limitations on the clients.

5. Revenue balance: While profits are not limited, the support test for certain nonprofits requires that revenues remain in balance and the test for associations usually requires that a substantial part of their revenues comes from membership dues.

6. Limited financial reward for managers: The financial rewards as a fixed salary are not the issue. Both for-profit and nonprofit managers are limited by the concept of reasonable reward. The issue is largely that the nonprofit manager cannot be paid in stocks and options. These two items have the potential of appreciating in value and can constitute the major part of the total earnings of for-profit managers.

7. Limitations on investments: For legal, moral, and sound investment reasons, a nonprofit is generally barred from undertaking highly risky investments unless its mission is to do so.

8. Limitations imposed by donors: A creditor can impose restrictions on both the nonprofit and the firm. A common stockholder of a minority share cannot tell the corporation how its money can be spent. But any individual donor can restrict how a nonprofit spends the money the individual or entity donates. Members, acting as a class, can limit the way an association uses their dues.

9. Limited creditworthiness: A firm's financial strength or credit worthiness is due in part to its ability to pledge assets to back a loan. It is also due to its ability to require, in the case of small corporations, that the borrower pledge personal assets in addition to the corporate assets. Furthermore, it can force an involuntary bankruptcy. None of this is as easily done (and occasionally not at all feasible) with a nonprofit corporation.

10. Public expectations: The misunderstanding and expectations of the public place severe and often irrational demands on the nonprofit corporation.

11. Tolerance of bad management: The tolerance of bad management and the willingness to substitute good intentions for efficient operation are eventually expressed in ruinous financial health of the organization.

In sum, the principal advantage of tax exemption is that the organization is allowed to keep a greater part of its revenues from conducting its mission, passive revenues from investment whether in securities or real estate or from royalties for use in its mission and its growth, than it would have if that portion had to be paid to the government—Federal, state, and local in the form of taxes. For a specific group of nonprofits, 501(c)(3)s, another tax benefit is derived from not only having that exemption, but from the fact that their donors can deduct the amount donated so that they are induced to give more. Tax exemption means more money to apply to the burden. It may come from (a) earnings from the burden if possible, (b) deductible contributions, (c) savings from not paying dividends or taxes, although all tax such as payroll taxes are not exempt.

How Is the Tax-Exempt Status Acquired? First at the Federal Level

Given that tax-exempt status has value, how is it acquired? Acquiring tax-exempt status begins with the IRS and in meeting its conditions. Once the IRS has granted tax exemption, most states will automatically follow with little other proof and when most states follow so do most localities, which piggyback their exempt policies on the states. Delaware is a notable exception because its exemption may be gotten either by first having the Federal exemption, or it can be gotten by the applicant merely declaring on its application that (a) it is a nonprofit, and (b) no part of the earnings will inure to individuals. Its exemption does not, however, extend to the Federal level or necessarily to other states.

To acquire tax exemption on the Federal level, the organization must pass three tests: the organizational test, the asset test, and the political test. Most states and jurisdictions are cognizant that those nonprofits that are to be free standing are better off passing the 501(c)(3) hurdles because that gives them the right to raise funds through charitable donations, that is, to induce donations because the donor gets a tax deduction. The tests are based on their attestations and the evidence drawn from their financial statements and the IRS Form 1023, which is required. For new organizations, the answers may only be an expectation but not hard evidence since they have not yet operated. Accordingly, a preliminary approval of exemption may be given pending the first couple years of operation where the evidence can be gathered and analyzed.

The Organizational Test

The *organizational test* states that the organization is organized (for example, as a corporation) and conducts an approved mission. For a 501(c)(3) that means health, education, serving the poor and the distressed, scientific, religious, the fostering of amateur sports, literary, preventing cruelty to animals and children, and for supporting other 501(c)(3) organizations. A key ingredient in the organization test is its *mission*. Each broad category, for example religious, is defined. To be religious means having a creed, religious activities and ceremonies, members and a clergy.

Moreover, within each broad category there are specific types of activities that qualify for exemption and from the list (Table 3.3). Note the abundance of choices under each broad category—all available under 501(c)(3) the same category as the traditional charitable organization if they meet the three-part test discussed in this chapter. Under what activity code in Table 3.3 would what you are contemplating fit? Can your idea of an organization meet the three-part test that would make the fit? Notice how many of these activities are detached from any traditional charitable purpose and to the functioning of governments and other citizen needs; codes 094,200, 480–484, 512, 524–525, 903, 924–926, and so on. While the traditional charitable function is extremely well represented in this table, so is the nontraditional and it is in this latter area where there may be considerable room for further growth or recognition of the creative utility of nonprofits along with variations of the traditional—a key assumption of this book.

Indeed, Table 3.3 is useful when applying for tax exemption, but it is critically useful in opportunity scanning for relieving the burden of government for everything listed is consistent with IRC Section 501(c)(3). Take a look at 525, 528, 907, 560, 524, 513, 382, 150, 063, 065, 165, 064, 417, and especially 915 for the erection and maintenance of municipal buildings an example to be used later in this book.

Table 3.3. Specifically Authorized Missions of Exempt Organizations: Candidates for Assumption of Government Burden if They Exist

Code	Code	Code
Religious Activities	042 Student housing	093 Cultural exchanges
001 Church, synagogue,	activities	with foreign country
etc.	043 Other student aid	094 Genealogical activities
002 Association or	044 Student exchange with	--- Achievement prizes or
convention of churches	foreign country	awards (use 914)
003 Religious order	045 Student operated	--- Gifts or grants to
004 Church auxiliary	business	individuals (use 561)
005 Mission	--- Financial support of	--- Financial support of
006 Missionary activities	schools, colleges, etc.	cultural organizations
007 Evangelism	(use 602)	(use 602)
008 Religious publishing	--- Achievement prizes or	119 Other cultural or
activities	awards (use 914)	historical activities
--- Bookstore (use 918)	--- Student bookstore	
--- Genealogical activities	(use 918)	Other Instruction and
(use 094)	--- Student travel	Training Activities
029 Other religious	(use 299)	120 Publishing activities
activities	--- Scientific research	121 Radio or television
	(see Scientific Research	broadcasting
Schools, Colleges, and	Activities)	122 Producing films
Related Activities	046 Private school	123 Discussion groups,
030 School, college, trade	059 Other school related	forums, panels,
school, etc.	activities	lectures, etc.
031 Special school for the		124 Study and research
blind, handicapped,	Cultural, Historical or Other	(nonscientific)
etc.	Educational Activities	125 Giving information or
032 Nursery school	060 Museum, zoo,	opinion (see also
--- Day care center	planetarium, etc.	Advocacy)
(use 574)	061 Library	126 Apprentice training
033 Faculty group	062 Historical site, records,	--- Travel tours (use 299)
034 Alumni association or	or reenactment	149 Other instruction and
group	063 Monument	training
035 Parent or parent-	064 Commemorative event	
teachers association	(centennial, festival,	Health Services and Related
036 Fraternity or sorority	pageant, etc.)	Activities
--- Key club (use 323)	065 Fair	150 Hospital
037 Other student society	088 Community theatrical	151 Hospital auxiliary
or group	group	152 Nursing or
038 School or college	089 Singing society or	convalescent home
athletic association	group	153 Care and housing for
039 Scholarships for	090 Cultural performances	the aged (see also 382)
children of employees	091 Art exhibit	154 Health clinic
040 Scholarships (other)	092 Literary activities	155 Rural medical facility
041 Student loans		156 Blood bank

Code		Code		Code	
157	Cooperative hospital service organization	203	Regulating business	---	Fair (use 065)
158	Rescue and emergency service	204	Promotion of fair business practices	236	Dairy herd improvement association
159	Nurses register or bureau	205	Professional association	237	Breeders association
160	Aid to the handicapped (see also 031)	206	Professional association auxiliary	249	Other farming and related activities
161	Scientific research (diseases)	207	Industry trade shows		
162	Other medical research	208	Convention displays	**Mutual Organizations**	
163	Health insurance (medical, dental, optical, etc.)	---	Testing products for public safety (use 905)	250	Mutual ditch, irrigation, telephone, electric company, or like organization
164	Prepared group health plan	209	Research, development, and testing	251	Credit union
165	Community health planning	210	Professional athletic league	252	Reserve funds or insurance for domestic building and loan association, cooperative bank, or mutual savings bank
166	Mental health care	---	Attracting new industry (use 403)		
167	Group medical practice association	---	Publishing activities (use 120)		
168	In-faculty group practice association	---	Insurance or other benefits for members (see Employee or Membership Benefit Organizations)	253	Mutual insurance company
169	Hospital pharmacy, parking facility, food services, etc.			254	Corporation organized under an Act of Congress (see also 904)
179	Other health services	211	Underwriting municipal insurance	---	Farmers cooperative marketing or purchasing (use 234)
		212	Assigned risk insurance activities		
Scientific Research Activities		213	Tourist bureau	---	Cooperative hospital service organization (use 157)
180	Contract or sponsored scientific research for industry	229	Other business or professional group		
181	Scientific research for government			259	Other mutual organization
---	Scientific research (diseases) (use 161)	**Farming and Related Activities**			
199	Other scientific research activities	230	Farming	**Employee or Membership Benefit Organizations**	
		231	Farm bureau	260	Fraternal beneficiary society, order, or association
Business and Professional Organizations		232	Agricultural group		
		233	Horticultural group	261	Improvement of conditions of workers
200	Business promotion (chamber of commerce, business league, etc.)	234	Farmers cooperative marketing or purchasing	262	Association of municipal employees
201	Real estate association	235	Financing crop operations	263	Association of employees
202	Board of trade	---	FFA, FHA, 4-H club, etc. (use 322)		

Code	Code	Code
264 Employee or member welfare association	Youth Activities	Housing Activities
265 Sick, accident, death, or similar benefits	320 Boy Scouts, Girl Scouts, etc.	380 Low-income housing
266 Strike benefits	321 Boys Club, Little League, etc.	381 Low and moderate income housing
267 Unemployment benefits	322 FFA, FHA, 4-H club, etc.	382 Housing for the aged (see also 153)
268 Pension or retirement benefits	323 Key club	——— Nursing or conva- lescent home (use 152)
269 Vacation benefits	324 YMCA, YWCA, YMHA, etc.	——— Student housing (use 042)
279 Other services or benefits to members or employees	325 Camp	——— Orphanage (use 326)
	326 Care and housing of children (orphanage, etc.)	398 Instruction and guidance on housing
Sports, Athletic, Recreational, and Social Activities	327 Prevention of cruelty to children	399 Other housing activities
280 Country club	328 Combat juvenile delinquency	
281 Hobby club	349 Other youth organi- zation or activities	Inner City or Community Activities
282 Dinner club		400 Area development, redevelopment, or renewal
283 Variety club		
284 Dog club	Conservation, Environmental, and Beautification Activities	——— Housing (see Housing Activities)
285 Women's club	350 Preservation of natural resources (conservation)	401 Homeowners association
——— Garden club (use 356)		
286 Hunting or fishing club	351 Combating or preventing pollution (air, water, etc.)	402 Other activity aimed at combating community deterioration
287 Swimming or tennis club		
288 Other sports club	352 Land acquisition for preservation	403 Attracting new industry or retaining industry in an area
——— Boys Club, Little League, etc. (use 321)	353 Soil or water conservation	
296 Community center	354 Preservation of scenic beauty	404 Community promotion
297 Community recreational facilities (park, playground, etc.)	——— Litigation (see Litigation and Legal Aid Activities)	——— Community recrea- tional facility (use 297)
298 Training in sports		——— Community center (use 296)
299 Travel tours	——— Combat community deterioration (use 402)	405 Loans or grants for minority businesses Job training, counseling, or assistance (use 566)
300 Amateur athletic association	355 Wildlife sanctuary or refuge	
——— School or college athletic association (use 038)	356 Garden club	
301 Fundraising athletic or sports event	379 Other conservation, environmental, or beautification activities	——— Day care center (use 574)
317 Other sports or athletic activities		——— Referral service (social agencies)(use 569)
318 Other recreational activities		
319 Other social activities		

Code	Code	Code
——— Legal aid to indigents (use 462)	483 Support, oppose, or rate political candidates	534 Busing students to achieve racial balance
406 Crime prevention		535 Racial integration
407 Voluntary firemen's organization or auxiliary	484 Provide facilities or services for political campaign activities	536 Use of intoxicating beverages
——— Rescue squad (use 158)	509 Other legislative and political activities	537 Use of drugs or narcotics
408 Community service organization		538 Use of tobacco
	Advocacy	539 Prohibition of erotica
429 Other inner city or community benefit activities	Attempt to influence public opinion concerning:	540 Sex education in public schools
	510 Firearms control	541 Population control
Civil Rights Activities	511 Selective Service System	542 Birth control methods
430 Defense of human and civil rights	512 National defense policy	543 Legalized abortion
	513 Weapons systems	559 Other matters
431 Elimination of prejudice and discrimination (race, religion, sex, national origin, etc.)	514 Government spending	
	515 Taxes or tax exemption	**Other Activities Directed to Individuals**
	516 Separation of church and state	560 Supplying money, goods, or services to the poor
432 Lessen neighborhood tensions	517 Government aid to parochial schools	561 Gifts or grants to individuals (other than scholarships)
449 Other civil rights activities	518 U.S. foreign policy	
	519 U.S. military involvement	——— Scholarships for children of employees (use 039)
Litigation and Legal Aid Activities	520 Pacifism and peace	——— Scholarships (other) (use 040)
460 Public interest litigation activities	521 Economic-political system of U.S.	——— Student loans (use 041)
461 Other litigation or support of litigation	522 Anti-communism	562 Other loans to individuals
	523 Right to work	
462 Legal aid to indigents	524 Zoning or rezoning	563 Marriage counseling
463 Providing bail	525 Location of highway or transportation system	564 Family planning
	526 Rights of criminal defendants	565 Credit counseling and assistance
Legislative and Political Activities	527 Capital punishment	566 Job training, counseling, or assistance
480 Propose, support, or oppose legislation	528 Stricter law enforcement	
481 Voter information on issues or candidates	529 Ecology or conservation	567 Draft counseling
	530 Protection of consumer interests	568 Vocational counseling
482 Voter education (mechanics of registering, voting, etc.)	531 Medical care service	569 Referral service (social agencies)
	532 Welfare system	572 Rehabilitating convicts or ex-convicts
	533 Urban renewal	

Code	Code	Code
573 Rehabilitating alcoholics, drug abusers, compulsive gamblers, etc.	902 Emergency or disaster aid fund	snack bar, food services, etc.
574 Day care center	903 Community trust or component	917 Thrift shop, retail outlet, etc.
575 Services for the aged (see also 153 and 382)	904 Government instrumentality or agency (see also 254)	918 Book, gift, or supply store
——— Training of or aid to the handicapped (see 031 and 160)	905 Testing products for public safety	919 Advertising
	906 Consumer interest group	920 Association of employees
Activities Directed to Other Organizations	907 Veterans activities	921 Loans or credit reporting
600 Community Chest, United Way, etc.	908 Patriotic activities	922 Endowment fund or financial services
601 Booster club	909 4947(a)(1) trust	923 Indians (tribes, cultures, etc.)
602 Gifts, grants, or loans to other organizations	910 Domestic organization with activities outside U.S.	924 Traffic or tariff bureau
603 Nonfinancial services or facilities to other organizations	911 Foreign organization	925 Section 501(c)(1) with 50% deductibility
	912 Title holding corporation	926 Government instrumentality other than section 501(c)
Other Purposes and Activities	913 Prevention of cruelty to animals	927 Fundraising
900 Cemetery or burial activities	914 Achievement prizes or awards	928 4947(a)(2) trust
901 Perpetual care fund (cemetery, columbarium, etc.)	915 Erection or maintenance of public building or works	931 Withdrawal liability payment fund
	916 Cafeteria, restaurant,	990 Section 501(k) child care organization

Another aspect of the organizational test is that the organization has a management and governance structure and any business or personal interrelationships between those who occupy these positions be identified and a conflict of interest policy be adopted and implemented. The terms of that statement must be reasonable, capable of putting a wall between those actual or potential conflicts, and be monitored and reported through various mechanisms of transparency. Yet another part of the organizational test is to determine who controls or can potentially control the organization and can conceivably subvert its purpose or cause it to be subservient to personal or business objectives even while conducting its principal mission. Is the source of that potential power, unequal voting power, financial support, or relationships to other key persons in the organization management or governance structure or support base? These questions are answered not only in the form of narratives, but by actual numbers; for example, how much did the top donors give and what proportion of the total support is from them? These are not trivial in many government-created nonprofits such as the National Park Foundation that seek large donations whether from firms, foundations, or individuals. Donors may have more than a causual interest between a nonprofit created for lessening the burden of government and presenting a favorable face to the government agency. This may be a call for transparency, not a prohibition on giving.

The Asset Test

The *asset test* states that no part of the assets or earnings of the organization shall inure to the benefit of, or be distributed to its members, trustees, officers, or other private persons except for reasonable compensation or to further the mission of the organization. Among other things, this provision prohibits the paying of dividends. Upon the dissolution of the nonprofit corporation, the assets may be distributed to and with an organization of similar mission and classification, or to the Federal, state or local government. Any asset not so distributed must be distributed by the county court in which the principal offices are located and only to organizations that are organized exclusively for the same purposes as the dissolved organization. The asset test goes beyond financial assets and includes tangible and intangible assets. Thus, the amount that top persons in governance, in management, in hired assistance, including contractors, receive from the organization as compensation, benefits, or the value in use, is used to determine if the assets are being used for the benefit of private persons. Such use is prohibited.

The Political Test

The *political test* states that no "substantial part of the activities of the corporation" can be for propaganda purposes, to influence legislation, and the organization may not participate in a political campaign on behalf of or in opposition to any specific candidate for public office. We shall discuss the subtleties of these concepts of politics, lobbying, and "substantial" as opposed to exclusive later because how much is permitted depends upon how the nonprofit is further classified once it falls within the tax exempt umbrella, Section 501(k) of the U.S. Tax Code. For example, with the 501(c)(3) designation, the most favored tax-exempt group, lobbying is permitted but limited, and the term *no substantial political use* (as opposed to none) is more applicable to a 501(c)(4) when it comes to *partisan* politics than it is to a 501(c)(3) which is not limited in nonpartisan education.

Tax-Exempt Status Acquired on the State and Local Levels

It is safe to conclude that if the federal government has granted income tax exemption to the organization the state and local government will as well. The federal exemption applies to corporate income tax. For each state and local government, the issue is whether such exemption is appropriate for their property and sales taxes as well. This has led to a wide variation in how state and local governments exempt nonprofits from property and sales taxes and what they consider to be a burden of government worth recognizing. The federal conditions for exemption under the theory of lessening the burden of government are given in the Preface of this book and in Louthian and Henchey (1998). But states and localities differ in (a) whether they consider the lessening of the burden of government sufficient for exemption from their particular taxes, and (b) what constitute a lessening of a burden to them.

For example, in Minnesota (2010) an organization must first qualify as a 501(c)(3) under the U.S. Tax Code. Then the following must be considered (note point 3 below):

1. Whether the stated purpose of the undertaking is to be helpful to others without immediate expectation of material reward;
2. Whether the institution of public charity is supported by material donations, gifts, or government grants for services to the public in whole or in part;
3. Whether a material number of the recipients of the charity receive benefits or services at reduced or no cost, or whether the organization provides ser-

vices to the public that alleviate burdens or responsibilities that would otherwise be borne by the government;

4. Whether the income received, including material gifts and donations, produces a profit to the charitable institution that is not distributed to private interests;
5. Whether the beneficiaries of the charity are restricted or unrestricted, and if restricted, whether the class of persons to whom the charity is made available is one having a reasonable relationship to the charitable objectives; and
6. Whether dividends, in form or substance, or assets upon dissolution, are not available to private interests.

All six of these requirements, in addition to first being a 501(c)(3) must be met, except that failing to meet 2, 3, and 5, that the organization provides acceptable justification to the assessor. Once exemption has been granted under these provisions, they cannot be removed except for material changes in the facts in the actual operation of the organization.

In Pennsylvania it is different. Large nonprofits in Allegheny County have worked out a formula for payments in lieu of taxes, called PILOT. Current state law based on the Pennsylvania Supreme Court ruling in the 2012 decision commonly known as *Pike County* (Mesivtah Eitz Chaim of Bobov, Inc. v. Pike County Board of Assessment Appeals, 2012) requires that the nonprofit first be deemed a "purely public charity" (but see point 3) by its having satisfied the following five-part criteria imposed by the Pennsylvania Supreme Court in Hospitalization Utilization Project in 1999 (known as HUP):

1. Advances a charitable purpose;
2. Donates or renders gratuitously a substantial portion of its services;
3. Benefits a substantial and indefinite class of persons who are legitimate subjects of charity;
4. Relieves the government of some of its burden; and
5. Operates entirely free from private profit motive.

Upon the satisfaction of this first test, the localities may employ the detailed methodology, definitions, and procedures that were adopted in the Institutions of Purely Public Charity Act of 1997 (IPPCA) to determine if the purely public charity qualifies for property and sales tax exemption. It cannot bypass or supplant step one by resorting to the definition of purely public charity that is in IPPCA (sometimes referred to as ACT 55)—which would allow the organization to qualify as a purely public charity if it operated primarily for the following in any combination—to relieve poverty, to advance education or religion, to prevent and treat disease or injury, to treat mental retardation and disorders, to fulfill a government purpose or a purpose of advancing moral, social, or physical objectives, and to place the burden of proof that it does not qualify on the authorities—explicitly given the presumption that it is to the organization itself. None of this can follow without first meeting the requirements of HUP, which was derived from distilling what case history in Pennsylvania indicated were the criteria used to determine if an organization was a purely public charity.

In Minnesota, where by its own admission the state toiled not only about property tax exemption to the point of surveying over a focus group of nonprofits, the state settled on these guidelines which is noteworthy because it specifically makes reference in point 3 to lessening the burden of government:

> Minnesota first requires that the nonprofit be exempt from the federal income tax under 501(c)(3). Then it requires that they meet the following conditions for exemption of property tax:
>
> (1) That the stated purpose of the undertaking is to be helpful to others without immediate expectation of material reward;
>
> (2) That the institution of public charity is supported by material donations, gifts, or government grants for services to the public in whole or in part;
>
> (3) That a material number of the recipients of the charity receive benefits or services at reduced or no cost, or whether the organization provides services to the public that alleviate burdens or responsibilities that would otherwise be borne by the government;
>
> (4) That the income received, including material gifts and donations, produces a profit to the charitable institution that is not distributed to private interests;
>
> (5) That the beneficiaries of the charity are restricted or unrestricted, and, if restricted, whether the class of persons to whom the charity is made available is one having a reasonable relationship to the charitable objectives; and
>
> (6) That dividends, in form or substance, or assets upon dissolution, are not available to private interests.
>
> A charitable organization must satisfy the factors in clauses (1) to (6) for its property to be exempt under this subdivision, unless there is a reasonable justification for failing to meet the factors in clause (2), (3), or (5), and the organization provides to the assessor the factual basis for that justification (http://www.minnesotanonprofits.org/mcn-at-the-capitol/Property-Tax-Final-Revenue-Bulletin.pdf).

In general, and where states do not use a blanket exemption, the current objection in cases in New Jersey, Pennsylvania, Minnesota, and Washington D.C. for example, is based on (a) whether the organization can be considered a purely public charity, and (b) whether the organization serves to reduce the burden of local government by providing a public service to the citizens in the locality in which they are located. The concept of pure charity or the evidence of service to the local public and whether the organization meets that test varies by state and locality and is always in dispute. Because of these state variations, the concept used throughout this book is the Federal rule, which most states have as a prerequisite.

What is the upshot of this section? Citizen-created nonprofits even for relieving the burden of government cannot assume that they will receive tax exemption at the local level. Every level of government determines its burden and whether the nonprofit lessens it in a way that is within the public's interest. Almost exactly these words appear in the Minnesota and Pennsylvania legislation referred to earlier in this section unless (a) they as the National Park Foundation, being a federally chartered nonprofit, is exempted by Congress in the organization's charter, (b) they are exempt by the specific state law, and (c) they meet the specific requirements of the local jurisdiction.

Some Factors that Threaten the Loss of Tax-Exampt Status Under 501(c)(3)

Just because a nonprofit is created to relieve a burden of government does not protect it from the threat of losing its exempt status. Most states, and consequently their localities, would not consider exempting a nonprofit in the first place or continue that exemption unless it can first demonstrate that the organization continues to be exempt by the Federal government. Therefore, we focus here on protecting the Federal exemption. What are the factors that place the nonprofit at risk so that the nonprofit loses its exemption?

The five principal reasons for the loss of tax-exempt (not the corporate) status are:

1. Significant departure from the mission.
2. Subversion of the assets to personal benefits including persistent corruption, self-dealing, and personal gains.
3. Excessive lobbying (see the discussion below for meaning).
4. Politicking: influencing politics in a nonpartisan way (see the discussion below).
5. Persistent failure to obey reporting requirements and to pay taxes including employment related taxes for which nonprofits are generally not exempt.

Note that the loss of exemption is not equivalent to a dissolution. In a dissolution, the corporation disappears. In the loss of an exemption, the corporation continues to exist and operate but without the benefit of whatever level of tax exemption it carried. Also note that at times rather than extract the exemption, the IRS on its discretion might impose an intermediate sanction—something between but not total removal of exemption.

Excessive Lobbying

A nonprofit that has assumed a burden of government is likely to have considerable contact with lobbying. But it is common that nonprofits created by government to lessen a burden of government are barred from lobbying and politicking. Virtually every one of the nonprofits created by government in this book has such clauses. Those created by citizens do often omit a lobbying prohibition but contain a politicking prohibition. Almost all of the citizen-created nonprofits in this book permit lobbying but not politicking. What is permitted that is not lobbying or politicking and therefore occur without the fear of penalty? Lobbying is the attempt to influence legislation through influencing the public and/or an attempt to influence legislation through influencing any member or employee of a legislative body or an employee of government who may participate in the formulation of legislation.

Certain actions common among nonprofits are not considered to be lobbying. These include:

1. Sharing the results of nonpartisan research
2. Studying or discussing social and economic problems
3. Providing technical assistance to a jurisdiction or governmental body when that assistance was requested in writing
4. Communicating or appearing before a legislative body on themes that may influence the organization, its mission, and its tax-exempt status
5. Communicating between the organization and its members on a proposed legislation unless the members are urged to take specific action or to encourage others to act
6. A communication with a government or legislative official when that is not intended to influence legislation

Politicking

Expenditures for political (partisan) purposes are, in general, prohibited for all 501(c)(3) organizations in particular but permitted in a limited way in others such as the 501(c)(4), and totally permitted as a sole purpose in those organizations known as Section 527s or political organizations and committees. Moreover, these expenditures are totally prohibited by government-created nonprofits. Political expenditures include those intended to promote or oppose a candidate, the control of such an organization by a candidate, the dissemination or propagation of a political philosophy or position with the aim of promoting a party or influencing a campaign. When these occur, in any amount, the organization and the managers are taxed. This tax can be avoided if the amount spent and the materials distributed are recovered and if safeguards are implemented to protect against political actions in the future.

Summary and Preview

The last chapter was about the key planks necessary for creating a functioning organization to lessen the burden of government. This chapter was about power and the provision of power in the legal design of the organization to exercise these powers to lessen the burden of government that is designed as its mission. The next chapters divide these organizations into groups according to their characteristics, exemption, and function. Some of these organizations are designed to be doers and others not; some can only be formed by government; some can be formed either by government or by citizens. There are material differences in form and in function.

Bibliography

Minnesota (2010). http://www.minnesotanonprofits.org/mcn-at-the-capitol/Property-Tax-Final-Revenue-Bulletin.pdf

Pike County (2012). http://www.lgc.state.pa.us/deskbook06/Issues_Taxation_and_Finance_04_Pennsylvania_Charitable_Exemptions.pdf and http://www.portal.state.pa.us/portal/server.pt/community/charities/1244

Institution of Purely Public Charity Act, 10 P.S. Sec. 371.et.seq. (1997). http://www.portal.state.pa.us/portal/server.pt/community/bureau_of_charitable_organizations/12444/the_institutions_of_purely_public_charity_act/571856#5

Louthian, Robert and Amy Henchey, "Lessening the Burdens of Government" (1993). https://www.irs.gov/pub/irs-tege/eotopicb93.pdf

Chapter 4 – Nonprofits as Doers in Reducing the Burden of Government

Central Park Conservancy, Inc. is a 501(c)(3). It is an official manager of New York City's Central Park. It does so with in-kind service contributions from the New York City government. It is responsible for the day-to-day maintenance and operation of the park—including landscaping, the preservation of the grounds and historic monuments, and the managing of visitors and programs. It is one of the most famous parks in the world. Over 90 percent of its total support of nearly $200 million in 2013 came from the public in the form of contributions, grants, fees and gifts. In the context of this book, it is a *doer* and 509(a)(1) as will be described in this chapter. Some doers are more dependent on contributions than others and this is significant in what they need to know and how they operate. This chapter will also distinguish *doers* from *facilitators*, and the various categories of each. How do they become so described, how do their networks help to lessen the burden of government?

One way of distinguishing one doer from another is whether it is more likely to attract contributions and be more dependent upon contributions than business income or whether or not it is capable of earning its own maintenance primarily through charging for what it provides. Knowing this helps to craft the organization so that it is well equipped with the fundraising or business income-generating powers to function sustainably. Another way of distinguishing them is whether they provide services directly to the public or through a membership group. This makes them different in how they operate, but also may affect the kind of exemption they will be given. These are also the subjects of this chapter.

The nonprofits described in the last chapter help reduce the burden of government and can be divided into two large groups: (a) there are doers—the ones most likely to assume and to carry out a burden of government, and (b) there are facilitators—those like the National Park Foundation that principally raise and finance activities within their mission, and those who facilitate in other ways such as being a catalyst or a coordinator so that others might directly and effectively lessen the burden of government. The IRS regulations provide for tax exemption for both doers and facilitators. All doers and all facilitators may not have the same exemption, however, not only because what they do and how they do it may differ, but especially because of how they finance the burden they have assumed. Again, some do it by charging and some by selling a service—business income from doing their mission. These are very different business models.

DOI 10.1515/9781501505799-005

Take the Internet Corporation for Assigned Names and Numbers (ICANN), a California 501(c)(3) that affects us all in the fields of commerce, communications, and technology—anyone using the Internet—because it assigns names, numbers, and domains on the Internet. It is an example of a doer that charges. It does not depend upon contributions, but on business income. In its own words:

ICANN's sole activity, to which it devotes 100% of its time and resources, is the administration and management of various technical and policy functions necessary to ensure the continued stability, interoperability and effective performance of the domain name system of the Internet, through the development of consensus concerning those issues... Because the domain name system is the collection of names and addresses that enables the Internet to properly route information, the purpose of this activity is to maintain and enhance the performance and availability of the Internet for the general public. The performance of these technical and policy functions furthers ICANN's tax-exempt purpose of lessening the burdens of government because, if it were not for ICANN's willingness to assume responsibility, the U.S. government would be obligated to continue to perform these functions so that the Internet would continue to be a viable and useful resource for individual and business users around the world.... ICANN is organized and operated exclusively for the charitable purpose of lessening the governmental burden of providing DNS management. ICANN [https://archive.icann.org/en/financials/tax/us/appendix-4.htm] qualifies as 501 (c)(3) to lessen a burden of government.

ICANN directly lessens a burden of government in the way it describes and its application for exemption gives "lessening the burden of government" as the reason for the exemption.

This chapter is about what qualifies an organization to be an independent, tax-exempt doer assuming a burden of government under the 501(c)(3) umbrella. ICANN above is an independent corporation, tax exempt under 501(c)(3) and earns over 90 percent of its revenues from fees it charges. The remainder it earns principally from investment. Nothing comes from the government. First, what is a doer?

A doer lessens the burden of government by implementing a policy that:

1. The government recognizes as a burden by statute, by implementing it, and by actively collaborating in its implementation. In its application for exemption, ICANN noted that if it didn't do its work the government would have had to continue doing it, and that the government was collaborating with it and sanctioning it through a working agreement.

2. The organization is capable of discharging the burden, shown with evidence. ICANN is a California nonprofit corporation with the powers, struc-

ture, and means of financing to perform the function as evidenced in the working agreement between it and the Department of Commerce.

3. The public is to be the beneficiary with no personal benefits inured to any private party; for example, dividends and special arrangements.

Thus, ICANN is a doer. It met the test of qualifying as a 501(c)(3) with the purpose of lessening the burden of government and the organizational, political, and assets tests, but where under Section 501(c)(3) does it fit?

The 501(c)(3) category has two major subdivisions of doers. One category must depend heavily on contributions to finance the burden they have assumed. The other relies heavily on business income—charging. They both can use a combination of business income and contributions. What distinguishes them is the relative weight of business income to contributions in how they are financed. Both categories differ from 501(c)(5) and (6) doers because these two cannot accept deductible contributions and rely on fees.

The Doers: Distinguishing Examples

Three examples of doers are described next. The first two are 501(c)(3)s. Note how they are financed differently from the 501(c)(6). Recall that to lessen the burden of government, the IRS recognizes 501(c)(3)s, (c)(4)s and (c)(6)s so that doers can be found in any of these categories. Since the money to finance the burden that the organization is assumed to likely come primarily from one or a combination of (a) contributions and (b) the sale of the service called business income, these organizations have to be designed to assume a burden that is compatible with their ability to access these sources.

It is clear that outside of the 501(c)(3) umbrella the burden is likely to be financed by business income since they do not have access to tax-deductible contributions. With the 501(c)(3) category, a combination is possible; so within this category burdens that must be paid for from contributions to burdens that can be paid for by business income can be assumed. The issue within the 501(c)(3) category, therefore, is the weight that an organization may have to put on contributions relative to business income. Here examples of these various categories:

The American Bureau of Shipping (ABS) is a 501(c)(6) membership organization that gets zero revenues from government or from contributions. In 2013, it earned $675 million of its $749 million from fees it charged for its inspection and certification services to shipping and marine related firms. This inspection would have been the responsibility of the U.S. Coast Guard to do. To carry out this burden, the ABS has some 220 affiliates in about 70 countries. They work under an agreement with the U.S. Coast Guard as the agency that would have had to carry out these duties. ABS is a doer financed solely from direct sales of its services.

Now, 501(c)(3)s are different. There are those that (a) rely almost completely on contributions or grants because they have clients who cannot afford to pay to cover full costs; and (b) those that rely on contributions but mostly their own earned business income because they have clients who are able and are willing to pay to cover more than full cost. Universities, hospitals, and museums are examples. What permits those that rely on contributions to do so is that the service they provide can attract donors because of some highly motivating reason such as patriotism, charity, altruism, the desire to preserve the environment, to cure, and so on.

The Vietnam Veterans Memorial Fund (VVMF) is a 501(c)(3) doer. This is a group of veterans who said to Congress: If you give us three acres of land on the National Mall, we will raise funds from private sources, design and build a memorial, and operate it all on private funds. They have almost maximally relieved a burden of the federal government of what is now known as "The Wall" or the Vietnam War Memorial. They not only raised the funds, but they do the work and maintain the project with the cooperation of the National Park Service.

VVMF raises its money principally from the public in the form of contributions. Some of its total support comes from private gifts and contributions from individuals, firms, and foundations together called the public. So it lessens a burden of government by paying for it primarily through contributions.

The American Red Cross (ARC) is a version of a 501(c)(3) also created by citizens, and eventually chartered by the United States Congress under the laws of the District of Columbia with the powers and structural design features discussed in the last two chapters. It reduces the disaster burden of government through the more purely charitable mode and does so through contributions of money, goods, and volunteer human services. It is out in the field of work, but it does more. It is the U.S. representative to and under the Geneva Conventions. The Conventions are a series of internationally agreed upon protocols about the treatment of combatants and civilians in conflict and in disasters. It is not an accident that when there is a domestic disaster and the President makes an appeal, it is to give to the ARC. So, the ARC does the work, making it a doer, and it affords these burden-lessening services through contributions. Yet, the amounts it gets from contributions is a fraction of what it earns as business income from the sale of blood-related products The combined annual business and investment income of ARC and its chapters is over $3 billion. The blood services are supported primarily by sales covered by a third party—insurance companies, the clients, and in some cases government. Therefore, it finances this burden primarily through sales—business income.

Categorizing 501(c)(3) Doers

The 501(c)(3) category is broken down into two major types of doers—the 509(a)(1) type that depend mostly on contributions and the 509(a)(2) type that depend mostly on business income. These two groups have exactly the same exemptions but different income compositions; and as they move more toward being heavily dependent upon business income, they may look like or behave more like firms, relying on business income, there are greater restrictions to restrain them assuming that they do not wish to be taxed as firms.

To enhance their ability to perform complex tasks and sustainably so, both of these 501(c)(3) groups may create subsidiaries, auxiliaries, and chapters that extend and deepen their reach and these units may also be exempt. Either may form by itself or in collaboration with another 501(c)(3) what is known as a 509(a)(3) which is a subsidiary or an auxiliary and assign it a role that provides the technical, marketing, or financial expertise, for example, fundraising or business service it is not proficient or sufficient at doing; and they may also form chapters or units that allow them to operate over an immense space. In general, they can do all of these things with greater flexibility than government can.

What is critical about these 509(a)(3)s is that they serve one purpose: facilitate and assist the 501(c)(3) parents in fulfilling their responsibilities. They are parts of an interlocking collaboration to fulfill the task of lessening the burden that was assumed by the performing 501(c)(3)s doers or combinations of them. With this, we can move to understanding not only the differences between these two major 501(c)(3) doers—those dependent more upon contributions and those more on business income and the supporting structure, but the 509(a)(3)s they can build to help them fulfill their promise to lessen the burden of government as their mission. Again, government does not have this flexiblity or access to voluntary money to support a burden or to create this type of structure that gives it the flexiblity in doing so; but nonprofits do.

Doers and Internal Networks

Now we have within the 501(c)(3) category two types of doers and their supporting structures. How does each differ from the other and what does each contribute? They differ in that one group depends more upon contributions than business income; and the other does just the reverse yet they both can serve the lessening of the burden of government.

In general, 509(a)(1)s contain the real charities—what they do mostly benefits the poor, the indigent, and the disadvantaged and usually at zero cost to them or at a nominal charge which often does not cover full cost. The legislative debate in some states—Minnesota, Pennsylvania, and New Jersey—has been stipulating that if you wish to relieve us of a burden, be a 501(c)(3) and specifically under that, a 509(a)(1); that is, serve the poor and raise the money from contributions to do so. And in so doing, be exempt under Section 170(b)(1)(A)(vi) which refers to public-supported charities—a broad category.

Yet, there are many, many nonprofits that fall into this 509(a)(1) category that serve all income levels. The Vietnam War Memorial is an example. Their principal source of income is contributions. This allows them to serve the undifferentiated general population—anybody, not necessarily those who can pay. This categorycontains those nonprofits that serve people across the income spectrum and without reference to income as a qualification for their services and whose services are not paid for by a direct charges to them as users. These nonprofits depend more heavily on contributions rather than business income. Contributions work well for them because of their mission, because they cannot put up a wall around the wall to effectively exclude those who do not pay, and because they wish to reach an infinite public including those who cannot pay.

They differ from the 509(a)(2)s because these can sustain themselves and deliver the benefits by charging a fee to do so and both this "charging to use, to play or to get" and the kinds of services they provide are the nontraditional within the meaning of charity: "You pay to play or to partake." It is the difference between getting soup in a soup kitchen and getting entry on a toll highway. Both categories can lessen the burden of government—one mostly through contributions and the other mostly through fees. The financing capability of the organization influenced by the nature of its mission and public should be reflected in the design and expectations of the organization. Both require a numerical hurdle that they are doing so with public support.

Demonstrating Public Support When Dependence Is on Contributions

The public demonstrates its acceptance of government policy and performance by voting. They reflect their approval of the performance of the nonprofit that is supposedly lessening the burden of government by what is known as pubic support—a quantitative metric backed by qualitative data of their monetary and nonmonetary contributions. This is the topic of this section. Can they demonstrate public support in doing what they are in order to lessen the burden of government?

When the nonprofit depends upon business income, price and total revenues are reasonable signals of its value to the public—that is, the amount and willingness of people and entities to pay for what they receive from the organization. But when the organization is one that cannot for whatever reason charge for full cost and relies upon contributions, an alternative measure is the extent to which its total revenues reflect such contributions. This ratio is another way of demonstrating that the nonprofit has public support for what it is doing. In this case, lessening the burden of government. Here is how that works for the two 501(c)(3) groups—the 509(a)(1) and (a)(2):

Proof of public support for 509(a)(1) organizations, those relying mostly on contributions, comes in the form of passing one of two tests: the one-third public financial support test, or the 10 percent financial support and facts and circumstances test. The facts and circumstances test shows that the organization operates in a public manner although it cannot demonstrate this by showing that at least one-third of its financial support is from the public.

To demonstrate that it "normally" has public support through the one-third test, a nonprofit must show that over the preceding four years, at least one-third of its financial support came from the government or the general public, foundations, corporations, or a combination of these. The words support, normal, and public are specifically defined.

Support includes gifts, contributions, membership fees (excluding the portion that is an assessment for special services), net income from unrelated businesses, gross investment income, revenues from taxes levied by the government for the benefit of the nonprofit, and the value of facilities furnished by the government free of charge if those facilities are usually rented or sold.

Note that 509(a)(1) support refers to income from unrelated business rather than to related business. This means that a nonprofit cannot include in its calculation of support any revenues it receives from an activity for which it is tax exempt if the payment benefits the payer. To illustrate, a nonprofit exempt as a day-care center cannot include as support fees from parents for caring for their children. These payments benefit the payors and are in conjunction with the tax-exempt purpose of the day-care center. If the daycare center owns a fast-food restaurant, an unrelated business catering to the general public, the net income from this business may be included in the calculation of support. If the parents made a contribution for assisting children other than their own who are members of the general public, this would be support. If the parents contributed services that are not deductible contributions, these contributions will not be included in the calculation of support. Do you see the rationale? It does not tempt the organization to penny-pinch poor people to show public support.

Membership dues qualify as support only after adjustment is made for the portion of the dues that is a payment for services, such as a magazine. It is only the portion that is for the general support of the organization that counts.

Facilities received by the organization from the government cannot be included as support unless the government usually charges for the use of these facilities or sells them.

Public means governmental units and the general population. A gift or contribution from a community trust, itself a tax-exempt nonprofit, is a contribution from the public if these trusts receive their funds primarily from contributions from the general public and are based on public participation. Earnings from an endowment created by public funds are also considered a public contribution. Obviously, contributions from foundations, persons, and firms are also public. It is the concentration of contributions from a few people that creates the problem.

The word *normally* also has a precise meaning. It spans the revenue-raising experience over the preceding four years. The classification of the nonprofit is determined for the current and the next year based on the performance of the organization over the four preceding years. It is publicly supported in years 2016 and 2017 if it passes the public support test in the years 2012 through 2015. It is publicly supported in 2017 and 2018 if it passes the test for the period 2013 to 2016, and so on. A nonprofit can have its classification changed depending on how it performed over the preceding four years. Since a classification is not given in perpetuity, a publicly supported organization will lose that favored status when it can no longer prove public support.

Calculation of Public Financial Support: 509(a)(1)

For a nonprofit to be classified as a public organization under 509(a)(1) as defined in Section 170(b)(1)(A) by proving it has public support, it must demonstrate that a portion of its total support is from the general public. How is this proved? One test requires that at least one-third of such support must come from the general public (government, foundations, firms, and people from the community at large). Alternatively, the nonprofit may show that at least 10 percent of its support comes from the general public, but that the facts and circumstances surrounding the operation of the organization prove that it encourages and involves public participation and that there is a continuous effort to attract public support, for example, through fundraising drives.

One focus in applying the 10 percent facts and circumstances test is on the source of the other 90 percent of income. Is there some reasonable way to say that the amount came indirectly from the public? Is the source of income, for example, from an endowment created by the public? If so, the nonprofit wins or maintains classification as a 509(a)(1) public organization.

If the interest and dividends are from the investment of funds in a publicly created endowment, the organization may be less likely to pass if that investment income is from a gift by a single individual. The circumstances are important.

The IRS may focus on the 10 percent rather than on the 90 percent. If this came from one or two individuals, lack of public support may be implied. Because the test is subjective, we cannot be sure how the given example will be interpreted. The nonprofit would probably be helped if a major source of funds is a publicly supported community chest.

The IRS has five factors that it considers in its facts and circumstances test— which it calls its "attraction of public support requirement":

1. *Percentage of financial support*: If the organization normally gets at least 10 percent of its financial support from the public, is this chiefly from an endowment or investment created by the public rather than from a few individuals?
2. *Sources of financial support*: Do the sources of the 10 percent represent government and a diversity of people rather than just a few?
3. *Composition of the governing board and open membership*: Is the board a cross-section of the community, including elected or appointed public officials? Is membership in the organization open to the general public?
4. *The availability of facilities or services factor*: Does the nonprofit open its facilities to the public, and does it conduct or participate in programs for the general public?
5. *Other factors representing broad community support*: Does the organization appeal to people who have some broad but common interest? Are the dues of the organization for individuals set so high that a substantial part of the public cannot enroll?

In short, the price the government is willing to pay in the form of exemption is contingent upon performance in receiving contributions and in deriving earnings from the sale of the service—all dependent upon the public's acceptance of the organization and what it does. The completely failed organization with no contributions or income derived from performing its purpose gets zero value out of having an exemption. This outcome repeats itself in another form with the 509(a)(2) since they are different but still must show public support.

Doers Depending Mostly on Business Income

The 509(a)(2)s, unlike the 509(a)(1)s, have clients who can pay for services, and these fees, rather than contributions, are a principal source of their income to finance the burden they have assumed from the government. These fees are virtually monopolistic market rates. They are *monopolistic* because frequently there are no competitors and *market* because the rates cover full cost, plus an allowance for reserve, replacement and repairs, and a margin. In short, the fees are so set that the organization is self-financing and sufficient.

Here is an example of a 509(a)(2) lessening the burden of a government entity:

The Retiree Resource Corporation (RRC) in Knoxville, Tennessee, is a 501(c)(3) and specifically a 509(a)(2), which means that it is principally a doer that can finance its projects through fees and the sales prices it charges its clients—not its members. These fees and prices are derived from transactions that are integral parts of its mission. The mission is to provide the Tennessee Valley Authority (TVA) with retired TVA workers and to provide the TVA with related services throughout the TVA operations including its watershed management, recreational, energy, environmental, and educational missions. RRC revenues from these activities were virtually 100 percent of all of the over $45 million they earned in 2014—the last period for which we could get data.

The Tennessee Valley Authority is a corporate agency of the United States that provides electricity for business customers and local power distributors serving 9 million people in parts of seven southeastern states. The TVA receives no taxpayer funding, deriving virtually all of its revenues from sales of electricity. In addition to operating and investing its revenues in its electric system, the TVA provides flood control, navigation, and land management for the Tennessee River system and assists local power companies and state and local governments with economic development and job creation.

The TVA is a wholly owned but self-funded agency of the United States government. It meets its funding needs with operating revenues and power program financing. TVA debt securities are issued only for power program purposes—including financing of existing debt—and are secured by revenues from its power system. The TVA issues a variety of debt securities: TVA Discount Notes have maturities of less than one year; TVA may also issue long-term bonds with final maturities of up to 50 years. These bonds and notes are available to investors through banks, brokers and investment dealers.

Because RRC is an organization that facilitates the TVA, it is in the context of this book classified as a *facilitator*—the subject of the next chapter. Thus, the concepts work here designate whether the organization is a doer or a facilitator.

ICANN, a doer, is also a 509(a)(2). Over 90 percent of its $232 million in revenues came from fees and it netted $85 million in 2014. ICANN is in the context of this book a doer. Therefore, the distinguishing characteristic of 509(a)(1) and 509(a)(2)s for the purpose of exemption is not whether they are doers or facilitators, but how they are financed. The latter is quite capable of doing it on its own; financing itself. Yet it needs to demonstrate some public support for what it does.

So, these are the rules. A 509(a)(2) is subject to two tests: the one-third public financial support test, the denominator of which is different from that of the 509(a)(1); and "the not more than one-third support" test, which has no 509(a)(1) counterpart. The 509(a)(2) organizations differ from 509(a)(1)s in what is included in the calculation of support (the denominator for calculating the one-third public support). Unlike 509(a)(1)s, they include not only unrelated business income but also related business income.

Related business income of a 509(a)(2) from any one source can only be the greater of $5,000 or 1 percent of the organization's total support. The effect of this is to recognize that, unlike the organizations under Section 509(a)(1), which tend to the needy who may not be able to pay, these organizations often function on the ability of their clients to pay a fee. But the rule limits the extent to which the charging of that fee to a few or a select class of people (clients) can substitute for the expression of public support.

A similar rule for these organizations says that a source's gift (not just fees) can only be counted as public to the extent that it is not more than the greater of $5,000 or 1 percent of the organization's support. Therefore, the organization cannot escape by turning to single donors.

To pass the second test, the 509(a)(2) must demonstrate that the sum of their gross investment income and their after-tax profits from unrelated businesses does not exceed one-third of their total support. This latter test has the effect of forcing the search for public financial support even for organizations that could be self-supporting. Since price is a measure of value in a commercial setting, public welfare is a measure of value with these types of nonprofits.

Gross investment income includes rents, royalties, interest, and dividends but does not include any income that would be classified as unrelated. As we shall see in Chapter 10, the effect of excluding unrelated business income in calculating gross investment income is that some investment could be denominated by the IRS as unrelated and, therefore, be double-counted if not for this rule.

In sum, both the 509(a)(1) and (a)(2) organizations must demonstrate public support, and in this sense they are both publicly supported nonprofits. Both must have a mission to advance public welfare and both may conduct related and unrelated businesses. The basic difference is that the 509(a)(2) organizations are financed more by business income, particularly related business income, than are the 509(a)(1) organizations. Museums are good examples because their support is heavily weighted in the direction of fees, subscription revenues for magazines, sales of related art products, and other business income, and depends less on contributions by individuals or foundations. The backbone of 509(a)(2) organizations is that they are good businesses conducting a public service and generating a substantial amount of their support through sales. They may operate in highly competitive or in monopolistic markets. Business acumen and perspective matter.

Subsidiaries, Affiliates, and Holding Companies as Internal Facilitators

Supporting organizations are a vital in the network of an organization lessening the burden of government. Some of these organizations directly help provide support for government agencies. The New York Public Library and the Library of Congress, have several such supporting organizations. St. Jude's Children's Hospital is able to provide such extensive free services to children with cancer, to their families, and to do the research and other work it does because of a supporting organization that raises all the funds for these services. A supporting organization may support one or several organizations dedicated to the same mission; for example, environmental care; or it may be designed to be integrated into part of the organization of one or the other of them such as being a subsidiary or free standing entity but yet tied to one or more supporting organizations because of its required annual contributions to them, which must be of significance to them and a significant part of the revenues of the supporting organization.

In general, supporting organizations lessen the burden of government by being facilitators enabling the finances of the doers' mission since the only mission of a supporting organization is to support a mission of the organization(s) which it supports. It can have no other mission. Supporting organizations enable the doer to focus on the quality, quantity, extension, and innovation of doing and less on direct fundraising. The East Baltimore Development Foundation is a 501(c)(3) which, in its own words, is a supporting organization to The East Baltimore Development Corporation. As a supporting organization, it too must meet the requirements of Section 501(c)(3) and file a Form 990. In 2014, its net assets were over $61 million. It is not a trivial contributor. It is also a Type I supporting organization meaning, in part, that it is dedicated to significantly supporting only the work of this one organization which also sits on its board.

Supporting organizations are tied to doers in a variety of ways. Principally through who appoints whom and how many to the board, with what operational, decision-making, and policy influences, and through the charter of the supporting organization. Here are some details that may influence the crafting of these 509(a)(3) organizations, supporting organizations, and their relationships to the doers. Do note the safeguards that exist so that the money flows from the supporting organization to the supported ones and their causes; that is, lessening the burden of government, and that under different crafting arrangements the supporting organization can do the appointments of the board of the supported organization or vice versa. The crafting of the board is important and discussed in Chapter 6.

1. Their exclusive purpose is to support 509(a)(1)s and (a)(2)s in their missions. They have no mission other than that.
2. In performing this support role, they may make grants to the organization they support, to another entity supporting the same organization as they do, or to individuals on behalf of the organization they support.
3. They cannot be controlled by a disqualified person; that is, a donor or a person with a significant economic interest in them.
4. They must have a delineated relationship to the organization(s) they support.
5. This defined relationship in Type I support organizations means that the organization is operated, supervised, or controlled by the supported organization which does so by appointing the majority members of the board of the supporting organization—making the latter subordinate or a subsidiary to the former; the former is like a parent to the latter. The charter of the Type I organization also names the organization or the mission it is supporting.
6. Type II also names the organizations or causes it is supporting but its entire board, or a majority of it, is made up of the members of the boards of those organizations. Therefore it is tightly controlled by the supported organization and the two are more tightly knit as brothers and sisters subject to the same persons in control of them both.
7. A Type III support relationship is yet different. It is not lateral (Type II) or one above the other (Type I) because it is independent in its organizational structure. The supported organization does not control its board. Furthermore, it need not state in its charter what organization or mission it intends to support. A Type III supporting organization has to (a) annually notify of the amount it sends the supported organization each year, send them a

copy of its Form 900, and a copy of its charter; (b) show that it is responsive to these organizations by virtue of the fact that these organizations have some representation on its board, or its board on theirs, or that a ranking officer of the supported organization is involved in their decision-making; (c) have the option of being functionally integrated doing fundraising itself, by itself, for transmittal to the supported organization—fundraising that had the supporting organization not existed the supported organization would have had to do to finance mission; or (d) be able to appoint the majority of the board and officers of the supported organization and to provide substantial direction over the decisions, programs, operations, and policies over the Type III organization; or (e) be non-functionally integrated, in which case it needs to make significant distributions annually to the supported organizations ammounting to about 10 percent of their support,or that induces their attention because of its size, or its importance, because without it, they could not have performed certain activities crucial to their mission.

8. A Type III organization may be created to support one or more government agencies by carrying out some of its activities that would have been carried out by the government agencies if the supporting organization didn't.

A Specific Statewide Example of Supporting Organization That Lessens the Burden of a Government Agency

By virtue of Section 258.015 of Florida law, citizen support organizations for the Florida Park Service are required to be incorporated and to be certified as 501(c)(3)s. Their boards do not have to have a park employee, but one must participate in their meetings. Park employees, not their family members, are barred from serving on the board of a Citizen Support Organization (CSO). Their mission is to support the park service through fundraising, volunteer work, programs, docents, tours, and otherwise as may be agreed upon with the top management of every park. They operate exclusively for the state park system and for the individual parks. Every such agreement has to be in writing and accompanied by a budget in which the CSO furnishes at least 60 percent of the funds. Each CSO submits an annual budget and plan of operations including fees to be charged. Moreover, they submit annual reports on governance, activities, and volunteer hours and submit audited reports as required. They and their volunteers are covered by the state liability insurance policy.

Title Holding Companies

A special form of subordinate corporation, a title holding company, may be formed by a 501(c)(3) to assist it in lessening the burden of government. A title holding company, a 501(c)(2), is one that not only holds the title to real property, but manages it, collects the rent, and transmits it to the 501(c)(3). This is particularly helpful in situations such as housing, community development, and conservation activities that the government requires, mandates, or is financially involved.

Other Categories of Doers

To this point, we have recognized the 501(c)(3) as a principal group of tax-exempt organizations designed to lessen the burden of government. The Internal Revenue Code also allows (c)(4)s and (c)(6)s.

This is significant because it means that a 501(c)(4) can do so not for charitable reasons but for civic and social betterment and it can do so by providing a service to its members without the façade of charity or poverty. And a 501(c) (6) can do so without a charity pretense and while enhancing a profit opportunity for its members.

Here is a 501(c)(4) IRS factual example taken from and used by the IRS itself. I have chosen it because it also exemplifies what it means to be lessening a burden of government:

The Case: An organization provides bus transportation during rush hours between a suburban community and the major employment centers in a metropolitan area because of inadequate bus services during those important hours. The membership of the organization is made up of residents of the suburban community. The organization contracts for buses and drivers, plans routes and schedules, and arranges for volunteers to collect fares. The service is provided to the community in general but is used mainly by the residents of the suburban community. The Board of Directors is elected by members of the suburban community and serve without compensation. All meetings of the board are publicized and open to the general public. Fares are not sufficient to cover the cost of operations and the organization solicits and receives financial assistance from local government to continue its operation of the bus service.

The Ruling: The organization provides a useful service to the community; the service is not commercially available and is open to all community residents, and the service is subsidized by governmental financial assistance. The activity is conducted by volunteers and, therefore, is not the conduct of a business with the general public in a manner similar to organizations that operate a bus service for a profit. The organization is promoting the common good and general welfare of the people of the community within the meaning of Treas. Reg.1.501(c)(4)-1(a)(2) and qualifies for exemption under IRC Section 501(c)(4). (Rev. Rul. 78-69, 1978-1 C.B. 156 (http://www.taxanalysts.com/www/freefiles. nsf/Files/EO%204.pdf/$file/EO%204.pdf).

Below are two examples of membership groups that can be described under 501(c)(6) that are doers, yet they represent professional and business interests and affect our lives every day. One is formed by private entities and one is formed by government. Observe how they reduce the burden of government by taking over an otherwise certain government function and operating through their members to benefit the general public. Moreover, they both work with written agreements with the government and neither takes a penny from it. Observe also that they are self-financing, a condition that will be addressed in Chapters 7–11. Notice also that the burdens are not charitable or philanthropic, and that all three remove a sizeable burden from government—meaning that this strategy: creating and engaging nonprofits to reduce the burden of government is not about trivial things that nonprofits can do. The burden, financial and operational, are removed. Because the members are the direct beneficiaries with the ability to pay, they can be charged a fee for the benefits they receive from the policy being implemented and from their membership in the organization in general. Because the members incorporate these benefits in what they offer the public, they get a superior product and service and are the ultimate beneficiary. The fees charged the individual members may be deductible as an ordinary and necessary expense, but not as a charitable deduction. In these two cases, the general public benefits from the removal of uncertainties and risks.

First, the Financial Industry Regulatory Authority (FINRA) is a 501(c)(6) that does the kind of work the Securities and Exchange Commission (SEC) is responsible for and oversees, but FINRA is not attached to the government. It relieves the government of the training, the overseeing, and the regulating of all persons doing securities business in the United States. It has its own board and staff and supports itself through fees and assessments of its members and earnings from its investments. It is not a creation of the government, but technically of its founding members—securities firms. It is not a government creation; but it does work the government requires and would have had to do consistent with the law. It relieves the burden of government by assuming an essential function FINRA is accountable first to its members and then to the SEC and the U.S. Congress; but it is controlled by its members, whose interests are served as is the public by market member transparency, rules of performance, and order. It qualifies under the theory that a demonstration that a government burden is being relieved is the dependence or cooperation of the government on the non-profit.

Second, the Securities Investors Protection Corporation (SIPC) is a 501(c)(6) tax-exempt nonprofit formed by the U.S. Congress by the laws of the District of Columbia and included as part of the Securities Exchange Act of 1934. It is a membership organization made up of broker-dealer firms in securities, and insures the public—investors—against specific acts of broker-dealer liquidity problems. It relies upon fees and assessments of its members, broker-dealers, and sets and enforces its own rules. It is not part of the government. It qualifies as reducing the burden of government under the theory that it was created by government for what would otherwise have been a governmental purpose. Like FINRA, it regulates members for the benefit of the public. But unlike FINRA, which gets its tax exemption by reference to a specific section of the IRS Code, SIPC get it's by writing the terms of the code into its charter.

A General Comparison of Doers

In all of the categories of doers discussed above, there are those that have memberships and those that do not; but the last two groups are especially noted for their membership tied together with a common identity or interest and their sole dependence upon some sort of fee either from their members and/or for their services for financing themselves and the burden they seek to lessen. They have no public support constraints like the 509(a)(1) or (2). They are responsive first to their membership—not the general public. The general public derives its benefits from the members. Some are doers and some facilitators. The common characteristics that distinguish them from the 501(c)(3)s are:

1. They do not cater to the general public.
2. They do not need the general public's support in money or in-kind.
3. The burdens they lessen are the ones that affect an identifiable group of people or entities and, through them, to an indefinite, general public.
4. They are able to bring substantial political and lobbying power to the cause of their members.
5. They are financed and the burden they finance is focused and often singular.
6. They rely almost exclusively on business income and investments with near if not zero contributions from the public.
7. They have zero or near zero contributions because they cannot accept deductible contributions and must make that known, but they can create affiliates and other 501(c)(3)s that can accept contributions.

8. These groups are not subject to the extent of public disclosure—the disclo-
    sure of Form 990—to the public as are 501(c)(3)s.

Their singular difference is that one is concerned with civic involvement and
welfare and can lessens the burden of government along those lines, but meeting the same criteria as to what constitutes lessening the burden of government,
and the other does it primarily through attacking business and professional
burdens.

As a general rule, what difference does it make in relieving the burden of
government? If the burden does not require some form of processing in order for
the general public to benefit, then a nonprofit that is not a membership group
would do. It implements the policy directly so that the general public is the
direct beneficiary. If the policy requires processing in order for the general public to benefit, then a membership group may be preferred. Processing involves
professional learning and sharing, shaping and refining the policy so that it is
readily applicable and receivable by the persons who implement the policy on
or for the benefit of the general public, and the formulation and enforcement of
rules and discipline of enforcement—peer (as opposed to state prosecutorial)
pressure—leading to greater acceptance and conformity. Membership is also
important when there is a need for confidence, where the involvement of the
public at large is not particularly helpful but expert knowledge is; when there is
an importance of focus and timeliness of response.

The general powers and authority to function given these groups is not unlike those in Chapters 2 and 3 except that these membership-related powers are
especially relevant:
1. Rules on qualification, rights, and responsibilities of members.
2. The organization's powers over members and membership.
3. Specific qualifications, number, and quorum of board of directors.
4. Rules limiting the liabilities of members and the organization to members.
5. Rules on amendments, dissolution, and reporting.

Lessening the Burden of Government: The Benefits and Justification of Tax Exemption

All of the nonprofit organizations in this and other chapters are beneficiaries of
tax exemption. All the 501(c)(3)s are tax exempt on gifts and donations they
receive and on revenues they receive from performing their missions; in this
case, lessening the burden of government in a specific way. The 501(c)(4)s and
(6)s mentioned above are not eligible for tax deductible contributions, so that

does not apply to them. However, they are eligible and do get tax exemption on their business revenues so long as it is related to their missions.

These exemptions are not gifts or subsidies; they should be thought of as compensation in a contractual sense, and a payment of part of the cost of producing the lessening of a burden. Contributions to these nonprofits and the income they derive from doing their missions, in this case, the lessening of the burden of government, have the effect of increasing the funds available for that purpose. For 501(c)(3)s it works this way:

1. Donations made to them are tax deductible by the donor—providing an incentive to give.
2. Contributions received by the organization are not considered taxable revenues making 100 percent of what was given available to the organization.
3. Revenues derived from selling that service are also not taxed making 100 percent of that also available for further use in lessening the burden of government.

Tax exemption is therefore neither a gift nor a reward. In contract terms, it is a payment by the government (foregone taxation) for the organization's lessening its burden. Therefore, the government rightfully has expectations that the organization that presents itself as lessening the burden of government is doing so and is neither misrepresenting truth nor being fraudulent in the extent to which it demonstrates public support (the public values what it is doing, so it is willing to support it).

Summary and Preview

Creating nonprofit organizations to lessen the burden of government involves specific things and specific sections of the Internal Revenue Code, principally 501(c)(3), (c)(4) and (c)(6). This chapter has been about the doers—the organizations that get the job done and their own internal subsidiary, auxiliary, or holding companies that serve as internal facilitators over which they have some direct control. Notice too that these doers need a measureable amount of public support annually to maintain their tax exemption—meaning that the public supports and values their performance. From this perspective, having the nonprofit lessen the burden of government by assuming certain missions leads to greater efficiency—all things equal.

The next chapter continues this line, but emphasizes the facilitators rather than the doers and how they not only support doers individually, but coordinate a collaborative effort to lessen the burden of government. Further, unlike this chapter, it emphasizes facilitators that are not beholden to the doers or any particular doer in a network of doers.

Chapter 5 – Nonprofit as Financiers and Facilitators in Reducing the Burden of Government

Federal, state, and local tax laws provide for tax-exempt nonprofits that lessen the burden of government directly—the *doers*—and for those who do so indirectly—the *facilitators*. The principal function of facilitators, the subject of this chapter, is to serve the doers making them more likely to succeed. They include nonprofits that finance the doers—the private foundations,and, in some cases, the community foundations some of which simply give and are known as private non-operating foundations. They also include others who both do and give and are principally self-financing This chapter breaks these groups out into those that facilitate through financing and those that facilitate through coordinating.

This chapter focuses on external facilitators: (a) those that are 501(c)(3)s that provide financing, (b) those that are government-created that provide both financing and facilitation particularly through the coordination of efforts of nonprofits, be they 501(c)(3)s, (c)(4)s, or (c)(6)s, and (c) those that are hybrids. They are all considered external to the network of doers because they are not controlled by any member of the network as discussed in Chapter 4. The doers cannot demand or order a response from these organizations with respect to finance or facilitation.

Two Government-Created Examples: To Be Close But Not Controlled

We begin with two government-created nonprofits that are closest to Type III supporting organizations (Chapter 4) and progress to facilitators that are completely unattached.

The National Park Foundation is not a subsidiary of the National Park Service. The Board of Regents of the University of California is not a subsidiary of the individual universities in the California university system. Article 9 of Section 9 (a) of the California Constitution says:

> The University of California shall constitute a public trust, to be administered by the existing corporation known as "The Regents of the University of California," with full powers of organization and government, subject only to such legislative control as may be neces-

DOI 10.1515/9781501505799-006

sary to insure the security of its funds and compliance with the terms of the endowments of the university...

The Regents of the University of California shall be vested with the legal title and the management and disposition of the property of the university and of property held for its benefit and shall have the power to take and hold, either by purchase or by donation, or gift, testamentary or otherwise, or in any other manner, without restriction, all real and personal property for the benefit of the university or incidentally to its conduct....

The Board of Regents of the University of California is a government-created facilitator. It is an independent trust with the powers of a corporation, but it is attached to the government. It may inherit, buy, hold and dispose of properties for the benefit and use of its member universities, each of which is a doer. But it also acts as a board of trustees, writing procedures and policies covering key issues such as academic hiring, promotion, retention, investment, admissions, fundraising, bonding, borrowing and debt issuance, risk management, and so on; but it does not do the work of research and teaching done by each campus, a corporation, with concomitant rights and powers. It is an independent nonprofit subject to its own ability to sue and be sued.

As discussed in previous chapters, the following should emerge in designing and engaging nonprofits to lessen the burden of governments:

1. What, conceptually, it means and requires to design a tax-exempt nonprofit corporation to reduce the burden of government.
2. What, conceptually, it means and requires for the organization to be a doer that actually performs the burden from one that plays a facilitating role. Both are admissible as tax-exempt.
3. What, conceptually, it means and takes for designing the organization to be a tax-exempt doer—especially one that creates its own facilitating organization that is subordinate to or an auxiliary to it.

Chapter 4 was about point 3. This chapter continues on the same line, the distinction between the doer and the facilitator, but with emphasis on the latter; and, as always, consistent with Sections 501(c)(3), (c)(4), and (c)(6) or exemption because of being an agency of government. This chapter divides the facilitators into two major groups—that of financier and that of coordinator or overseer. These may be independent of or superior to the doer in the organizational chart of what becomes the creation of a system, if that is desired, for lessening the burden of government. This is exemplified by the California Board of Regents, described above. But all arrangements do not have to be government-created or similarly attached. What is significant is the design of the individual unit as financier or coordinator (or both) to be operative and to meet the tax-exempt hurdle.

The Nonprofit Financers

The principal function (the mission) of nonprofit financers is to finance the doers. When the principal purpose of the nonprofit created either by government or by private citizens is to raise funds, whether it is called an endowment, a corporation, a trust or a foundation, it is subject to the private foundation rules. These rules are intended to protect the assets from overly aggressive investments—equivalent to what we shall see in a later chapter as a protection of donors against misrepresentation, and yet another chapter protecting the assets against corruption. It is also to protect against self-dealing and the use of the might of the foundation for political or business purposes or over investment in a single business. Moreover, the private sources often used in the charters created to lessen the burden of government is without exception a reference to private foundations whether formed by citizens, governments, or corporations, giving rise to the relevance of this discussion.

What is the private foundation?

A private foundation is a 501(c)(3) that does not have to meet the public support test as discussed in earlier chapters. This means it can be funded by a single individual, family, or corporation or small group of them. The basic strategy of the private foundation is to receive tax deductible donations, invest them, and distribute them according to a plan that would enable the foundation to live into perpetuity or to the specific period of time set by its board.

There are two types of private foundations.

First, there are the private operating foundations which only finance qualified projects, that is, projects operated by 501(c)(3)s, makes some program related investments particularly in high-risk ventures, and provides seed money for the doers. More often than not, private foundations provide some funding for nonprofits designed to relieve the burden of government even those that are formed by government. The National Park Foundation is an example of this type of foundation, as is the Fairfax County (Virginia) Park Foundation.

But citizen-created private foundations also play a critical role in lessening the burden of government often through funding or co-funding programs for which the government would otherwise have been responsible (if the programs were at all undertaken. In 2016, for example, the Bill and Melinda Gates Foundation made direct gifts to the Shasta County Office of Education and the Tubare County Superintendent of Schools totaling over $3 million for network education in those Washington State Counties. It also gave the Kentucky Department of Education over $6.6 million for improving education in grades K-12. The Annie E. Casey Foundation, a Baltimore private foundation, describes itself as making grants that help Federal agencies, states, counties, cities and neighborhoods across the country to create more innovative, cost-effective responses to the issues that negatively affect children: poverty, unnecessary disconnection from family, and communities with limited access to opportunity (http://www.aecf.org/about/). In the context of this book, it helps to lessen the burden of government by financing social and administrative innovation. In one of its program-related investments, the Annie E. Casey Foundation guaranteed a $15 million dollar loan to a Baltimore 501(c)(3) to help it finance an area revitalization program.

The point being made is that relieving a burden of government with private foundations can occur (a) through a foundation dedicated to that purpose, or (b) a foundation dedicated to a larger purpose. Furthermore, private foundations created by citizens are a principal source of revenues of the doers including those created by government.

The other type of private foundation is the operating foundation—of which there are relatively few—less than 10 percent of all foundations. They, too, are 501(c)(3)s that do not have the burden of demonstrating public support. The distinction here is that they are not required to make distributions to the doers, as the private non-operating foundations are required to do, and to report annually; rather, they self-finance much of what they do as doers.

Endowments operate very much like private, non-operating foundations; except their funds come from a variety of donors—many using highly sophisticated methods made available to them through the endowment. These will be discussed later in the book. When the government or private citizens create a doer, they would invariably give the doer the power to set up an endowment and require the trustees to oversee it, hire auditors and financial advisors, receive audit and other reports, and set and revise investment policies. Furthermore, the endowment may be separately incorporated and with its own management within the corpus of the doer or the financial facilitator. That management reports to the board and is not necessarily subordinated to the management of the nonprofit doer or financial facilitator.

The central and common problem faced by all of these are (a) maximizing the contributions to them, (b) maximizing the returns on the investments they make with these, and (c) making distributions based on capital budgeting techniques of the amount that will be distributed to the doers.

In general, the way private foundations serve to lessen the burdens of government are:

1. Created and financed by a corporation, individuals, or a small group with the sole intent of financing public organizations, such as public charities, and without the desire to demonstrate public support or a close alignment with a group of publicly supported organizations

2. Created by governments to raise funds from private sources including private foundations started by citizens
3. Created by these same parties to discharge a mission that qualifies under Section 501(c)(3), lessening the burden of government, but with the intent of having the organization be principally self-supporting and not dependent on further public contributions than that which created it

The Rules of Foundation Operation

Private foundations, including those created for lessening the burden of government, operate under the nonprofit rules as described under IRC Section 501(c)(3) and the rules of trust in the state where they were incorporated. These latter rules stipulate governance and governance structures, reporting and fiduciary requirements, liabilities and indemnification agreements, and the levels of risk tolerance or risk exposures that may be taken. Why are these rules important? Please go back to the descriptions and missions of the organizations described in the previous sections and see how vulnerable they are, absent these rules, to acts of corruption and misuse of the assets of the organization. The Federal tax exemption rules are fairly straightforward and hold across states. They are as follows:

Disqualified Persons and Self-Dealing

The concept of a disqualified person is about self-dealing. This rule reduces the risk that well-placed persons would take economic advantage of an organization. The key to understanding self-dealing from the perspective of a private foundation is the term *disqualified person*. This is a person or entity that is barred from having a business relationship with a private foundation. One such person is a *substantial contributor* to the private foundation. A substantial contributor is a person or entity who gives a total of $5,000 or more if this amounts to at least two percent of all contributions received by the foundation since its beginning. But the law does not stop here.

- The spouse, children, parents, and grandchildren of a substantial contributor are also substantial contributors, even if they did not contribute a penny. Based on the legal principle of attribution, the theory is that close relatives such as spouse and children are subject to the control and influence of the contributor. In the eyes of the law, they are all one. Oddly, brothers and sisters are excluded from the taint of attribution for private foundation purposes.

- Attribution also extends to businesses in which the substantial contributor owns 20 percent or more of the voting interests. If the business is a substantial contributor, so is the owner or owners. Attribution runs both ways.
- Management or anyone who has authority to set policy is also a disqualified person. The attribution rule also applies to the family of the managers of the nonprofit and their businesses and disqualifies them from engaging in certain business transactions with the organization.
- Government officials are also disqualified persons, including elected as well as appointed officials and at every level of government and in every branch, judicial, legislative, or executive. The same attribution rule is applied. Government officials are included among disqualified persons to preclude the use of the private foundation to influence these officials. The conditions under which government officials may receive benefits from private foundations are generally restricted to nonmonetary awards, annuities associated with employee programs during periods that the government official previously worked for the foundation, reimbursement for travel costs if the purpose of the travel was consistent with the tax-exempt purpose of the private foundation, and payment in anticipation of employing the government official if such payment is made within ninety days of termination from government service.

Self-Dealing

Direct or indirect business transactions between the private foundation and disqualified persons as defined above can lead to penalties imposed by the state and the IRS for self-dealing. What kinds of transactions lead to charges of self-dealing? Hiring, loans, the sale and purchase of assets, paying excessive compensation or reimbursement of expenses, providing facilities to disqualified persons, and the leasing of space by a disqualified person to the private foundation are all subject to charges of self-dealing.

There are some exceptions worth noting. A lease by a disqualified person to a private foundation is not self-dealing if no rental fees are involved. Self-dealing is not incurred if the transaction is for less than $5,000 in one year or if the transaction is generally favorable to the organization. The basic way to avoid issues of self-dealing when a disqualified person must be engaged in a business transaction of any type is to be sure that the transaction is ordinary for such a private foundation and is necessary to discharge its duties, the good or service could not otherwise have been provided more favorably by dealing with a qualified person, and the private foundation was appreciably the net beneficiary of the transaction. We shall return to self-dealing in Chapter 6 as it pertains to trustees and Chapter 13 as to compensation.

A penalty for self-dealing may be imposed on the self-dealer as well as the foundation management if it can be shown that the management participated in the action or could reasonably be expected to have known about it, did not try to stop it, engaged in it, or remained silent. The penalty to the self-dealer can rise to 200 percent of the value of the transaction. The penalty can rise to 50 percent of that amount for the manager.

While these penalties are imposed by the IRS, an individual may bring civil charges. Revenue Letter 9047001 presents an example of a combination of terms we have used. About half the space of a building owned by a private foundation is occupied by a for-profit company owned by the foundation manager. The company was a disqualified person with respect to the foundation because of its ownership by the foundation manager. It did not matter that the property leasing was done by a property management company with which the manager had no association. The foundation had veto powers over leases and guess who exercised that veto power on behalf of the foundation? The manager. This was declared self-dealing.

Distribution of Income

Unlike public organizations, private foundations are required to distribute their income annually. These rules are intended to force the facilitator, especially the financiers, to spend a minimum annually to help doers. Three types of distribution meet the qualification.

The private foundation may distribute funds for paying expenses and for making grants to public organizations [509(a)(1), (a)(2), and (a)(3)] for conducting those activities for which the private foundation is tax exempt. These may be grants, but they can also be loans. These loans are called program-related investments.

A second type of distribution that qualifies is a set aside to purchase assets to be used in the tax-exempt purpose if such set asides are absolutely necessary (as they are in a building program) and if the funds will be used within sixty months. Set asides or accumulations must be approved by the IRS.

A third type of qualifying distribution is the amount spent to purchase assets to be used by the private foundation in its tax-exempt mission or other charitable purpose. These latter amounts, unlike the set asides, do not have to receive prior IRS approval.

The actual dollar amount that a private foundation must distribute is technically determined. Basically, it is substantially all (although 85 percent is acceptable) of the greater of either its minimum investment return or its adjusted net income. Its minimum investment return is the fair market value of its assets not used for tax-exempt purposes, minus the debt associated with those assets, multiplied by five percent. Its adjusted net income is all income, including those from unrelated businesses, minus the expenses associated with producing that income.

The failure to distribute the correct amount can lead to stiff penalties, starting at 15 percent of the amount that should be distributed and rising to 100 percent if the distribution is not made in the time allotted for correction. Fortunately, unlike the self-dealing tax, this tax does not fall on the management but on the private foundation itself. When in doubt, a distribution is often preferable, since any such amounts may be carried over the next five years.

Jeopardy of Investments

Private foundations and their managers are prohibited from making investments that would jeopardize the financial well-being of the organization. These rules are intended to safeguard against the reckless and imprudent use of assets intended for the lessening the burden of government. Included among the prohibited actions are certain investment strategies, such as buying puts and calls, warrants, buying stocks on margin, selling short, and trading in commodities futures or in futures markets in general. This poses a problem of interpretation, since some of these actions, such as buying a put, are viewed in some investment quarters as defensive and conservative in the sense that they may put a limit on losses. Interpretation of the motives for certain transactions is subjective based on the investment intent and strategy, the frequency with which they are used, and so on. States may restrict the type of securities or the companies whose securities may be bought.

Certain investment risks are acceptable and encouraged if they are program related. Offering loans to individuals (or nonprofits) deemed to be among the least preferred risks by a commercial lender is acceptable as long as the making of such loans is within the tax-exempt mission of the nonprofit.

If this rule is violated, a five percent tax is imposed on the foundation and another five percent on the manager who is aware of or participates in the investment decision. In a case such as this, the finance or investment committee of the board of directors, the president, and the investment officers of the organization could all be held responsible.

Excess Business Holdings

There is a limit on the business holdings of a private foundation. No more than 20 percent of the voting stock or interest of a single business may be owned by a private foundation and all its disqualified persons combined. These rules are intended to reduce the risk that the facilitator will hold excess business interests, not directly related to the lessening of the burden for which it was founded, even if the interest was acquired through a gift and is profitable. Some types of businesses are unaffected by this rule. These are program-related businesses and businesses that make their income through dividends, royalties, rents, interest, or so-called passive income rather than by sale of goods and services. In addition, some foundations, such as Kellogg and Hershey, are exempt from this rule.

Where the nonprofit and its disqualified persons combined do not own (control) 20 percent of the voting stock, they may own unlimited amounts of nonvoting stocks. Their holding could exceed the 20 percent of voting stocks and move up to 35 percent if it is clear that someone other than the disqualified person effectively controls the corporation.

In the case of partnerships, the rules are exactly the same as they are for corporations. However, partnerships do not issue stocks. So the words "profit interest" are substituted for voting stock and the words "capital interests" are substituted for nonvoting stocks.

What does the foundation do if it receives a gift that causes an excess of business holdings? In general, it has five to twelve years (five plus an extension of seven if granted) to divest itself of such holdings. Private foundations have had to divest themselves of department stores, public utilities, aircraft manufacturers, automobile companies, golf courses and social clubs, newspapers, hotels, to name a few. This is not hard to understand. Many of their holdings came in the form of bequests of stocks by principal shareholders of these companies.

A private foundation cannot own a sole proprietorship unless obtained by bequest or prior to 1969. The reader should not confuse a sole proprietorship with sole ownership of a corporation or unrelated business as previously described. The term sole proprietorship simply means that the business is owned by a human and unincorporated. The nonprofit would be totally liable for any failures of the business. If sole proprietorships were allowed, all the assets of the foundation would be exposed to claims by creditors of the business. A large claim against the business that it could not meet by itself would lead to claims against the assets of the foundation.

Should the rule on excess business holdings be broken, the penalty is five percent of the value of the excess holdings. This penalty is imposed on the foundation, not the management. The penalty could rise to 200 percent if left uncorrected in the time allotted.

Prohibited Expenditures

Some expenditures by private foundations, such as those aimed at influencing legislation, can lead to tax penalties. Legislation includes any action by a legislative body at any level of government. School boards, commissions, and authorities such as housing or economic development on any level are considered administrative bodies rather than legislative bodies and expenditures to influence them are not prohibited. In addition, expert testimony in response to a written request by a legislative body or nonpartisan studies that are made public are not construed to be attempts to influence legislation and are not prohibited. These rules are intended to reduce the risk that the assets and specifically the cash of the organization would be used to apply pressure on the government or for political reasons.

Expenditures to influence the outcome of any election are prohibited. Such expenditures include producing or distributing supporting literature or paying campaign workers or providing facilities for campaigns. Critically, any expenditure such as voter registration is also prohibited if it is centered in a specific geographical area. This prohibition is not violated

1. If the private foundation makes a contribution to an organization that is exempt under Section 501(c)(3)
2. If the activities of that receiving organization are nonpartisan and are conducted over more than one election period and in at least five states
3. If the organization spends most (at least 85 percent) of its income on the tax-exempt purposes for which it is organized
4. If 85 percent of its support is from the public (government units and the general public)
5. If the contributions from the private foundation are not used solely for a specific election or geographic area

The prohibition against political activities gave way to a strategy used in the presidential elections in the 1980s—a resurgence in the form of fundraising by political action committees. Supporters of political candidates would form a nonprofit group under Section 501(c)(3)—not to support the candidate, but to do research and disseminate information on subjects close to the heart of the potential candidate and even to support the potential candidate's travel to speak (not campaign) on these subjects. Some of these foundations even gave money to public charities. Under this guise, the organization did not become involved in politics because its activities were "educational."

There were several advantages to going this route:

1. The contributions to a nonprofit were deductible and did not suffer the same limitations on giving as contributions to a political campaign.
2. The nonprofit organization had several cost advantages, including the lower postal rate.
3. Gifts to foundations are not subject to public disclosure, as are contributions to political campaigns.
4. Many persons who may not otherwise contribute to a candidate may contribute to a foundation.
5. It gave an unannounced candidate a platform and a way of being identified with an issue in a nonpartisan light.
6. It was a source of information and dissemination of information with which the potential candidate could be identified.
7. The foundation can support foundation-related speaking engagements for the candidate that simultaneously coincide with the issues with which the candidate seeks identity and in the communities in which the candidate needs exposure.

Another category of prohibited expenditures is grants to individuals. Here the intent is to be certain that grants to individuals are intended to assist them in meeting some measurable objective, such as writing a book or earning a degree, are a bona fide prize or award, are nondiscriminatory (that is, not targeted as a payoff or bribe), or aim at improving skills. Many private foundations shy away from making grants to individuals due to this rule.

Expenditures to carry out missions that are not religious, scientific, or charitable, or to foster those activities that permit an organization to qualify under 501(c)(3) are also prohibited.

Finally, private foundations may not make grants to organizations other than those 509(a)(1)s, (a)(2)s, and (a)(3)s previously discussed unless the foundation takes responsibility for how these funds are used by the donee. The rule means that private foundations must be sure the funds are used only for the purposes for which they are given, keep proper and thorough records, and report expenditures to the IRS.

Violation of these rules against prohibited expenditures leads to a 10 percent tax penalty based on the amount involved on both the foundation and its management. An additional tax of 100 percent may be imposed on the foundation and 50 percent on the manager if they fail to correct the situation during the allotted time.

Investment Income

Finally, private foundations have to pay a two percent tax on net investment income if they fail to make sufficient distributon to qualified nonprofits during any year. Net investment income is the total of all income, including rents, royalties, dividends, interest, and business income, plus net capital gains. This rule is to reduce the risk that the nonprofit would focus on maximizing investment income and not make substantial disbursements of financial assistance to the doers.

The Key Characteristics of the Facilitator

A facilitator may be external to the doer organization or its network or it may be part of the affiliate network of the doer organization such as the 509(a)(3). No matter, the rules apply the same as they apply for facilitator organizations whether formed by citizens, the government, or the doer organizations. When the facilitator is outside of the doer network, it is free to choose which doer it will assist and which missions (including those not lessening the burden of government) it will assist.

Back to the central theme, citizens or governments may create a nonprofit organization with the mission of facilitating other players in accomplishing a mission of lessening a burden of government. The Economic Development Corporation of Kansas City (EDCKC) is a 501(c)(4) civic organization without the need to directly deal with the public and created by government to coordinate the economic development activities of six statutory agencies—their members— to which it is accountable and through them, the public by facilitating or "coordinating."

O ther (less obvious) examples of facilitators are some local economic development corporations. They do not so much do local development as they are catalysts for getting it done. Local economic development corporations qualify for 501(c)(3) status because, even though they provide and improve profit opportunities for firms, they provide a coordinated benefit to the lessening of the burden of government that significantly exceeds the profits of any of its participants. Their constituents are the public (not agencies as in the case of the EDCKC) and they are focused on activities qualifying under Section 501(c)(3).

For example, see the State of New York Not-for-Profit Corporation Law, Section 1411. It provides for local municipalities to create local development corporations that are designed to qualify as 501(c)(3)s for lessening the burden of the local government through reducing unemployment, promoting and enhancing employment opportunities, job training and skill improvements, conducting scientific research to attract and retain firms, and lessening the burdens of government in the public interest. The powers of the local development corporation in furtherance of this are;

> a local development corporation incorporated or reincorporated under this section shall have the following powers: to construct, acquire, rehabilitate and improve for use by others industrial or manufacturing plants in the territory in which its operations are principally to be conducted,
> to assist financially in such construction, acquisition, rehabilitation and improvement, to maintain such plants for others in such territory, to disseminate information and furnish advice, technical assistance and liaison with federal, state and local authorities with respect thereto, to acquire by purchase, lease, gift, bequest, devise or otherwise real or personal property or interests therein,
>
> to borrow money and to issue negotiable bonds, notes and other obligations therefor, and notwithstanding section 510 (Disposition of all or substantially all assets) without leave of the court,
>
> to sell, lease, mortgage or otherwise dispose of or encumber any such plants or any of its real or personal property or any interest therein upon such terms as it may determine and, in connection with loans from the New York job development authority,
>
> to enter into covenants and agreements and to comply with all the terms, conditions and provisions thereof, and otherwise to carry out its corporate purposes and to foster and encourage the location or expansion of industrial or manufacturing plants in the territory in which the operations of such corporation are principally to be conducted,
>
> provided, however, that no such corporation shall attempt to influence legislation by propaganda or otherwise, or participate or intervene, directly or indirectly, in any political campaign on behalf of or in opposition to any candidate for public office. – See more at: http://codes.findlaw.com/ny/notforprofit-corporation-law/npc-sect-1411.html#sthash. 9I0fYTOw.dpuf

Further, notice the power of the LDC to acquire land:

> The local legislative body of a county, city, town or village or, if there is a board of estimate in a city, then the board of estimate, may by resolution determine that specifically described real property owned by the county, city, town or village is not required for use by such county, city, town or village and authorize the county, city, town or village to sell or lease such real property to a local development corporation incorporated or reincorporated under this article; provided, however, that title to such land be not declared inalienable as a forest preserve or a parkland.
>
> Notwithstanding the provisions of any general, special or local law, charter or ordinance to the contrary, such sale or lease may be made without appraisal, public notice, (except

as provided in subparagraph (4)) or public bidding for such price or rental and upon such terms as may be agreed upon between the county, city, town or village and said local development corporation; provided, however, that in case of a lease the term may not exceed ninety-nine years and provided, further, that in cities having a population of one million or more, no such sale or lease shall be made without the approval of a majority of the members of the borough improvement board of the borough in which such real property is located.

Before any sale or lease to a local development corporation incorporated or reincorporated under this article shall be authorized, a public hearing shall be held by the local legislative body, or by the board of estimate, as the case may be, to consider the proposed sale or lease.

Notice of such hearing shall be published at least ten days before the date set for the hearing in such publication and in such manner as may be designated by the local legislative body, or the board of estimate as the case may be.

A local development corporation, incorporated or reincorporated under this section, which purchases or leases real property from a county, city, town or village, shall not, without the written approval of the county, city, town or village, use such real property for any purpose except the purposes set forth in the certificate of incorporation or reincorporation of said local development corporation. In the event such real property is used in violation of the restrictions of this paragraph, the attorney-general may bring an action or special proceeding to enjoin the unauthorized use.

See more at: http://codes.findlaw.com/ny/notforprofit-corporation-law/npc-sect-1411.html# sthash.9I0fYTOw.dpuf

Notice that all these powers point to enabling the LDC to facilitate local economic development through actions of others reacting to their facilitation whether it is by incentive, providing space, or an available work force and that while the corporation has these powers, it is also the role of public hearings and that these LDCs fall under the Public Authorities Accountability Act and individually, they are described in the New York State Authorities Budget Office.

Hybrids: Private Operating Foundations

There is a small set of organizations that both facilitate *and* do. They accomplish this mainly by self-financing but with the option of financing others. These are *private operating foundations*. The private operating foundation is a facilitator, but it is also a hybrid because it is both a doer and a financier. However, it only finances those things which it does itself or which it does in collaboration with another doer. It cannot just finance (as does the private non-operating foundation) and do nothing. "In collaboration" means that it is directly and actively involved in a joint effort. Its involvement may vary from actually doing to actively coordinating. An operating foundation is indicated when the government or citizens wish to carry on a burden of government on the outside because of its costs, its need for focus, and its need for highly technical skill and additional financing. It is also indicated where the intent is not to dissipate available resources by a compulsory requirement to fund others (such as the case of the private non-operating foundation) or to raise funds or to involve the participation in funding or in engagement of a wide number of persons to show public support such as the 501(c)(3) doers.

While the operating foundation is not required to support other doers, it may elect to do so but must participate and is required to use its assets and earnings in furtherance of its tax exempt mission. In this connection, a citizen-created operating foundation can relieve the burden of government by providing technical staffing at a government facility or by permitting the use of its facility for government purposes.

Incubators are examples of what an operating foundation could be. Their mission is to encourage entrepreneurship by bringing entrepreneurs together to take advantage of a network agglomeration. Incubators are nonprofits, often self-financing, that are formed by governments. Another quite different example is a major research institute steeped in theoretical and applied physics, including the large campuses of the Jefferson Laboratory founded by the Department of Energy, but supported both physically and financially, in part, by state and local governments, and involving scientists and students from various universities across the countries in basic physics—science being one of the fields qualifying for 501(c)(3) status, as is economic development (in the case of the incubators). It is managed outside of the government by an educational consortium.

An operating foundation for lessening the burden of government is indicated when:

(a) there is one individual or one family of donors,
(b) who wishes to be intimately involved and wishes the foundation to be directly involved in the carrying out of a mission or project,
(c) so that the operating foundation emphasizes its intimate involvement through collaboration rather than by making grants,
(d) which wants to leverage both its grant-making and receiving to a single line of interest,
(e) to involve corporations even to the extent of significant ownership stakes,
(f) that does not wish to occupy itself with fundraising or grant-making, which it needs or to demonstrate public support,
(g) can satisfy the two tests and one condition for qualifying for lessening the burden of government, and

(h) has the technical staff to do the work in which it represents itself as partici-
pating or collaborating in doing.

In this vein, Jacobs Family Foundation in San Diego, California, describes itself
in the spirit of an operating foundation. It is attached to a single family and only
funds projects in a distressed area of the city, such is the family and foundation
involvement. It promotes collaboration among the various interests and attracts
investment to the area.

Summary and Preview

We have divided the nonprofits lessening the burden of government into the
doers and the facilitators. The previous chapter dealt with the doers whether
they are included in Sections 501(c)(3), (4) or (6). These classes are very different
in the types of government-related mission they can undertake effectively and
very different in the types of exemption they enjoy. Exemption is a contract
price the public pays for the agreement to shift their burdens from government
to a nonprofit where it is presumably less expensive and likely more efficient.
Proof of relevance and performance are required.

In this chapter, the focus was on facilitators—those who facilitate the doers
in their mission but are not part of their constructed organizational network.
Some facilitators provide money from their own treasuries and others raise
money from private sources. They, too, are tax exempt and most can be found in
the 501(c)(3) category, these are relegated only to help the doers in this (c)(3)
category. The facilitators in this chapter are largely unattached to a doer or a
specific internal network of a doer. Here there is competition for their attention
and responsiveness.

There is a particular group discussed in this chapter that are not only doers
but self-finance and may also have access to other facilitators. They are generally formed by a wealthy family or individual who is dedicated to a specific interest and wish the nonprofit to proceed with dedicated attention to that interest
whether that be parks, memorials, transportation and community development,
or research and technology—all of which provide opportunities for lessening the
burden of government.

Chapter 6 – Government Created Nonprofits to Lessen the Burden of Government

The Tennessee Valley Authority (TVA) is a *corporate agency* (an independent nonprofit tax-exempt corporation) of the United States that provides electricity for business customers and local power distributors serving 9 million people in parts of seven southeastern states. TVA receives no taxpayer funding, deriving virtually all of its revenues from sales of electricity. In addition to operating and investing its revenues in its electric system, TVA provides flood control, navigation, and land management for the Tennessee River system and assists local power companies and state and local governments with economic development and job creation. In 2015, it produced $3.315 billion in cash, and because it is nonprofit and tax exempt this profit cannot be paid in dividends and must be used to make the communities it serves progressively better.

The TVA is a wholly owned but self-funded agency of the United States government, created and incorporated by Congress pursuant to the Tennessee Valley Authority Act of 1933. It meets its funding needs with operating revenues and power program financing. TVA debt securities are issued only for power program purposes—including financing of existing debt—and are secured by revenues from its power system. TVA issues a variety of debt securities: TVA Discount Notes have maturities of less than one year; TVA may also issue long-term bonds with final maturities of up to 50 years. These bonds and notes are available to investors through banks, brokers, and investment dealers (https://www.tva.gov/About-TVA/Investor-Relations).

The TVA represents an optimal arrangement: the burden of operating, planning, and financing this vast operation is off the backs of the taxpayers. Not all authorities are so designed. What are the essentials in the design of such an arrangement? This is the basic question of this chapter, a continuation of the discussion of creating and designing the nonprofit specifically to meet the terms of lessening the burden of government. It will culminate with the conditions that allow the complete burden—planning, capacity, construction, operating, management, and financing—to be removed from the corpus of the government in one nonprofit tax exemption.

Some designs may be smaller but just as skillfully done. The Northern Kentucky Tri-County Economic Development Corporation 501(c)(6) and Tri-County Economic Development Foundation, a 501(c)(3), have a common local development interest and shared boards. The corporation receives a significant percentage of its revenues from motor vehicle rental license fees but as a 501(c)(6) does not receive grants and deductible contributions. The Foundation, however,

DOI 10.1515/9781501505799-007

does and receives grants from each of its three members Boone, Campbell, and Kenton counties and is set up to receive such contributions from others and through fundraising events as any other foundation. Most of the Foundation's expenditures are used to purchase an entrepreneurial start up program and related marketing provided by the Corporation. The Foundation has no staff. The Corporation is a facilitator of regional economic development and the Foundation is its structurally connected financial facilitator (http://www. northernkentuckyusa.com/about/2014-annual-report.aspx).

Nonprofits Created by Governments to Lessen Their Own Burdens

The two preceding examples are of nonprofits created by government, Federal in the first case and three local governments in the second case. A nonprofit created to reduce the burden of government can be created by private citizens or entities or by one or more governments and they can qualify for tax exemption under IRC Section 501(c)(3) as long as their purpose is to conduct one or more of the missions—-health, education, science, culture and arts, housing, preventing cruelty to animals, and promoting some amateur sports that qualify under 501(c)(3); and that they also comply with the other provisions to which any other organization under that title would have to comply, are separate, and do not mimic or exercise the powers of government (https://www.irs.gov/pub/irs-tege/eotopic184.pdf).

There is a significant difference, however, between those created by government and those created by citizens in terms of meeting the qualification that a burden of the Federal, state, or local government is being relieved. This is a huge issue. An organization formed in any state under its laws is presumed to de facto meet the qualifications, and need not prove that it is relieving a burden of the State, and that it has the organizational structure to do so within that state (http://www.irs.gov/irm/part7/irm_07-025-003-cont03.html).

Although created by the state, and therefore evidence is presumed that it assumes a burden of the state, it must also prove that it relieves that burden in fact, is separate from the state (that is, a bona fide corporation as in Chapter 2), and does not fully exercise any of the sovereign powers of the state. If it fully exercises a sovereign power, it is considered a state agency or instrumentality and not an autonomous or independent nonprofit. Sovereign powers include the power to set and collect taxes, the policing power, the power of eminent domain, and judicial powers. Thus, the police at a college can direct traffic on the campus, give parking tickets, carry a weapon, arrest someone; but not try to incarcerate that person, and, if there is a murder or rape on the campus, it has to call in the local police jurisdiction. An instrumentality or agency could be assigned these powers as does the local police force.

So why would public policy provide for governments to create organizations that qualify for tax exemption, not as instrumentalities, but as 501(c)(3)s?

1. It reduces the specific financial and operating burden from the government.
2. It reduces the administrative burden from the government, and it shields the government from the risks associated with the project. Not only does the government shift project-related liabilities to the organization, but the organization cannot shift its liability to the government.
3. It increases the voluntary funding from private sources—firms, foundations, individual investors, and donors (see the discussion on Sec. 170 in Chapters 2 and 3).
4. It increases the direct participation of private citizens and entities that can participate in governance without being named by the government, and that have direct interest to win or to lose in the activity.
5. It can be localized and benefit from local identity and information.
6. It increases the opportunities for "ownership," creativity and imagination, and involvement unconstrained by the government bureaucracy and its rules. Yet ownership does not translate to private or personal inurement unless by specific performance contracts.
7. The sustainability and longevity of the organization is independent, not tied to political changes and procedures, legislative appropriations and endorsement, and is perpetual. The government may create it, but it can't close it down except for reasons that it can close any nonprofit subsequent to a court decision (see Chapters 1 and 2).
8. The organization can hire its own management and oversee its own governance as required by state law, the charter, and the bylaws that the government as creator initially designs. When the Federal government creates or charters a nonprofit it does so subject to the laws of the District of Columbia. Each state and its jurisdictions will do so subject to the laws of that state.
9. The organization is subject to the same accountability and transparency rules of all 501(c)(3)s and in many ways has greater exposure than if it were embedded in the budget and organizational chart of a government and protected by the informational protection of the government. Furthermore, when created by the government it is usually a single product or service entity with a single location.
10. The organization does not have the immunity of government and the workers are not protected by civil service rules. Workers are free to unionize and

to strike depending upon state laws—creating a framework of discipline different from what is found in government.

11. In time-sensitive transactions where parties are of interest and exposed to considerable losses (or gains). Dealing with a nonprofit is far more efficient than dealing with government.

12. Reducing the debt burden of the jurisdiction, or at least avoiding increasing it by the debt cost of a large project means: (a) other essential needs are not crowded out because of the inability of the government to borrow when it has to do so; (b) the entire population is not put at risk as if a bond were used by the government or guaranteed by it, which means its taxing base; (c) it does not cause the cost of issuing or servicing bonds by the government to rise; (d) given the IRS and international accounting rules, it is hard to create these just to avoid debt limits. The debt limit of a state or local government is not like the debt limit of a firm, family, or the Federal government. State governments cannot change their debt limits, but for time-consuming constitutional action. The Federal government can change its debt limit every year. Most states and local jurisdictions cannot. So relieving the burden of a state and local government often means the difference between the project getting done, delayed, or denied.

The sum of these can be explained in three current examples, (1) the problem that Puerto Rico has because of the incompetence of the Government Development Bank for Puerto Rico and the failure to have separated it from the government so that the weight of their combined problems brings them both down; (2) the problem of the City of Harrisburg, Pennsylvania, to properly craft the bond terms for its waste infrastructure and that its inability to cover it brings both down; and (3) the same problem likely in Atlantic City, New Jersey.

Qualifications of a Government-Created 501(c)(3)

A government may create a full range of nonprofits but not all will qualify for exemption as a 501(c)(3), (4) or (6) even if the intent is to lessen the burden of government. Some will not qualify because they are not separate corporations and 501(c)(3) rules require both separation and a corporate body (or a body with most of the characteristics of a corporation except the profit motive). Whether the nonprofits have a corporate status is not too difficult to verify—they are either incorporated or not and they have corporate characteristics or not. But are these entities in fact separate? Revenue Ruling 57-128, 1957-1 C.B. 311, is helpful here. These considerations help to determine for the nonprofit:

1. If it is used for a governmental purpose and performs a sovereign function
2. If it does so on behalf of one or more states or political subdivisions
3. If the only interests involved are governmental
4. If control and supervision of the organization is vested in a public authority
5. If a statutory authority, expressed or implied, was necessary to create it
6. The degree of financial autonomy and the source of its operating expenses

In general, the more control government has on the organization, the more dependent it is on them, and the more it carries out functions on behalf of the government—especially sovereign functions—taxation, eminent domain, policing—the more likely it is not to qualify for a 501(c) status because none of these is inherently consistent with what that status calls for, and the more they are likely to be considered as an instrumentality of government and tax exempt as such.

A 501(c)(3) created by government, by private citizens, or by other private entities must past the organizational test; that is, have an acceptable operating structure (a corporation association, or trust with powers of a corporation) according to that state's law, and that what they plan to do is a burden of the state, and that it can be relieved by them and allowed to do so by the state, as well as pass the asset test as described in Chapters 1 to 3. They must do so both for Federal tax exemption and for state and local exemption. In Pennsylvania, for example, many nonprofits, while exempt for this purpose at the Federal level, have been denied such exemption on the local level from property tax. This has also been true in Minnesota.

The heat revolves around the term "reducing a government burden." Federal law recognizes several areas in which a nonprofit could qualify under this rubric. It could build and operate transportation systems, it could operate parks and recreation facilities, it could build and operate educational facilities, it could be involved in urban economic development, and so on. On the other hand, there are things called sovereign responsibilities, and no government can allow or transfer these to a nongovernmental entity. These involve writing of laws, writing of regulations, running of courts, determining and imposing taxes, enforcing an arrest, engaging in foreign policy, issuing of passports. Therefore no organization formed by citizens or by government can qualify as reducing the burden of government by doing these things.

Those other functions that the Federal government easily recognizes may not be recognized by an individual locality. That has been the crux of the problem in Pennsylvania and Minnesota where localities have denied property tax exemption on the grounds that the nonprofit was not relieving them of any burden. Consequently, they have set specific rules for a nonprofit, though qualifying under Federal and state laws, to which they must conform in order to qualify for local property tax exemption (see Chapter 2).

Note, as we shall see below, all nonprofit organizations created by government do not have to qualify for 501(c)(3) status to be tax exempt. Those not qualifying can obtain exemption as long as they are part of the jurisdiction or state since these are tax exempt. They are deemed part of the state if they carry out any state or sovereign function with the same scope as a jurisdiction; that is, policing, eminent domain, judicial function, and taxation being the primary ones. Nonprofits known as public authorities are a range of organizational designs fulfilling a range of missions. It may be independent or an extension of the jurisdiction. The characteristics of this independence matter in how much of a burden lessened. See the chart at the end of this chapter.

Public Authorities as Government-Created Nonprofits to Relieve Government Burden

Public authorities are government-created nonprofit tax-exempt entities to do, to manage, or to fund large projects. But not all authorities are alike in the degree of independence from the government and not all have 501(c)(3) status. Either way, the authority might be exempt from taxes—either as a 501(c)(3) or as an agency of the government. The difference is important in determining, as we shall see below, the extent to which debt incurred by the nonprofit is attributed to the government and therefore reduces its capacity to further borrow, in addition to dealing with project risks and liabilities. How fully is the burden relieved?

In general, authorities are created to provide large-scale infrastructure projects—toll roads, water and sewer systems, housing and community development, construction of buildings, university and hospital systems, airports and sea ports, and so on for the community. An *authority* is a nonprofit corporation created by a state, local, or Federal government to conduct some function of that government which is not a sovereign function but which benefits the public. Sovereign powers include the power to impose taxes, general powers of policing and of eminent domain, judicial powers over crime, and so on. They are powers only a jurisdiction can exercise.

Why create an authority? A central motive is to reduce the burden on government to finance, construct, and deliver a specific product or service to the public to satisfy a recognizable public need of substantial scale, and, thus, reduce the impact of that function on government fiscally and/or operationally. It reduces the financial burden principally by entering into debt for capital purposes to finance projects, debt the government would otherwise have had to incur—creating a fiscal burden for the government. These projects may be for general public use or for the use of the government itself (for example, a municipal building).

Because it can borrow very large sums, depending upon its creditworthiness which is based on its ability to charge fees for its services and cover the debt service plus a margin, the properly designed authority relieves the capital burden of the government as its borrowing does not count against the government's debt limit. The authority takes out the debt, assumes all risks, and liabilities thereby fully relieving the government of that debt and associated expenses. Therefore, that debt does not appear on the government's balance sheet— providing room for the government to satisfy other capital needs that require borrowing, and operating needs that would have had to be satisfied through annual taxation or fees because the need for annual interest and principal payments would have been avoided.

Not all authorities are designed to bring this complete outcome; some lack the organizational independence or competence, the operational skill or resources, and the power (by decision of the legislative drafting of the charter) to charge sufficient fees not to need a government subsidy, or they lack the capacity to borrow independently without government backing or guarantee to the creditors of the authority. Thus, authorities vary not only in their functions, but in their dependence upon government and therefore the degree to which they relieve that government of its burden. The ultimate relief comes from the organizational ability and authority to (a) issue and to completely cover debt— principal, interest, and fees with a margin for reserves, (b) operate the infrastructure efficiently and profitably, and (c) self-governance. The weaker the authority is on any of these dimensions, the lower the amount of government burden it can carry.

An optimal design, one that completely removes the operational and fiscal burden and their related risks from the government and yet provide service beneficial to the public is in the details of the charter and bylaws of the nonprofit as they are decided upon by government (see Chapter 1). Accounting, tax, and credit analyses are not impressed by the concept of "authority" or the concept "an autonomous agency" or any other use of the words autonomous or independent. They look at the organizational design details and its faculty to perform as in Chapters 1 and 2.

This chapter will show what is required in the organizational design of the nonprofit to achieve this optimal relief of burden to the government, noting that this is a legislative, administrative, and rule-making function of the government itself when it creates a nonprofit to serve the public and to relieve its burden.

Chapter 13 will describe the debt and the conditions for making that debt tax exempt and some of the misplaced comments about this strategy, government created nonprofits for the purpose of relieving it of burden and for serving the government by relieving it of a debt burden.

The U.S. Census Bureau reports that there are 32,000 government-created nonprofit organizations, not including those involved in education. New York State alone has over 6,000 authorities with different levels of independence or dependence on government. Here are other state examples:

In Section 22–21–71 of its code, Alabama authorizes several of its counties to organize public corporations for the purposes of acquiring, owning, and operating public hospitals and other health care–related facilities. This allows the governments to fulfill their responsibilities to the community but off the public budget and outside of the public bureaucracy. To accomplish this, Alabama municipalities can elect to transfer all or parts of its hospital and health-related assets to this corporation. These assets are both tangible and intangible, and they may well be assets that were to have been received in the future, such as government or patient payments. So the initial capitalization of this authority is the pool of assets transferred from all of these hospitals—many of them on the brink of economic disaster.

In Florida's Industrial Development Financing Act, the state created a number of industrial development authorities and granted them powers because they "will be for the benefit of the people of the state, for the increase of their industry and prosperity, for improvement of their health and living conditions, and for the provision of gainful employment and will constitute the performance of essential functions."

This Act continues, "The ... agency will not be required to pay any taxes on any project... ." Further, "The bonds issued under the provisions of this part, their transfer, and the income therefrom (including any profit made on the sale thereof), and all notes, mortgages, security agreements, letters of credit, or other instruments which arise out of or are given to secure the repayment of bonds issued in connection with a project financed ... shall at all times be free from taxation by the state or any local unit, political subdivision, or other instrumentality of the state." The earnings of the bonds (revenue bonds discussed in this book) issued by the authority are exempt from tax by the state. Incidentally, they are tax-exempt by the Federal government as long as the money raised from selling the bonds is used exclusively (not less than 95 percent) for public purposes or for purposes of the environment or for pollution abatement.

The powers of the authority do not include the ability to tax. Authorities do not have taxing powers. Florida statute 159.48 gives the board of commissioners (legislature) the power to levy an *ad valorem* tax for the purpose of helping their industrial development authority carry out their mission but specifies that no part of this tax may be used to pay off the indebtedness by these authorities. Notice that the authorities do not have the power to levy a tax. The municipal government does and may earmark these for the authority.

The authorities can "fix, charge, and collect rents, fees, and charges for the use of any project." It is these revenues that pay off the bonds. Therefore, the principal sources of financing an authority are the revenue bonds, fees, and charges.

Ports and Powers

Two examples of government-created nonprofits that are not 501(c)(3)s that significantly reduce the burden of government are discussed below—one a city (the Chesapeake Port Authority in Chesapeake, Virginia), and another a foreign example, the Panama Canal.

Chesapeake Port Authority

The Chesapeake Port Authority, Chesapeake, Virginia, is created as a nonprofit (Section 14) but as a political subdivision (Section 1) of the Commonwealth of Virginia: This means that is it a government agency and its exemption is obtained because it is carrying out a government function (one that the government would otherwise have to do); there is no need to qualify under Section 501(c)(3) from the Federal government and the state can award this status for itself and its localities. It is a government-created nonprofit to lessen governmental burden by carrying out a government function (Section 13).

The exercise of the powers granted by this act shall be in all respects for the benefit of the inhabitants of the Commonwealth, for the increase of their commerce, and for the promotion of their safety, health, welfare, convenience and prosperity, and is hereby deemed to be performing essential governmental functions. Accordingly, the Authority shall not be required to pay any taxes or assessments upon any Authority facility or any property acquired or used by the Authority under the provisions of this act or upon the income therefrom; nor shall the agents, lessees, sublessees or users of tangible personal property owned by or leased to the Authority be required to pay any sales or use tax upon such property or the revenue derived therefrom; and the bonds issued under the provisions of this act, their transfer and the income therefrom including any profit made on the sale thereof, shall at all times be free and exempt from taxation by the Commonwealth and by any municipality, county or other political subdivision thereof.

The mission is expressed in Section 3 that also defines the public (the inhabitants of the City and Commonwealth) to benefit and how:

> It is the intent of the General Assembly in passing this act to facilitate the improvement and development of Authority facilities in the City for the purpose of increasing trade and commerce beneficial to the economy, prosperity and welfare of the City and the Commonwealth; to promote the development and operation of adequate, modern and efficient seaports and harbors through such aids and other such encouragement as may be authorized by the General Assembly; and to promote and encourage the acquisition, construction, operation and management of Authority facilities.

The management is described in Section 5 as a five-person board who must be residents of the city and appointed by the City Council.

The money for funding the authority comes from fees and charges, debt, and commercial transactions but not from the imposition of taxes. Section 6 is a recitation of these and various powers highlighted in Chapters 2 and 3. The exception here is that the authority also has the power of eminent domain if that is necessary to carry out its mission which also allows it.

> 10. To acquire, lease, construct, maintain, operate and sell landings, wharves, docks, piers and quays, and the approaches to and appurtenances thereof, ships, tracks, spurs, crossings, switchings, terminals, warehouses, elevators, compressors, refrigerated storage plants, and terminal facilities of every kind necessary or useful in the transportation and storage of goods, to perform any services at such facilities in connection with the receipt, delivery, shipment and transfer in transit, weighing, marking, tagging, ventilating, fumigating, refrigerating, icing, storing and handling of goods, to prescribe and collect charges from vessels using any landings, wharves, docks and piers, operated and maintained by the Authority and from persons using any of its other facilities, and to lease or sell any and all of such facilities or any concessions properly incident thereto for the maintenance and operation of any or all thereof on such terms as it may deem proper (http://law.lis.virginia.gov/authorities/chesapeake-port-authority).

Panama Canal Authority

The Panama Canal Authority is a foreign example. With nearly 15,000 transits per year, accounting for six percent of the country's GDP, the Panama Canal Authority is an independent authority that finances itself through fees, receives no transfers or subsidies from the Panamanian government, issues its own debt (recently $5 billion to cover the canal expansion) with no government guarantees. It pays an annual fee to the government as royalties and interest, and at its own discretion and calculation it pays the government an annual "dividend." It sets transit rates and collects them; and because it is independent, those rates have to cover the full cost, the need for reserves, plus more. For international canal users, its independence separates the authority from the politics and bureaucracy of the government—reducing their risks of use. To the creditors it reduces risk of default and corruption. Transparency and accountability are also improved because the authority's numbers are not hidden in or dependent upon the reporting of any other agency. Lenders can hold the authority directly responsible and accountable and may require information as the lenders deem necessary. Among other reports, the authority files an annual public report (financial and otherwise) on the operation of the authority. Because of this, the canal authority has a higher credit rating than the government.

Three-Part Typology of Authorities

Is the authority independent, autonomous, is it part of government? These questions matter because they determines the extent to which a burden is lessened by taking it out from government completely or if it is lessened by its reallocation to a dedicated unit of government and because it has corporate powers shields the remainder of the government. Section 8 of the Chesapeake Port Authority above gives the authority the power to issue bonds at its own discretion but states:

> Neither the Commissioners of the Authority nor any person executing any bonds issued under the provisions of this act shall be liable personally on the bonds by reason of the issuance thereof. The bonds of the Authority, and such bonds shall so state on their face, shall not be a debt of the Commonwealth or any political subdivision thereof, and neither the Commonwealth nor any political subdivision thereof other than the Authority shall be liable thereon, nor shall such bonds be payable out of any funds or properties other than those of the Authority. The bonds shall not constitute an indebtedness within the meaning of any debt limitation or restriction.

Authorities, including those described above, are created by legislative bodies and signed into law by the executive of the political jurisdiction at their discretion. The legislators in their wisdom assign not only the purpose, but the powers of the authority, and the amount of control the jurisdiction will have over the organization—the amount of fiscal and operational dependence between the authority and the government. The legislators also decide if there are to be flows of cash from the government to the organization and vice versa and, if so, for what purpose. Thus, the level of independence and powers granted are a matter of organizational design and policy.

The level of independence determines the amount of fiscal and operational burden the authority removes from the government and supposedly frees it to deal with other pressing problems. It does this less to the extent that the government has to finance it, cover its debts, pay its workers, and negotiate its contracts. When the authority is truly independent, the government only oversees the authority, and only in the public interest. The authority, being a nonprofit, cannot pay dividends to private persons but can, by the terms at its creation, make annual transfers for the public welfare to the government from its net income and after keeping prudent financial reserves for its future operations. This amount, not being a tax, is paid in the sum and at the times determined by the trustees of the authority. This has the advantages of public accountability and of avoiding excess accumulations by the authority.

Authorities fall into three groups according to their levels of independence as in Table 6.1:

Table 6.1. Three-Part Typology of Public Authorities

Political subdivision: Carries one or more sovereign powers (such as the power of eminent domain) and operates as if it were an independent political corporation such as a city, county, or municipality, or within the government itself. Tax exemption is based on its being in fact government or a government agency. Tax deduction is available to contributions made for their use; for example, build a facility as opposed to service to clients.

Instrumentality: A nonprofit to lessen the burden of government, but which does so involving the exercise of one or more sovereign powers or by facilitating the government in the exercise of such powers and is controlled by government; for example, through financial or operating dependence, even if it is a separate corporation. Its exemption is based on it being an agency of government and contributions for its use; for example, acquisition of a facility, rather than service to clients, are tax deductible. It is an organizational entity (instrumentality) through which the government conducts a function. It is not the government itself, but a corporate channel through which the government (including political subdivisions) act.

Independent or autonomous: A nonprofit corporation created by government but not controlled by it or dependent on it other than by usual contracting, that carries out no substantial sovereign function and that qualifies as a 501(c)(3), 509(a)(1), (a)(2), or (a)(3), and treated as such for deductible contributions which increases its range of fundraising as tax deductions are higher, private foundations and corporations are more willing to give to it, it is able to operate and fulfill its mission with greater discretion. It operates, including managing and financing, itself with its own borrowing and earnings and is solely responsible for these. It is an independent corporation having all the powers of a nonprofit corporation described earlier. Therefore, even though it is created by government it is not a government agency, either in the eyes of tax law or international accounting rules.

Source: Author as compiled from: http://www.irs.gov/pub/irs-tege/eotopice90.pdf

Some authorities are incorporated by jurisdiction(s) as political subdivisions, others are instrumentalities of government, and there are those that are independent or autonomous of government. According to the IRS rules, and the rules of both U.S. and international government accounting and corporate law, an authority is not considered to be autonomous or independent of government if it is in any way dependent upon government or government guarantee or if the authority carries out a sovereign function of government such as writing laws, general public regulations, police and judicial functions, eminent domain or imposition of taxes.

An independent authority fulfills its mission under its own discretion, is overseen by its own independent board beholden to it and not to government even if some are government functionaries, its workers and staff are not government employees. It does not depend upon government for financing or financing guarantees (receive other than an arms-length loan) for assistance in its operations and in its hiring, in determining its prices or revenues, in its defense in the case of lawsuit and labor dispute, in the determination of its contracts or purchasing. It issues its own debt, negotiates the terms with its creditors, pays the interest and principal on its own and sets its own prices to meet its operating, capital, and reserve financial needs.

Keys to Determining Independence or Autonomy

It follows that the key criterion, independence or autonomy, is determined by the facts and circumstances of the powers and how the organization operates in fact—not whether or not such words are used in its name. Using the Governmental Accounting Standards Board (GASB), the International Accounting Standards Board (IASB), and the IRS rules, legislators could design authorities with such elements that could be called independent and therefore maximally reduce the burden of government. Bear in mind that to be truly independent in carrying out a function, one must have not only the fiscal means, but the corporate power to function as an independent entity. When these are put together we get Table 6.2.

When an authority is independent depends upon on the preponderance of facts and circumstances; and if it is independent, as long as the law permits, it can issue debt and have liabilities that are not obligations of the government, permitting what is called off-balance-sheet financing, and the debt does not count against the jurisdiction, allowing it to borrow for the financing of other urgent needs such as schools and roads. The key to this is that it has its own corporate identity, an independent way of earning income to cover all expenses including the debt, and it can manage itself.

Table 6.2. A Design Guide for Independent Authority

Elements of Design	Description
Public Interest	The project should be of general and significant public interest to justify the government involvement in the creation of an independent agency to finance and manage it.
Basic Design	The determinative questions are: Can the created organization function on its own? To the extent that it cannot, is it dependent and just a part of the government as an organization—an agency or instrumentality? The key to the organizational design therefore is to make evident independence—the absence of direction, assistance, or control by the government. This is basic.
Incorporation	For the entity, in this case the public authority, to be independent, it has to have to have a legal standing and identity, and is therefore qualified to carry on basic functions and assume basic liabilities without benefit of government guarantee; that is, it has to be a legal person (see Chapter 2).
For-Profit or Nonprofit	A nonprofit authority cannot be beholden to private owners or persons and therefore cannot raise funds through the sale of equity (ownership) in the infrastructure avoiding leakages such as dividends to private investors. As a nonprofit, its principal purpose by definition, is advancing the public welfare. Thus, there is no limitation on the profits it makes as long as those go toward self-financing, including the payment of debt, being able to provide for future operating and capital expenses, and other contingencies. The remainder may be channeled to the public; for example, regular annual payments to the government for public use. A truly independent entity determines this amount in the same way that a firm declares and determines the amount and timing of its dividend payments. The government cannot stipulate this amount, although it may negotiate any service or royalty fees it charges the authority, but all these must be treated as hands-off, separate, and traceable and accountable as sales (purchases) just as if the authority were a firm.
Self-Financing	To be independent, the projects of the authority have to be able to finance it. This means that the authority has to be deemed creditworthy on its own. It has to have a reliable flow of earnings to cover all debt service and to keep the operation financially sound over a long period of time so that debt service and other expenses can be covered. This also means that the management must be able to set prices and reliably collect fees, make payments and be liable for payments, as well performance. To the extent that the authority can do none of these, it is a dependent agency.

Debt	Only governments can issue general obligation bonds; therefore, if the authority is dependent on general obligation bonds is prima facie evidence that it is dependent upon government. Authorities would issue revenue (not general obligation since it is not a political jurisdiction) bonds of the type not guaranteed by the State. To the extent that the revenue bond is guaranteed by the state, the authority is not independent of the state. The authority may borrow using its own assets such as its buildings, equipment, and inventory as collateral, but may not do so using the assets or backing of the state or the infrastructure as collateral for a loan. Loans to the independent agency are non-recourse loans—meaning that creditors do not have recourse to the government if the loan fails. These loans are also subject (as most loans are) to indenture (a written contract) in which the potential creditor is clearly told that the loans are non-recourse loans. They lend based on their faith in the authority.
Taxes and Fees	The independent authority has no power to impose taxes. It will also not receive tax dollars except as it might occur because the government collects a user "tax" in lieu of having the users pay directly to the independent agency and passes it on to the authority. This is often done for the purposes of efficiency. The independent authority sets and collects fees from those it serves. In multi-jurisdictional arrangements, each jurisdiction may pay regular assessments as if they were members without implying their control.
Management	The independent authority has its own management—though the board and the chief executive officer may be named by the government and removed by it for cause and with due process. In this capacity, their duty is to the authority, but no member of the management is a government employee. A minority of board members may be government officials. They serve to protect and express the public interest and to facilitate transactions with the principal agencies with which the independent authority interacts. Their participation also ensures a level of transparency and accountability. Their first duty is, however, to the operation and sustainability of the infrastructure and the authority. They are not paid separately for this service.
Hiring	The independent authority is not part of the government civil service. It hires, fires, assigns, and negotiates worker contracts (set terms of employment) and settles worker disputes on its own but within the country's labor laws unless specific exceptions are made.
Tax Exemption	All public authorities are not tax exempt. To be so, the authority must be formed as a nonprofit and given tax exemption as a privilege on specific income streams such as those derived from performing its mission and on passive income such as interest, dividends, and rentals. However, an independent authority does not require tax exemption, but it supports the case because in addition to providing financial resources, it eliminates the potential use of the government of its power to tax as a tool of control.

Budgets	The budget of the independent authority is independently determined by its management and not by the executive or legislative branches. However, because they are overseeing a public asset in the interest of the public, the government may have the right to call into question, but not design, control, or manage the budget or its individual items. Any member of the public has this same right. They may question if a particular activity is within the public interest, within the boundaries or mission of the independent agency, or within the approved rules to avoid misconduct or inferences of government obligation. They can deny approval, which only means that the authority, being independent, continues to operate but under the previous budget. Budget stalemates cannot close down operations as they could with a dependent agency.
Audits	The independent authority chooses its own auditors who report to the board. The audit is public information and the government may use such information or request in its oversight role.
Contracting	An independent authority has its own rules and guidelines on contracting, designs its own contracts, negotiates them, monitors them, makes payments and receives refunds or credits, settles contract disputes without resort to government. The contracts are between them and the other parties who would generally have no recourse to government. The authority is not a representative of the government in these contracts or the government of them.
Acquisition and Disposition of Property	Part of infrastructure development and operation is the acquisition of property and other assets to facilitate efficiency, and to dispose of them when no longer necessary or useful; and, similarly, to accumulate inventory and to dispose of it on a timely basis at the discretion of the authority. To the extent that the authority cannot do this, assuming that it is following a protocol including one to discourage corruption, it is not independent. An independent authority, however, may be restricted from acquiring property unrelated to its operation. A restriction on the disposition of these assets could produce inefficiency and increase holding costs of unnecessary items.
To Sue and Be Sued	An agency of the government has the protection of the government's immunity. It also has the advantage of the government's defense and a right to defense by the government. This is clearly not so with an independent authority. Being nonprofit however, does give it the benefits of whatever nonprofit shield or defense that might be available but this may be less than any immunity a dependent agency might have as an extension of government.
Joint Ventures and Partnerships	A truly independent authority is free to enter into any formal partnership its board deems appropriate and will be both accountable and liable in the form and extent that the partnership agreement stipulates. This is less true of a dependent agency since its involvement exposes the government or the part of the government to which it is dependently attached.

To Use Its Own Property as Collateral for a Loan (There May Be Limitations on the Use of the Property)	A truly independent authority can acquire its own property in support of its operation and dispose of it at its discretion. It might choose to use that property to collateralize debt, but their claims never extend to the government; if they can, the authority is not independent. There may be restrictions on use or disposition of the property it acquired through the government, or as deemed essential to the infrastructure, or the infrastructure itself as these may be deemed to be public property or part of the national wealth held in the public's interest. In this case, the authority is not the owner but the custodian and operator of the property.
To Obey the General Law and Not to Pretend to Be Government	An independent authority may have policing power within its boundaries, but not general policing powers, judicial authority, passport provision, or any other sovereign powers. An independent authority can be limited in its powers and scope of authority in the same way as a dependent authority. An independent authority may be required to state this limitation when dealing with a third party. Even within its boundaries any part of its sovereign powers (for example, policing) is not superior to the state's interest and responsibilities. An independent authority is not above the law although for certain purposes that allow it to do its job, it may have specific exemptions. It may, as any other entity, be dependent upon government for generally accepted government functions; for example, the detention of persons, the imposition of taxes, the contribution of taxes such as social welfare contributions, the issuing of passports, sanitation, and so on.
Government Oversight and Public Accountability	It is up to legislative and executive bodies to determine the extent of public oversight that is necessary on a firm, an independent authority, or a dependent agency. Some sectors of firms have extensive oversight, reporting, and public disclosure responsibilities. This is true with utilities, where public exposure to certain risks are likely, hospitals, and enterprises that have a key role in the health, welfare, and safety of the community. The thin line is that the oversight should be exhaustive enough to protect the public's interest, to give voice to the public, to be sure that the assets are used prudently, and yet should not be controlling. This seemingly impossible task is done routinely with public utilities.

Public authorities are extremely flexible in their organizational designs. They may be crafted for various purposes, to serve populations of different sizes, with a variety of governance structures and sizes, a range of independence and control, they may be formed as trusts (see Oklahoma Statutes, Title 60) or as corporations. Among the common themes are these:

1. They are formed to produce a product or service, organizationally at least, outside of the core bureaucracy.
2. The product or service is singularly focused even though it may provide various program routes toward meeting that end.

3. The focus is always to meet a stipulated public purpose of significance. While the beneficiary of the service is a public, the residual or beneficiary interest in the assets lies in the government. This means, among other things, that if the authority is terminated, the assets remain with the government and the government may impose certain restrictions or prohibitions on the disposition of the assets; that is, their sale.
4. While their governance structure may differ, especially in size, their directors or trustees are appointed.
5. The appointments may be made by any combination of the legislature or the executive.
6. Their appointees always include one or more offices of government whoever the incumbent might be. It is the office that is appointed—not the person of the incumbent.
7. Exemption from Federal, state, and local taxes is generally by virtue of being an entity of government without the need for a 501(c)(3) designation; but the latter may be elected providing the conditions can be met.
8. For almost all of them, the lessening of the burden of government is a reason for their creation. The burden may be the operational, planning, financing, or any combination of these.
9. They have the powers of a corporation (even if they are unincorporated or are a trust) for without these they cannot function. These powers are discussed in Chapter 2.
10. In addition to corporate powers, they have other powers depending upon their purposes. Often these are limited sovereign powers including the power of eminent domain.

The TVA discussed in the last chapter is an example of an authority with vast regional reach and powers—cutting across states. The Blanchard Municipal Improvement Authority (BMIA) is one configured totally differently for a small municipality. Blanchard is a town of approximately 8,000 people in Oklahoma. It formed the Blanchard Municipal Improvement Authority with the purpose of acquiring, holding and operating essential public services (for example, public utilities) for the benefit of the residents and those in the nearby area for the purposes of lessening the burden of government. It refers to the burden of local, state and federal governments. The trustees of the authority are the members of the council. The executive director is the city manager, the attorney is the city attorney, and the clerk is the secretary. It was formed pursuant to Oklahoma Statutes, Title 60, especially Section 176–180, which not only specifies the board composition of nonprofit entities such as BMIA, but states how it would operate and renders it the types of powers discusses in Chapter 2 as well as the power of eminent domain and of issuing debt for the benefit of the government. Districts, such as school districts, and special districts are authorities for small areas within a municipality that may be just a couple of blocks. All are formal nonprofit entities incorporated under the State's nonprofit corporation laws and are eligible for exemption as a state entity as long as they actually operate that way.

Are Authorities Doers or Financers?

They are both. Some states have authorities that simply issue debt to raise funds for other agencies or private users such as disadvantaged or small entrepreneurs unable to raise funds in the capital market on their own. Other authorities are doers. The Virginia Port Authority (VPA) coordinates ports, but the daily administrative, price-setting, negotiating and fee setting, and collecting are all chores done by a nonprofit, the Virginia International Terminals, LLC, a tax-exempt entity under the Virginia Port Authority (VPA), which gets virtually no state funds but turns all of its profits over to the VPA and is its principal source of income. Authorities are flexible as states may design them with great latitude (Thynne and Wettenhall, 2004).

Summary and Preview

Governments may create nonprofits that are tax exempt as government entities or they may create 501(c)(3)s that are exempt because they are in fulfillment of the terms of that section of the code for privately created nonprofits. In either case, the exemption applies to income related to their mission and unrelated business income is taxed. We shall explore the differences between these two types of income later. Further, while some government entities may receive deductible charitable gifts under Section 170(b)(1)(A)(v), they are not likely to be as effective as 501(c)(3)s in accessing the private market for donations. Moreover, they do not remove the operational burden from government.

For an entity to claim or to be treated as a 501(c)(3), it has to be de facto independent. This independence is determined by law and accounting principles by the facts and circumstances. Absent certain obvious powers, the entity cannot be deemed independent and is an agency of the state. These powers are given in this chapter because they help in designing the 501(c)(3) or truly independent agency. The author has extracted these from the discussions documents of the IRS and the international accounting agency for setting the rules and the author's own experience as a trustee for these bonds, authorizing their terms and issuance, and signing the prospectus as a legal trustee for them overseeing their performance. When an authority is truly separate it can remove the burden of government both in its operations and in its financing.

We shall return to this in Chapter 11, but moreso in the last chapter of this book because there is some serious misunderstanding as to why governments do this—it isn't to "hide" debt. It is efficient. It is also equitable because debt service falls on users rather than on the general population, and often this arrangement provides considerably more transparency. The principal contribution of this chapter on this matter is how must an authority be designed to optimally lessen the burden of government—given the accounting and tax rules that mitigate shenanigans.

When the government creates a nonprofit to lessen its burden or accepts a citizen-created one, a stipulation is made regarding the existence of a functioning board, one made up of specific categories of persons. This is less about democracy than it is about effective representation on decision-making of the board and keeping the board and the consequent operation of the organization aligned with the burden the organization is supposedly relieving.

Bibliography

Reilly, John Francis and Barbara A. Braig Allen. "Political Campaign and Lobbying Activities of IRC 501(c)(4), (c)(5), and (c)(6) Organizations," *Exempt Organizations-Technical Instruction Program for FY 2003.*

Thynne, Ian. "Making Sense of Organizations in Public Management: A Back-to-Basics Approach," *Public Organization Review*, vol. 2, Issue 3,, pp. 317–332 (2003).

Thynne, Ian and Roger Wettenhall, "Public Management and Organizational Autonomy: The Continuing Relevance of Significance of Earlier Knowledge," *International Review of Administrative Sciences*, Vol. 70, No. 4, pp. 808–821 (December 2004).

United Nations Economic Commission for Europe (UNECE), Guidebook on Promoting Good Governance in Public-Private Partnerships, United Nations: New York and Geneva (2008).

Wettenhall, Roger. "Explaining Types of Public Sector Organizations: Past Experience," *Public Organization Review*, Vol. 3, 2003, pp 219–245 (2003a).

http://www.ag.ny.gov/press-release/ag-schneiderman-adopts-new-disclosure-requirements-nonprofits-engage-electioneering

http://www.irs.gov/irm/part7/irm_07-025-003-cont03.html

In New York State, there are over 6,000 government created authorities. DiNapoli, Thomas, New York State Office of the State Comptroller https://www.osc.state.ny.us/pubauth/whatisauthority.htm

http://www.panynj.gov/corporate-information/pdf/2014-budget.pdf

Government Accounting Standards Board GASB, Exposure Draft, the Financial Reporting Entity: An Amendment of GASB Statements No. 14 and No. 34, especially paragraphs 24/53, 2010.

International Public Accounting Standards Board https://www.ifac.org/sites/default/files/publications/files/ipsas-6-consolidated-and-1.pdf.

Chapter 7 – Decision-Making and Governance Structure in Lessening the Burden of Government

Nonprofit boards that lessen the burden of government have very different profiles, purposes, and significantly more exposures to charges of organizational control, self-dealing, and directors' conflicts of interests and political cronyism; the need to address these concepts is important in the organizational design strategies—particularly of the way their boards are constructed to meet the requirements of lessening the burden of government. How and why to do this are the topics of this chapter.

To be incorporated, to get a tax exemption, and to be considered by the IRS to be relieving a burden of government, the nonprofit needs a governing board. It also needs a governing board to sign certain formal documents, to authorize and to enter into agreements, to receive certain institutional gifts and to hire top executives and independent contractors such as auditors and corporate counsel. But for nonprofits claiming to be lessening the burdens of government, the board needs a particular profile. The Federal rules in this connection are not about demography, diversity, or democracy. A core concept is that those who are at risk must be more than nominally represented in the governing body and the agencies of government whose burdens are being lessened should be as well. This is true whether the organization is a doer or a facilitator.

Because the governing body is highly if not exclusively populated with persons and entities at risk with clear personal, professional, and commercial interests (and in the case of governments politically appointed) certain concepts have a magnified significance. These include the concepts of control, interlocking interests, conflicts of interest, possibilities of disloyal or even illegal and corrupt behavior in the pursuit of self-interest or the interests of family or business associates, making policies and strategies toward concepts particularly relevant. Some of these concepts will be discussed in this chapter and some in Chapter 11. It all begins with how the governing board is usually chosen—not from the general population but from the population at risk.

The Board

In order to qualify for exemption as lessening the burden of government, boards created by government as well as those created by citizens must not only meet

DOI 10.1515/9781501505799-008

the requirements of their individual state laws, but the requirements of the Internal Revenue Service.

1. That their boards contain persons and entities in the community or jurisdiction they serve.
2. That their boards contain locally elected or appointed officials.
3. That their boards contain persons named by the government they serve.
4. That their boards contain persons and entities representing those at risk of being affected by what policies and programs the organization pursues.

In general, these boards are populated by persons and entities representing local businesses, local residents, the local government, and any group at risk to be affected by the mission of the nonprofit that is lessening the burden of government. Therefore, they may magnify the risk of conflicts of interest, political cronyism, self-dealing, and even what Brody, (2004), writing in a different context, referred to as parochialism paternalism—meaning focused almost exclusively on the local community; and paternalism—meaning that the attorney general and the state having an unusually keen interest in how the organization operates.

The boards of nonprofits that lessen the burden of government may have more turnover than other boards. This turnover may be present whether the nonprofit is created by government or by citizens. A prime reason for this is that they tend to have members appointed in conjunction with their official capacities; therefore, they leave their position when they are no longer in that official capacity, for whatever reason—dismissed, voluntary resignation, transfer, their end of term, or the replacement of their political parties. This turnover also occurs with other community members on the board serving in their capacity as residents, business or civic persons, or as a person appointed by the state or local government.

Yet, the board, as with all other nonprofit boards, must function. When the board is not functional or a member of the board is not functional, either the board or the individual members may be removed (a) by the board itself according to its bylaws, (b) by a vote of the membership, or (c) involuntarily by the attorney general of the state.

Specific Functions of the Board

The principal role of the governing body (directors or trustees) is to represent the public's interest in the organization, to assure conformity with the mission and all other contracts, to provide for the efficient and ethical operation of the organization, to assure conformity with the law, to oversee and to protect the assets of the organization—including the organization itself, and to give management the best of its insight and guide it with relevant policies and decisions. Thus, a functioning board will among other things do these essentials:

1. Approve the budget
2. Review, sign and assure submission of annual reports
3. Review and authorize personnel policies relevant to hiring, promotion, dismissal, compensation, whistleblowers, independent contractors, key employees, sexual harassment, and fairness to the disabled and other groups
4. Meet annually and as needed, even if only electronically
5. Review and approve plans of reorganization, growth, and contraction
6. Review and approve plans for major asset sales and acquisition
7. Review and approve major gifts including the terms of the gifts
8. Review and approve the organization's plans to do major borrowing
9. Review and approve the organization's investment policy, plans to open banking and other financial accounts
10. Review and approve major changes in retirement, benefits, and compensation for all employees with special focus on reasonableness of top executives
11. Review and approve amendments to the bylaws
12. Provide and be prepared to receive complaints, allegations of wrongdoing that affect the senior staff—its omission or commission including conflicts of interest
13. Discharge and replace its members for reasons authorized by the bylaws
14. Create committees and hire consultants
15. Write policy and review status of its own membership for independence, conflict of interest, self-dealing, competence, performance of duties, and compensation
16. Be prepared to authorize lawsuits by the organization, receive them and dispose of them by settlement agreed upon by them, if necessary
17. Authorizing liability, bonding, and other insurance and indemnification
18. Authorize collaborations, other commitments of the organization and their terms
19. Require accountability, transparency, loyalty, and conformity by key employees and to protect the identity and integrity of the organization
20. Request dissolution and to carry out its terms
21. Approve changes in the organization's name and address
22. Approve changes in the number, composition, qualifications, authority, or duties of the governing body's voting members; in the number, composition, qualifications, authority, or duties of the organization's officers or key employees
23. State the requirements of a quorum or for any class of issue

24. State the conditions and procedures for calling emergency meetings
25. Keep records of its activities

When the mission is to lessen the burden of government, the board must reflect those whose interests are at risk. In local economic or area development this means that local residents of the specific area, business entities, and officials must be on the board in their capacities as such persons. They lose their board seats once they are no longer in these specified capacities and replaced by another who is. Their absence is cause to put the application of the organization for exemption into jeopardy.

Board membership occurs mainly by appointment and by designation as in the bylaws. The terms are also in the bylaws. Unless the bylaws stipulate otherwise, the board by its majority vote determines acceptance, removal, and denial of membership.

In order to carry out its work, the board may divide itself into as many committees and subcommittees, permanent or ad hoc as it sees useful. Three committees—the audit, governance, and compensation committees—play especially central roles.

An *audit committee* (or its function) is required. It appoints both the internal and external auditors who report directly to the audit committee and through them to the board and through them to the organization or the authorities or partners as required. It engages auditors in discussions about the accounting practices used by the organization and in a discussion of the methods and procedures used by the organization to financially obligate itself, record that obligation, discharge it and display it. Based on all these, the audit committee not only helps to ensure accuracy and transparency of financial reports, but it helps to protect the organization against excessive transactions and self-dealing, corrupt acts, and by maintaining its good standing by reporting on time and in the manner required. It is common to require that the chair of the audit committee be an independent director (discussed below).

The *governance committee* is charged with ensuring that the organization maintains best industry practices in how it is managed and how it operates. The governance committee's emphasis is on methods of decision-making, methods of execution, employee-organization and employee-management interaction. It oversees rules including those on political participation discussed in Chapter 6. It is the body that oversees over the trustees themselves, their modus operandi, their relationship to the CEO and other managers, and the organization's relationship to the public. The governance committee oversees channels of communication and the way information is transmitted and travels through the organization. It establishes how complaints and recommendations are received, processed, and stored. The governance committee oversees disclosures, management reports, and the procedures through which these are developed. They also oversee how the bylaws are enforced. In some organizations where there is no formal nominating or appointments committee this committee also oversees appointments and removal from the board and the hiring and discharging of the very senior managers.

The *compensation committee* oversees executive appointments and compensation, but it also oversees the compensation of other key persons including independent contractors. The intent is to reduce self-serving and self-dealing that is not only contrary to law but that are not in accord with industry or ethical norms of the organization and the specific challenges it faces for an organization of its size, purpose and composition. This means consideration of salaries, bonuses, perks, loans, privileges, usually of the top 5 percent of those who receive compensations from the organization—including some independent contractors. The committee is also charged with avoiding discrimination in appointments and nepotism and cronyism. This committee along with the governance committee may also be involved in setting the terms of appointment and retention. This committee, like the audit committee, may be required to report the votes by independent or non-independent status.

Interlocking Directorates

An *interlocking directorate* is one in which one or more persons serve on two or more related boards, thus linking them. In terms of this book, particularly Chapter 3, this linkage has significance for determining whether the organization is an affiliate, subsidiary, who controls whom, and placement of loyalty and priorities. It also speaks to issues of taxation (see Chapter 9).

In Chapter 3 we saw that in a supporting organization, a 509(a)(3), an interlocking directorate is a positive signal to express the supporting and internal facilitating role among organizations forming an internal support network purposefully binding them in a brother-sister or a parent-child relationship to assure collaboration, responsiveness, and even subordination of one to the other. This is done by bylaws requiring them to share the same board members. Furthermore, the organizations in these networks share a common goal. Specifically, supporting organizations share a common goal with the organization they support. This common goal is reinforced by sharing an interlocking board.

In the case of two related nonprofits, each carrying out a different mission, an interlocking board of trustees would imply that one is controlled by the other. Hence, the receipt of income (especially interest and rental) from the controlled organization by the organization that is in control would expose that income to taxation.

Interlocking directorates also apply to collaborations such as joint ventures or other "disregarded" (the legal term for joint ventures, limited liability companies, and other for-profits in which the organization may be the sole member and therefore its activities are not separately reported but included as part of the organization's calculation of its own performance). Joint ventures, partnerships, and other such collaborations frequently share the boards of their parents in some agreed upon ratio. By definition, the joint venture is a shared and common goal among the partners and an interlocking board reinforces that joint interest.

Conflict of Interest, Independence, and Board Members

None of the above completely removes the possibilities of concern for the conflict of interest, a concept which focuses on personal or private gains from a specific transaction; or the independence of a board member, a concept which refers to the relationship of the board member to the organization. Is he or she a part of the organization and therefore likely biased in favor of the organization rather than objective?

The fact that a member may be non-independent does not necessarily mean that the member has a conflict of interest. But it can raise the question: Is the person's view likely tainted or biased? When a board member is not independent, that has to be recorded; it is not prohibited. Interlocking directorates may therefore have several members who are not independent, but not necessarily self-dealing. For a member of the board to be considered independent all four of the following conditions must be met:

1. The member must not be a compensated officer or employee of the organization, its affiliate, or other related organization, or any other with which the filing one does business.
2. The member must not have received compensation exceeding $10,000 from any of the above during the reporting year.
3. Neither the member nor a member of his or her family must have had an economic transaction with the organization or its affiliated or related organizations during the year.
4. Neither the member nor a member of his or her family must have had an economic transaction during the year with an organization doing business with the filing organization or its affiliates.

A member is not considered to be notindependent just because:
1. The member receives compensation from the organization contingent upon his or her being a member of a recipient group of the organization.
2. The voting member is a donor of any amount to the organization.

Obviously, these concepts of conflict of interest, independence and self-dealing need to be given further and keener attention in the design of a nonprofit to lessen the burden of government. Table 7.1 helps explain.

Table 7.1. Conflicts of Interest, Non-Independence, and Self-Dealing

---

Conflict of Interest: This concept relates to specific transactions. Who in a particular transaction may be exposed to a conflict of interest (regardless of remuneration from any party) because of direct or indirect ties to parties standing to gain (and also lose) from the transaction directly or indirectly? If not the person, is it relatives, associates, or businesses? A conflict of interest policy should apply to employees (especially those in senior management) as well some independent contractors (especially those that are integrally a part of the nonprofit operation; for example, doctors in a hospital).

Independent or Non-independent Director or Trustees: This concept applies primarily to voting trustees—those who by their actions can influence the decisions and direction of the organization. A person is not an independent trustee if the person receives remuneration from the organization (other than from being a trustee), or his or her relatives, businesses, and associates do business with the organization and any of its affiliates. Being a donor of any amount does not make a trustee non-independent.

Self-Dealing: This concept applies to donors and other benefactors of the organization. It also applies to trustees and senior management when (a) there is excessive or prohibited transactions, (b) transactions to which a donor or member of the management can benefit or whether they, their relatives, associates, or businesses can benefit. This type of violation, unlike the two above, comes with financial penalties to management.

Except for self-dealing, where penalties may apply, the reliance is on transparency and good judgment. A policy on any or all of these should be part of the annual orientation of managers and especially of trustees principally because it is possible to be inadvertently trapped. Policy should be refreshed annually with a simple question: "Have there been any changes in your condition, those of your relatives, associates, and businesses that could expose you to being classified as a disqualified person (to whom the concept of self-dealing applies), in conflict of interest, or as a non-independent trustee?" Let us deal with each of these potential problems.

Dealing With Possible Conflicts of Interest

A conflict of interest occurs when a person stands to gain from decisions he or she makes that are likely to benefit him or her self, family, or business associates at the expense of the benefit to the organization. A non-independent board member may not necessarily have a conflict of interest with a particular transaction. A conflict of interest with a transaction may just as easily occur (if not more so) with a member who is an independent member of the board. A conflict of interest implies that the person has subordinated or is at the risk of subordinating his or her duty (loyalty) to the organization on an organizational matter to his or her own gain or the gain of a family member or business associate.

Every nonprofit organization needs to consider ways to avoid conflicts between the interests of the organization and those individuals in management, governance, and decision-making roles in the organization. The IRS has recommended that organizations consider adopting a conflict of interest policy that includes provisions to which these individuals should conform when considering transactions in which they have a potential, actual, direct, or indirect financial interest. The policy might require:

1. Disclosures by interested persons of these financial interests and the facts that are material to them
2. Procedures for determining whether the financial interest could result in a conflict
3. Procedures such as abstaining from a vote or excusing one's self from discussion on matters related to the transaction
4. Procedures for taking corrective action should such a conflict occur
5. Procedures for recording discussions and decisions, including votes
6. Procedures for being sure that each trustee has received, read, and understood the policy

Managing the Risk of Self-Dealing

Self-dealing is invariably a consequence of a conflict of interest. If the latter were the signal of a likely opportunity, the former is the action that takes advantage of the opportunity for personal, family, or business-related gains or the gains of another manager or independent contractor (such as excessive compensation). California's Section 5233 clearly defines self-dealing as any transaction involving the organization and in which one or more trustees or officers have a material financial benefit, unless (1) the attorney general gave approval, (2) the organization entered into the transaction for its own benefit, (3) the transaction was fair and reasonable for the organization, (4) it was favorably voted for by the majority of the board, not including the affected members, and (5) the board had information that more reasonable terms were not available; (6) if the action was taken in an emergency, the board must approve it in its next meeting. The penalty for the infraction of self-dealing may include the return of the property with interest, payment of the amount by which the property appreciated, and a fee for the use of the property. It may also include a disciplinary penalty for the fraudulent use of the assets of the organization.

Again, self-dealing does not bar an honest, arm's length transaction that benefits the nonprofit and does not unduly favor the trustee or officer over others. These types of transactions should always be approached with very careful legal and ethical scrutiny and within the scope of a carefully crafted and existing policy. Discussions involving the questioning of the involved parties as well as decisions, and the supporting or exculpatory information should always be kept.

Dealing With Non-Independence

Each member of the board has to be classified as independent or not and, if not, why and how. Moreover, there is no prejudgment that is correct about the relevance of non-independence. A key employee may be non-independent and a member may be non-independent from business ties; this does not mean that their votes may be similar, but knowing "where they may be coming from" is important.

Standards at the Root of All Trustee Actions

At the root of independence, conflict of interest, and self-dealing are three simple standards: Together, the terms loyalty, care, and obedience define the fiduciary responsibility of the trustees and the officers of a nonprofit, both of whom can be held personally liable for monetary damages for breaching these duties. A trustee who behaves in conformity with these standards escapes personal liability for his or her action on behalf of the organization even if the result is an error so serious as to cause the organization to lose its status. The standards guide actions; they do not judge their brilliance or consequences.

These standards recognize the possibility of error, so they judge only unintentional negligence—not whether the decision was fruitful or intelligent. The application of these principles in a court of law prohibits second-guessing as long as the trustees made their decisions in good faith. This is called the business judgment rule. What follows is an explanation of the three.

Duty of Loyalty

The duty of loyalty means that while acting in the capacity of a trustee or manager of a nonprofit, a person ought to be motivated not by personal, business, or private interest, but by what is good for the organization. The use of the assets or goodwill of the organization to promote a private interest at the expense of the nonprofit is an example of disloyalty; in such cases, an individual places the nonprofit in a subordinate position relative to his or her own interest. The nonprofit is being used. One purpose of annual reporting referred to above is to check on self-dealing.

Self-dealing is a form of disloyalty. Again, self-dealing means using the organization to advance personal benefits when it is clear that the personal gains outweigh the gains to the organization. A trustee is not prohibited from engaging in an economic or commercial activity with the organization; but such a transaction can be construed as self-dealing if it can be shown that the trustee gained at the expense of the nonprofit, that the trustee offered the nonprofit a deal inferior to what is offered to others, or what the nonprofit could acquire on the open market, or that the nonprofit was put in a position of assuming risks on behalf of the trustee. A numerical amount, $5,000 or more, makes the self-dealing an illegal—not just an ethical—infraction.

Another form of self-dealing can occur when two or more nonprofits merge assets or transfer assets from one to the other and they have the same trustees. Here the issue is whether a good purpose is being served. Therefore, before consummating a merger or any major transaction, it is wise to set a barrier against self-dealing.

One common way the board of trustees must defend the nonprofit organization against self-dealing is not in cases of corporate officers abusing their trustee status for the benefit of their firms; rather, it is against the founders of these organizations. It is not unusual to find that after years of personal sacrifice in calling the public's attention to a good cause, founders of organizations confuse the assets of the nonprofit with their own, confuse the interest of the organization with their own, and begin to take dominion over these assets, or install themselves or relatives into highly favorable tenured positions. Operating under the burden of loyalty, boards must separate these persons from the organization.

Duty of Care

The duty of care requires trustees of nonprofits to act in a manner of someone who truly cares. This means that meetings must be attended, the trustees should be informed and take appropriate action, and the decisions must be prudent.

The test of prudence depends on state law. In many states, the trustees of nonprofits are held under the same rules that govern trustees of for-profit corporations. In these states, prudence can be construed to mean making decisions not unlike those expected of any other group of trustees faced with relatively the same "business" facts and circumstances. In other states, nonprofit trustees are held to a higher standard where prudence means using the same wisdom and judgment that one would if his or her personal assets were at stake. The first is called the corporate model and the second is called the trust model.

The duty of care can deny using ignorance as a defense. Therefore, it is inconsistent with this responsibility to allege that a trustee or manager does not hold any responsibility merely because he or she does not know. To know *is* the duty. It is this duty that makes many compassionate but busy people reluctant to serve on nonprofit boards. In a real sense, they can't care enough—not in the legal sense.

Duty of Obedience

The duty of obedience holds the trustee responsible for keeping the organization on course. The organization must be made to stick to its mission. We are reminded throughout this book that the mission of a nonprofit is unlike the mission of a firm. The mission is the basis upon which the nonprofit and tax-exempt status are conferred. Unlike a firm, a nonprofit cannot simply change its mission without the threat of losing either its nonprofit or tax-exempt status or both.

Economic Transactions and the Trustees

In the section below, we enumerate certain economic transactions that require decisions by the trustees; and, therefore, ones that have the possibilities of conflict of interest, self-dealing, corruption, malfeasance, and personal penalties on the trustees for failure to comply with the duties of loyalty, care, and obedience. The member may not be excluded from participation, but may recuse him or herself or require a vote or permission by the board for his or her participation. Furthermore, these transactions come with the right of the trustees to know and to be informed by the operating managers of the organization and may even require the approval of the trustee either by bylaws, state laws, or by the other parties to the transaction. They are listed in Table 7.2 below. They are inescapable in the role of being a trustee.

Table 7.2. Economic Transactions that Require Decisions by Trustees

1.	Changes in financial advisors or institutions
2.	Changes in the mission of the organization whether by amendment, interpretation, or by emphasis
3.	The allocation of the annual budget, both costs and expenditures
4.	The sale of the organization's assets
5.	The acquisition of capital assets or initiation of programs
6.	The annual performance of the organization—financially and in terms of its output
7.	Hiring, departure, or transfers in the top-tier of the organization
8.	The signing of contracts on independent contractors as well as key employees
9.	Major collaborations or partnership arrangements involving the organization
10.	The leasing of major assets by the organization whether as lessor or lessee
11.	Disputes in which the organization is likely to be involved, whether by clients, employees, or others
12.	Planned changes or agreement to any compensation schemes of employees, executives, and independent contractors—excessive compensation
13.	Independent assessment of financial activities and performances of the organization
14.	Specific performances of endowments and other funds subject to restrictions—dealing separately with restrictions imposed by donors from restrictions imposed by the trustees
15.	A projection of earnings and expenses by source with caveats of a projection and the identification of any uncertainty, twists, turns, and plans for more than a year if that is feasible and requested
16.	A discussion of diversion of funds and taking action
17.	The written authorization of debt and of any specific borrowing arrangement
18.	The written authorization of fundraising campaigns and contracts and choice of firm
19.	The hiring of auditors, receiving of their reports, and requiring organizational response
20.	The discussion prior to acceptance of large gifts whether outright or deferred and their terms
21.	Claims and potential settlements of corruption, discrimination, negligence or harassment
22.	Any legal action against the organization including failure to file proper documents
23.	Establishment and monitoring of internal control
24.	Approval of major advertising or use of the organization's logo or reputation
25.	Decide on dissolution, major collaboration, mergers, and other reorganizations
26.	Setting investment policies for unnecessary risk exposure and investment protection
27.	The assessment of purchasing contracts
28.	An assessment of the organization's business income stream and alliances
29.	Any cross-subsidization or subsidization of one program by another or by the organization that is tenuous
30.	Minimization of self-dealing, conflict of interest, personal inurement, and manipulation, fraud, and failure to comply

Excessive Economic Transactions and Due Diligence

Every economic transaction has the potential for some form of compensation where by a lack of exercising their duties of loyal, care, obedience, and the additional duty of due diligence, the trustees agree to or put forward a compensation that is offensively excessive. This occurs with compensation of key employees, the trustees themselves, and with independent contractors and vendors.

Trustees are responsible for negotiating and agreeing to executive compensation or key employee contracts. Key employees satisfy two criteria: (a) their full aggregate compensation of all types from the organization, its subsidiaries, its affiliates and disregarded groups (joint ventures and corporations that the nonprofit is sole member of and must include in their 990 reports) exceeds $150,000 annually, and (b) they hold a position of responsibility for making the decisions in any of the key employees. The Federal law, informally known as the intermediate sanction rule or "Taxpayer Bill of Rights 2," makes trustees disqualified persons. For purposes of compensation, a disqualified person is any trustee, manager, donor, or entity (and in the case of hospitals, physicians) who has substantial influence over the organization in the five years preceding the date of the "excess transaction." Any corporation in which a disqualified person owns or controls 35 percent or more of the stocks is also disqualified in a 501(c)(3) or (c)(4) organization.

Any such disqualified person who obtains excess benefits can be subject to an excise tax of 25 percent of such an excess, and any disqualified person who knowingly participated in this agreement would also be subject to an excise tax of 10 percent of the excess up to $10,000. The focus of this law is on executive compensation but it applies to all kinds of transactions, including the payment of trustees or any other disqualified person as defined above or the payment in a sale of a product or service rendered by them. The law considers excessive compensation to any disqualified person to be self-dealing; for example, using the assets of the organization for personal benefit.

Participation in self-dealing is willful if the disqualified person engaged in the act voluntarily, intentionally, and consciously. But liability also arises from silence and the lack of action to stop or to record objection to an excess benefits transaction unless there is reasonable cause to believe that the trustee or other disqualified persons did not know of the transaction, and did not know that the transaction would be deemed self-dealing. Failure to have inquired about whether the transaction was an act of self-dealing, where this inquiry is clearly indicated, does constitute an act of negligence and could likewise result in being penalized by the imposition of the excise tax.

But when is compensation excessive? When the compensation exceeds the economic value of the benefit the organization got in return, or when the compensation is calibrated to the organization's revenues or reflects personal inurement.

The law does provide for the organization to indemnify or insure the disqualified person against the cost of any penalty or taxes due to an "excess transaction." It does, however, also require that this insurance or indemnification be included in the compensation. Hence, the more the organization covers for the disqualified person, the greater the tax or penalty on all disqualified persons found to have knowingly participated in the transaction.

The principal defense against excessive economic transactions is comparable compensation information. Do comparable organizations justify what is being accepted or offered?

Duty of Organizations to Trustees and Their Rights

Trustees have the right to expect that the nonprofit organization has exactly the same duty to them as they have to the organization. They should expect obedience to their policies that are consistent with the mission of the organization. Trustees share liability for infractions; therefore, they should expect that their directions will be obeyed. It is they, rather than the employees, who represent the public interest. These are their first defenses against unwitting self-dealing, conflict of interest, and general failure to perform their duties of loyalty, care, and obedience.

Accordingly, they should expect a duty of care directed toward them. As their duty of care toward the organization means that they need to be informed and to act prudently on behalf of the organization, they should expect that they will be kept informed about those things that matter. These include being kept up to date on major changes in the organization's direction or assets, annual budgets and financial statements, changes in key employees, new risks to which the organization is exposed, employee compensation packages, and an evaluation of the organization's performance.

The duty to the trustees also encompasses loyalty. This concept implies a protection of the trustees. Trustees have a right to presume that the relationship between them and the organization is aboveboard (so to speak), at reasonable arm's length, and that the organization does not expose any trustee to personal or professional risks—even if it forewarned him or her that such risks might be present. Put simply, they have a right to expect that they are not being used or "set up" and that the information given them to form the basis of their decisions is as clear, complete, correct, and relevant as possible, and that the organization will not act imprudently.

Consistent with the exercise of prudence, trustees may rely on information they obtain from appropriately assigned employees, accountants, lawyers, engineers, and other experts. Relying on the expertise of such persons is an act of prudence and not necessarily a skirting or shifting of responsibility.

The Attorney General of New Hampshire brought suit against the board of trustees and president of a nonprofit organization for violation of the rights of trustees. Here is a list of specific rights of trustees that were involved:

1. To have a copy of the articles of organization (incorporation or deed), bylaws, and other documents that are necessary to understand the operations of the organization.
2. To inquire about an orientation session for board members and about a board manual containing the policies and procedures for the organization.
3. To have reasonable access to management and reasonable access to internal information about the organization.
4. To have reasonable access to the organization's principal advisors, including auditors and consultants on executive compensation.
5. To hire outside advisors at the organization's expense.

Observe that these rights are consistent with exercising the duty of care, and with the law's protection of trustees and officers if they rely on the expert judgment of persons such as auditors and accountants, lawyers, and investment advisors. They are also consistent with the duties of the organization to the trustees.

These rights translate to the right to know, to be informed, and to have their actions followed. Some of these are required by law, such as trustee approval of amendments, some are required by practice such as a bank's requirement that a trustee resolution by supplied before it extends a loan, some of these are subtle such as informing trustees about major transactions so that they can determine if there is a potential conflict of interest, some of these are early warnings or pleas for help such as giving a projection (not simply of the annual data) but what they may look like under certain projections such as if they continue to operate as they have been.

Liability of Trustees

No matter how much protective action is taken, there is always the possibility of a trustee being sued or involved in a lawsuit against the organization. How does the organization protect the trustee? First, by timely information as discussed above, so that the trustee can take adequate action. Second, by covering the trustee through insurance and indemnification. Third, by disclosures (to be discussed in the next section).

The board of trustees of a nonprofit organization may be sued by (1) the members in a so-called "derivative suit," whereby the members are suing the trustee on behalf of the greater good of the organization, (2) a third private party, (3) a government, and (4) one of its own members or employees. Liability may arise either for actions taken or for the failure to act. Furthermore, in some instances, liability may arise because of the actions of other trustees or officers. For example, a trustee can be held liable for failing to block an inappropriate action by other trustees or by management. The duties of care and loyalty mean that a trustee cannot choose to look the other way when an officer or another trustee may be involved in actions that are wrong.

This liability threat would discourage many good people from serving nonprofits. If the trustee can be held personally liable, then he or she faces the possibility of being sued and having to pay monetary damages out of personal resources. Even if monetary damages are not assessed, the trustee faces the unpleasant possibility of having to spend time and resources in a personal defense. In addition, there are the emotional and social costs.

Recognizing this deterrent, many states have taken actions to limit a trustee's personal liability. For volunteers as well as trustees, states range from no protection to protection only if the act was not intentional, the result of negligence or breach of fiduciary responsibilities, or a knowing violation of the law, or a result of a reckless action or done in bad faith.

In general, an officer or trustee is immune from civil suit for conducting the affairs of a nonprofit unless the action taken is willful or wanton misconduct or fraud, or gross negligence or that the person personally (or through a relative or associate) benefited from the action taken.

A trustee is liable for unlawful distributions of the assets of the organization. An unlawful distribution can be one that is inconsistent with the mission of the organization, inconsistent with the bylaws and tax-exempt laws, outside of the powers of the organization, and for private gains of the trustee of associates. A loan to a trustee is just one type of unlawful distribution. Using the assets for political purposes is another, and so is excessive executive compensation.

Not only are the trustees who voted in favor of the unlawful distribution liable, but so, are all other directors who failed to voice an objection. Arizona 10–3833 requires that objections be noted in the minutes of the meeting when the act was taken, or by 5:00 P.M. the day after. It further states that "the right to dissent does not apply to a director who voted in favor of the action." Still further, any trustee found liable for the unlawful distribution can collect from all trustees who voted affirmatively, all trustees and members who shared in the distribution, and all who failed to dissent in the manner proscribed by law.

Even though the nonprofit has the power to indemnify a trustee or officer, some states specify the conditions under which such indemnification can be offered. In Mississippi 79–11–281, indemnification can be offered only if the trustee (1) conducted him- or herself in good faith, and (2) believed that the conduct was in the best interest of the organization or at least not contrary to its best interest or those of its members.

The nonprofit may not indemnify the trustee or officer when he or she is judged to be liable to the nonprofit or in any situation where he or she benefited improperly. Indemnification may be limited to reasonable expenses incurred. Generally, reimbursement may occur only after the case is disposed, but Mississippi, as an example, provides for payment in advance. However, the trustee must provide a written statement attesting to having undertaken the action in question in good faith, the trustee promises to repay the sum if the judgment is against him or her, and the act is not one that would otherwise preclude indemnification. A trustee that is entitled to indemnification may turn to the court to have such indemnification paid by the nonprofit. If the proceeding is against the organization, rather than against the trustee, the trustee may be indemnified by the organization for his or her expenses. This is so if the trustee acted in good faith.

Annual Disclosures of Involvement of Current and Past Trustees and Senior Management

Disclosures are required about trustees, their current and past involvement professionally, business-wise, or their affiliation with other members, and with top executive officers and donors. This is to reduce the possibility of conflict of interest, the appearance and actuality of self-dealing, especially by a person who should have been known to have been a disqualified person, and for avoiding embarrassment or disgruntlement especially in membership organizations. The following are required disclosures on present and past trustees and of senior management:

1. Business or financial transactions between them and the organization or between the organization and the family members of these persons.
2. Grants from the organization to any of these people or members of their families.
3. Receivables, credits, loans, or payables to any of these or members of their families or business relations.

4. The size of the board, which members are independent, whether there is a difference in the voting power.
5. The member's contact information.
6. Whether the board members were required to disclose possible conflicts of interest.
7. The compensation received by any trustee not only from the organization, but from any entity related to the organization or any unrelated entity but for the benefit of the organization.
8. Whether each board member saw the 990 Form before it was filed.

The fact that the organization is required to disclose these is the first step. In some states, it may be followed by a suit from the district attorney if the transaction is prohibited on the state level. Moreover, to the extent that the board member, a member of his or her family, or business associate received benefits, this too could cause a problem because these are usually, as the member, classified as a disqualified person—meaning that any transaction of $5,000 or above must clearly show the nonprofit, not the person, as the key beneficiary. It also opens the question of conflict of interest which could trigger a state or Federal level investigation and consequences against not only the member with the conflict but other members of the board that did not explicitly object to it. Abstention or absence is denied as a defense.

Summary and Preview

Because of the rules to qualify for the lessening of the burden of government, the boards of these organizations are vulnerable to charges of self-interest, self-dealing, being non-independent and therefore biased, and conflicts of interest. They could also be charged with cronyism since those formed by governments are overloaded with government functionaries who are commonly political appointees to a government office. The defense against the latter is reduced by making the appointments of incumbents in an office—not the person. The defense of the others is more than writing policies, it is understanding what is involved and why some types of appointments are helpful. For example, a common requirement is that a substantial part of the board is comprised of individuals or entities that are at risk. It is also understanding the meaning of being a non-independent contract. This chapter has covered these issues as well as the duty of the organization to shield the trustees against the pitfalls of committing them.

Bibliography

Brody, Evelyn Whose Public? Parochialism and Paternalism in State Charity Law Enforcement, 79 Ind. L.J. 937, 985–999 (2004)

IRS Private Letter 8948034.

Hoover, Stewart P. "Nonprofit Corporations and Maryland's Director and Officer Liability Statute: A Study of the Mechanics of Maryland's Statutory Corporate Law," *University of Baltimore Law Review*, 18, no. 2 (Winter 1989), pp. 384–402.

Hanks, James J., Jr., and Larry P. Scriggins, "Let Stockholders Decide: The Origins of the Maryland Director and Officer Liability Statute of 1988," *University of Baltimore Law Review*, 18, no. 2 (Winter 1989), pp. 235–253.

Chapter 8 – Financing the Burden through Contributions

The Vietnam Veterans Memorial Fund, Inc., is a 501(c)(3) created by the U.S. Congress in 1980 to build and operate the Vietnam Veterans Memorial in Washington, DC, arguably one of the nation's most visited and spectacular memorials even in its simplicity. It gets no funds from the U.S. government but over 85 percent of its annual revenues come from contributions of the types discussed in this chapter and in the next chapter. The remainder is from investments and fees. The National Park Foundation is also a 501(c)(3) created by the U.S. Congress. Its sole purpose is to use these techniques to help support the National Park Service. It successfully raises a lot of money for the benefit of the public. It is obvious both were formed to relieve a burden of government and they do so successfully through contributions, the subject of this and the next chapter.

Contributions are important because (a) they help to finance the organization and the burden of government it assumed; (b) they are a metric of public support for what the organization is doing; (c) while the importance of contributions as a source of revenues vary across nonprofits that bear the burden of government, for some it helps to finance capital (such as buildings) as well as financing operating projects. Having been empowered to raise funds through this mechanism, the successful implementation of this strategy will depend on a mastery of the tools that are available , the powers to solicit , and a perspective about contributions. As generous as Americans are, they do not give simply to help lessen the burden of government. By my own calculations, gifts to reduce the federal debt annually do not exceed 2 percent of that debt. So what would motivate giving to a nonprofit that exists to lessen the burden of government?

A General Picture of Contributions and the Sector

Chapter 1 reveals that, on average, charitable donations account for roughly 50 percent of all 501(c)(3) revenues and this is just sufficient to cover about 50 percent of expenses. Clearly, there is variation among organizations within the 501(c)(3) group. A disproportionate share of all charitable contributions goes to the largest organizations. Nonprofits vary in the success of receiving contributions as well as perhaps why people give to them. We take note of this as we proceed.

DOI 10.1515/9781501505799-009

Why People Give: Aside From Tax and Purely Charitable Reasons

Bekkers and Wiepking (2011) found that people are inspired to give because of their awareness of a need, the solicitation effort, their perception of costs and benefits including psychological benefits to themselves, their sense of altruism, their values, and the efficacy with which they can do so. Trust is important as an inducement to give, but not without the base ingredient of commitment by the individual to the organization or cause (Sargeant and Lee, 2004), or an emotional or service involvement (Sargeant, Ford, and Hudson, 2008). The ability to identify with the organization that they hold in great esteem (Crosson, and Shang 2009), and an identity with a high moral purpose, matters to donors. For such persons, additional awards or recognition may not be necessary incentives (Winterich, Mittal, and Aquino, 2013). This speaks to contributions relating to government burdens such as parks and memorials, examples of which have been given in past chapters.

Studies on motives for giving cover a variety of reasons summarized by Bekkers and Wiepking (2011) from self-benefit (White and Peloza, 2009), to the perception of government contribution (Van Slyke and Brooks, 2005), which may help us to infer why donors give to the organizations that are formed to lessen the burden of government. It may depend clearly on the specific burden, their identity to its stature and representation, their being incentivized by others whom they respect, and whether they feel that there is a need measured in part by the burden itself and the contribution of others, including government.

Turning to experimental studies reported in Andreoni, James and Abigail Payne, and in Raj Chetty, Martin Feldstein, Emmanuel Saez (2013) one is left with the following insights:

1. Two motives found for giving are (a) pure altruism and (b) "warm glow." In the first, individuals give purely because of their individual emotional response to a problem—pure altruism. In the second, the individual gives in order to be a part of the effort—warm glow. In the first, the emphasis of the message is on a problem manageable by the donor's contribution. In the second, the message is on a problem in which the donor's contribution is marginal, but is critical to the sum and to the "warm glow" emanated by other donors and the problem of which the donor is being called to be a part.

2. People can enjoy supporting a cause either through taxation (through the government) or when giving voluntarily to a nonprofit, but they are likely to give more and to enjoy it more when giving voluntarily. An implication of this is that some programs are likely to do better when they can accurately be presented as publicly supported rather than government supported even

if the latter receives some government funds. It is the former that is the stronger stimulus for giving. This leads many researchers to wonder if government funding "crowds out" private giving. More importantly it suggests that the strategy to use nonprofit tax-exempt organizations to reduce the financial burden of government is an appealing concept.

In a separate effort, Lichtenstein, Drumwright and Braig (2004) in summarizing four studies, conclude that consumers support and identify with firms with corporate social responsibility and are more inclined to donate to those charities which the corporation supports. Further consumers are more likely to support a corporation even when it had no previous record of social responsibility. Why this happens begs the question: Why do corporations give?

Why Corporations Give Beyond the Tax Reasons

Among the nontax reasons for corporate giving is that it stimulates goodwill with workers, clients, and the community, and improves and protects the corporate market by being a good citizen (Harris and Klepper, 1977). It also represents what Baumol (1971) called "enlightened self-interest." This views corporate giving as a combination of corporate citizenship, prudent investment, the desire to take a leadership role in an activity, to encourage others to give, and to be identified with project success.

Corporations may say no because of the asset involved:

1. *Stocks*: More than a token gift by the corporation of its own stock could require shareholder approval and probably SEC filings. Appeal to the individual as a stockholder—not to the corporation for its stocks.

    To get the controlling shares of a privately held corporation is also to assume the company's liabilities and problems.

    Stocks will have to be appraised if they are not publicly traded (that is, on the stock market) and have an estimated value in excess of $10,000. Officers and directors of corporations cannot give stock based on the anticipation that the price of the stock is about to decline so that they can maximize their deductions. This is insider trading, which is illegal. Moreover, some stocks acquired by the officers of a corporation are subject for a time to restrictions against their sale or transfer, even in the form of a charitable gift.

2. *Real property*: This is buildings and land. The corporation would have to consider tax implications, particularly the depreciation and investment tax credit it took on the property or its improvements. It would also have to consider easements—prohibitions about what it can and cannot do with the

property, covenants or agreements with creditors who placed restrictions on the disposition of the property, its exposure to environmental hazard liability, future use of the land in corporate long-range plans, resale price, and the donee's use of the land or building, which affects the amount of the deduction they can take.

3. *Bonds*: When a corporation issues a bond, it does so to raise capital from creditors. Giving these away would most certainly create legal problems. The best source is a holder of the bond.

4. *Equipment*: Often the corporation does not own their equipment. It is leased. When the property is owned, it may be possible that the tax benefits to be obtained from selling the equipment at a loss are greater than could be gained from a charitable deduction. Moreover, the equipment has trade-in value. The corporation may also be required to hold the equipment to meet the holding requirements for depreciation and investment tax credit. Also, the equipment may be subject to a lien.

   Even if the equipment is not fully depreciated, the concern of the firm may be if that equipment is used in an unrelated business of the organization, its value for tax deduction purposes would have to be recorded at zero.

5. *Inventory*: Except for small corporations, small donations, groceries, and restaurant food, gifts of inventory may have to be appraised and discounted for spoilage and obsolescence. They must also meet legal quality standards. For many nonperishables, selling at a discount may yield greater gains for the corporation than giving it away. Moreover, the inventory may not be owned by the corporation. Many retailers use trust receipts. This means that the inventory is actually owned by their wholesaler-distributor or by a financing company.

   In addition, in calculating the value of inventory, the firm has to subtract any gain from the fair market value. This means that the amount the firm can deduct is its cost of that inventory. For public affairs purposes, however, firms announce their donations in the higher retail value.

   There is also liability. Idaho Title 6–1301 states that a donor or a gleaner (one who harvests a donor's perishable crops for free distribution to a charity) cannot be liable for the perishable food as long as it was given in good faith and apparently fit for consumption by human beings. The exception to this occurs when an injury is due to the gross negligence, recklessness, or intentional misconduct of the donor or gleaner. Perishable foods include bakery products, fruits, vegetables, poultry, seafood, dairy products, and frozen or refrigerated products but do not include canned foods. They may be fit for human consumption even though their appearance, freshness, or grade does not make them marketable. It is important to remember, even when the gleaner or donor may not be held liable, the nonprofit can be so held.

Work-in-progress inventory, which means materials, supplies, and unfinished goods, is not available because it is used in the production activities of the firm. Even if such materials are flawed or damaged, it might be better to sell them at a discount or under some other brand name or no brand name at all, as is sometimes done with clothing and bad wine.

If the value of the inventory is already included by the corporation as cost of goods sold, its charitable deduction for that inventory is zero.

6. *Employee*: Several companies assign employees to nonprofit organizations and encourage others to volunteer. The company gets no charitable deduction but continues to pay wages and benefits to these employees and deducts their salaries and benefits as normal business expenses. The deduction is not the issue, it is whether the company can afford the loss of services of an individual it continues to pay and whether that individual wishes to do the job.

7. *Cash*: This is the easiest for the company to give. The company considers alternative uses of cash, including paying off debt, the paying of dividends to stockholders, employee benefits and executive bonuses, stock repurchases, increasing cash balances, and reinvestment. Companies have missions to which they commit themselves. Some companies prefer giving in their local or corporate communities. Some prefer the arts, education, or health.

Corporations may say no for other reasons:
1. *Proposed use*: A United States corporation cannot take a charitable deduction for a donation that is to be used abroad. It will have to lower its deduction if a donated personal tangible asset (a tangible asset other than real estate) is used by the organization for activities unrelated to the tax-exempt purpose of the organization or if the asset is sold.

2. *Mission*: The request may fall outside of the purposes targeted by the directors of the corporation and may be inimical to the marketing strategy of the firm.

3. *Losses*: A corporation cannot take a charitable deduction on a donation that contributes to its having a loss for the year. The corporation must be profitable to take advantage of a charitable deduction.

4. *Limits*: A corporation may have reached its 10 percent net-income legal limit for charitable deductions, or whatever limit it might have elected for charitable gifts that year. The corporation may not carry back or forward losses due to charitable contributions. Furthermore, there is a limit to how a cor-

poration may utilize its different types of deductions before the corporation is required to pay the alternative minimum tax. When this happens, the value of charitable contributions—especially those made in the form of property—have to be reduced.

5. *Lobbying*: A corporation cannot take a business or a charitable deduction for contributions made to a nonprofit that lobbies on matters beneficial to the corporation.

6. *Partying*: A corporation may not take a charitable or business deduction for a contribution to any organization that has a principal purpose of entertainment of its members.

7. *Disclosure and publicity*: The organization may not wish the publicity attendant to its gift.

8. *Disqualified persons*: The organization may be disqualified because of its previous gifts or because of the ownership of its shares by the organization or others associated with it. This by itself should not stop the corporation, but may place conditions on its gift.

9. *Taint of impropriety*: Corporations such as accounting firms need to protect against the taint that they have bought business with the organization.

10. *Opportunity cost*: Every dollar given to charity comes from some alternative corporate use of that dollar.

Dangers in Accepting Gifts

Some gifts are simply not worth taking. Others require caution:

1. *Land*: Beware of easements, restrictions on how all or parts of the land may be used, outstanding debt, hazardous waste and environmental conditions, liabilities, liens held by creditors using the property as security, new restrictions imposed by donor and local zoning laws, unrelated business income tax depending on use, and the cost and risks of holding unimproved land.

2. *Appreciated property*: Beware of becoming a co-conspirator in a fraudulently inflated appraisal. Art, securities, jewelry, real estate, and historical artifacts are common types of appreciated property.

3. *Unappreciated or worthless property*: Accepting junk leads to disposal costs and potential liability if others are placed at risk.

4. *Real estate*: Beware of all the same considerations as in 1 through 3 above. Determine costs of maintenance and improvements, income stream to support, feasible use and disposition.

5. *Cash*: Beware of the impact on the organization, such as changing its character to a private foundation, changing its mission, or causing its image or 501(c)(3) status to be lost. Check out the source and beware of undue influence of the donor on the organization.
6. *Short-term gifts*: The organization must comply with reporting requirements for gifts it disposes of within two years of acquisition.
7. *Long-term and future interest gifts*: Be sure that maintenance and operating costs are projected and can be met, and that the item will be transferred without impediment and loss of value.
8. *Gifts subject to debt*: Who will pay off the debt? Beware of unrelated business income tax and valuation problems.
9. *Insurance*: Who owns the policy? Who will collect? Who will pay premiums? The beneficiary status is no assurance.
10. *Testamentary gifts*: Be prepared for delay if the will is challenged. The person may change his or her mind prior to death.
11. *Stocks*: Is this a minority or controlling interest, and if a private foundation, does this represent excess business holdings? Should the stock be sold to protect against loss of value?
12. *Large gifts*: Does this change the status of the organization?
13. *Gifts subject to donor restrictions*: Can you meet the conditions? Are there encumbrances and are these consistent with the mission of the organization or its plans? Were these encumbrances cleared before the gift was made and accepted? These are different to item 1 above because these are claims (for example, liens) that others might have restricting the transfer of the property. They may also be encumbrances based on a lawsuit, a court judgment or a prior designation as a historic site. If the item was subject to tax, are the taxes paid? Is there a tax lien?

Restrictions and Encumbrances

Some gifts create expenses. Some gifts come with temporary or permanent donor restrictions on their use and these restrictions are contractual. Some gifts are contingent upon matching funds. These challenge grants, as they are called, may push the organization in a specific direction. All of these factors must be taken into account by the trustees. Be cautious about accepting large gifts without a predetermined plan of their use and disposition, or without thinking through how they might affect the organization's exempt status (see Chapter 2).

A sensible strategy is to sell properties immediately that are received as donations. This frees the organization from risks and expenses. The cash can be folded into ongoing plans already approved by the trustees. Remember there is a reporting requirement. There is also a disclosure required by many corporations, their deduction may be affected.

Requirements of a Tax-Deductible Gift

Based on Venni v. Commissioner, Davis v. Commissioner, and Magin v. Commissioner and similar cases, a tax-deductible gift is an irrevocable transfer of property or cash from a qualified donor to a qualified donee for less than full consideration. The property or cash must be accepted by the donee without any retained remainder, or partial rights belonging to the donor. The donor must not maintain control or influence over the property and may not continue to receive economic benefits from it. Now we will discuss the details.

Cash or Property

Deductible gifts must be in the form of property or cash, not services or free rent. Although services are not gifts, expenses such as unreimbursed meals or transportation costs that are necessary and directly related to providing the service are deductible.

If the nonprofit sells a property that it received as a donation and that has a value of $500 or more within two years after it was received, it must report the sale on IRS Form 8282. Exceptions are those properties sold for less than $500 and those that are distributed or consumed without charge and in conducting the nonprofit's mission such as thrift shops and soup kitchens.

Transfer

Deductible transfers must be voluntary, purposeful, and complete. A transfer that is clearly the result of a misunderstanding is also not a gift; neither is a transfer when the donor is not mentally or legally competent. A transfer made in expectation of death is not a gift if the person survives.

A pledge or a promise is not a gift until it is reasonably certain that it would be collected. A promise of a gift constitutes no legal obligation. The nonprofit cannot enforce payment unless the promise to give is contractual or the failure to keep the promise results in economic harm.

State and local laws specify how some properties are to be legally transferred. For example: Suppose Elaine gave the nonprofit her automobile. She must also sign, date, and complete the information required on the car title and hand the title over to the nonprofit and the license plate to the state.

Real property, land, and buildings require a title be completed, conveyed, and the transaction recorded. A person who holds stock certificates must endorse and deliver them to the nonprofit or its agents if the gift is to be complete. Gifts of U.S. Savings Bonds must follow rules prescribed by the federal government. In some cases, the bond may have to be cashed. Gifts of creative work must be accompanied by gifts of their copyrights.

Irrevocable

A transfer must be irrevocable to be a gift. There can be no way in which the donor may repossess the property other than by arm's-length purchase. Any transfer with the intent or with conditions to permit repossession even by purchase is not a gift.

Retained Rights

There are times when a potential donor wishes to make a gift of property but also wishes to retain certain rights over the property to enjoy it. Let us couple the concept of retained rights with that of irrevocability and see the results: Shauna makes an irrevocable gift of her horse to a riding academy with the stipulation that she has use of it on Saturdays. The gift is irrevocable if there are no conditions by which she may recapture ownership of the horse. However, she has retained rights over its use. The consequence is that the gift is partial from the point of view of the IRS and therefore there is no tax deduction. It is, however, legally irretrievable. The horse belongs to the academy. In a similar vein, the retention of a copyright would lead to the same results as it did with the United Artists gifts of films to the Library of Congress.

Remainder Rights

Sometimes potential donors would consider making a transfer to a nonprofit with the condition that after some event or passage of time, all or some portion of the property would be returned. These are remainder rights and doable only within a trust discussed in the next chapter.

Present Interests

A donor may choose to make a gift at some time in the future. This is a future-interest gift, which is not deductible unless placed in a trust as described in the next chapter. A gift has to be of present interest to be deductible. This means that the nonprofit must acquire immediate and full control and ownership of the property or cash without restrictions. By inference, a future-interest gift becomes deductible only at the time that full control becomes effective, that is, when the conditions of future interest no longer exist so that the future interest is now a present interest.

There is an important exception to the present-interest rule when the gift is of real property, such as a building or a house. This exception will be discussed later in this chapter. Remember that as far as tangible personal property (property other than real estate and intangibles) is concerned, future interests are not deductible until all the contingencies of control, either by the donor or someone authorized by the donor (such as a successor) are removed.

Options

Gifts of options have no value until the option is exercised. The option is worthless whenever the market value of the property is lower than the purchase price allowed by the option.

Exceptions to Incomplete Transfers

In general, a transfer must be complete and of present interest to be deductible. This means that the donee must acquire complete and immediate control of the gift. The donor must maintain no retained, revocable, partial, or remainder rights.

There are notable exceptions to the general rule. One exception pertains to a situation in which the donor owns less than 100 percent of a property and is therefore unable to give the entire property. Under these conditions, the donor must give an undivided share of his or her total interest in a property if such a gift is to be deducted. To understand this exception, consider the following example: Shauna owns a one-half interest in a property consisting of a stable and ten horses. Her undivided interest is one-half of the property, as it is comprised. Therefore, the maximum she can give and take a deduction for is one-half of the property. One-half is 100 percent of what she owns of each horse. She may give less than 100 percent, but the amount she gives must be undivided; that is, the property, in this case, is the stable and horses together. She cannot divide the property such that she gives some of the horses and none of the stable. The key is how the property is defined. The horse cannot be separated from its legs and still be the same horse.

A second exception to the general rule refers specifically and only to a personal (not necessarily a principal) residence or a farm. A personal residence may include a vacation home or condominium. A person may make a future-interest gift of either of these two types of properties to a qualified nonprofit and get an immediate tax deduction. Accordingly, someone could get an immediate tax deduction on a gift of a home to a favorite nonprofit while continuing to live in it.

A third exception to the complete transfer rule relates to gifts of real property for qualified conservation purposes. Qualified conservation purposes include preservation of land area, protection of natural habitat, preservation of open space, and preservation of a historic site for public benefit. The gift of the property must be accompanied by some easement that will permanently restrict the future use of the land for any purpose other than for conservation. The donor may continue to use the property until some date in the future when it passes to the qualified organization.

The other exceptions to the requirement that gifts be complete and of present interest require the use of a trust.

Qualified Donor

Gifts can only be made by qualified donors who must be of age, of sound mind, and own the property. The most straightforward form of ownership is fee simple. In this case, the person owns all rights to the property and is free donate it.

Some properties are owned as tenants in the entireties. It means that neither party may give the property without the express consent of the other. Many homes are owned in this form and therefore no single spouse may, under normal circumstances, give the property away without the affirmative approval of the other.

Other properties may be owned as tenants in common. This means that either party may make a gift, but only of that share of the property that he or she owns. When a percentage of ownership is not specified, it is assumed that each cotenant has an equal share. This might be a little trickier than tenants in the entirety, where one-half ownership by each owner over the entire property is presumed. In the case of tenants in common, an unequal share or only a specified piece of the property may be owned by the donor.

Property may be owned in the form of joint tenants with the right of survivorship. The objective is to be sure that upon death the property is passed directly to a designated person outside of probate, that at the time of death ownership passes automatically to the survivor.

In the states where ownership exists as "community property," it is presumed that any property bought during marriage is owned on an equal basis by both spouses. The laws on the transfer of community property differ by state, but in general a person is only free to give the one-half of the property owned.

A person may have ownership that terminated upon death, such as a life estate. This form of ownership is obviously temporary. The owner of the life estate can give only the earnings received during his or her life, but cannot give the property that yields those earnings. That property must be passed on to another beneficiary when that person dies. Furthermore, the person with the life estate is obligated to preserve the property so that it may be transferred. For example, Marisa may own the earnings of a rental unit through a bequest from her mother, who stipulated that the unit should belong to Marisa's sister. Marisa can donate the earnings, but not the property. However, she cannot donate the earnings if by doing so there are no funds to repair and maintain the unit to transfer it to her sister in good condition. In the same vein, Marisa's sister cannot give away the rental unit while Marisa is still alive, particularly if by giving it, Marisa's flow of income would be terminated. Properties such as this are best given through a trust as we shall see in the next chapter.

Ownership may be contingent or non-vested. In these cases, ownership takes place only after some condition is fulfilled. Until those conditions are recognized as being satisfied, the "owner" has no legal power to give the property. A common contingency is the passage of time. If, for example, ten years must pass before ownership of the amount in a pension account is vested, then prior to that time the person in whose name the account appears has no power to give those funds, even though they appear in his or her name.

Acceptance or Substantiation

Gifts must be acknowledged for more than courtesy purposes. To illustrate, if Enrique gives $250 or more to the Felicia-Deborah Center for the Handicapped, he cannot deduct it unless the gift is substantiated (acknowledged) by the donee organization. The substantiation must be in writing and must be contemporaneous with the gift. It must state the amount of the gift, and whether the organization gave the donor something in return for the gift. If so, what was given by the organization must also be described and it must give an estimate of what it gave the donor unless what it gave is worth less than $75, pertained to membership privileges worth less than $75 per year, or if what it gave were certain privileges to the donor's employees or partners. If the organization received a gift of more than $75 and it gave something in return, then it must disclose what it gave the donor and its value in the letter of substantiation to the donor. The written substantiation must contain an estimate of the value of what the organization gave the donor and inform the donor that the charitable contribution is limited to an amount equaling the donor's contribution minus what the organization gave in return. This is very common in fundraising dinners, entertainment, and other events. Insubstantial donations include jugs, pencils, pens, hats, umbrellas, and the like.

Substantiation, as stated above, must be contemporaneous. This means that it must occur on the earlier of the due date for filing the donor's tax returns for the year the gift was made, or the date the donor files the original (not amended) tax return for that year.

Qualified Donee

Organizations formed to reduce the burden of government are qualified donees as long as they also qualify as 501(c)(3)s without regard to whether they were created by citizens or government.

Less than Full Consideration

A key concept in defining a gift is that the transfer must be for less than full consideration. Simply, this means that the donation must exceed the value of anything the nonprofit may give the donor as an inducement or in appreciation for the gift. The gift is the difference between the market price and the amount received by the donor in the transfer.

A gift also occurs when one pays more than the value of a service. It is a gift when one buys a banquet or dinner ticket for more than the cost of the food and entertainment, or the cost of any preference or special privilege given the donor.

Problems of Accepting Gifts Subject to Debt

Many properties are bought with credit. The purchaser borrows to acquire the property so that part of the dollar value of the property represents ownership or equity; the other part is debt. Raymond owns a home subject to a mortgage. The fair market value of the home is $50,000 and the home is subject to a $30,000 mortgage, meaning that Raymond's equity is $20,000 from his income-tax perspective. That is all he can deduct, even though the fair market value of the house is $50,000 and the nonprofit may carry such value on its books and even honor him for making a gift of that amount. But who is going to pay the bank the $30,000 that Raymond owes? Suppose that the nonprofit decides to assume the mortgage. In that case, Raymond has made a gift for which he gets a tax deduction, but he now has to report income. The relieving of his $30,000 debt is income to him even though he has not received a dime. If he agrees to pay off the debt, then this payment is included as part of the deductible gift. Note that the principal of the debt is deductible as a gift, but not the interest if deducted otherwise.

Let us assume that the debt is not paid by Raymond. The nonprofit has obtained a piece of property worth $50,000 for which it has only to pay the $30,000 of outstanding debt over a period of years. In addition to assuming a debt, it must now pay operating costs. If it rents the house, it must pay taxes, since the property is subject to debt. If it tries to sell the house, it may be subject to tax, for the property is subject to debt. If the building has declined in value, the nonprofit must support an asset with a diminishing market value. Raymond may offer to pay the mortgage. If he defaults, the nonprofit pays the bill or loses the property.

Bargain Sales as a Solution

Raymond may contemplate a different strategy. He may resort to a bargain sale. Assume that he paid $50,000 cash for the home and owns it fee simple. He has no debts and may do as he wishes with the property. Assume further that the property is in an attractive neighborhood so that rather than declining in price, it appreciated to $100,000. He may decide to give it to his favorite nonprofit through a bargain sale. Instead of the nonprofit paying $100,000, it pays $50,000. Since he receives less than full consideration, the difference between what he gets and the fair market value ($50,000) is a gift. A gift?

The bargain sale is part gift and part sale. Its effects on an unsuspecting donor can be devastating. In the above example, the gift amounts to $50,000, which is one-half of the fair market value. Therefore, Raymond gave away one-half of what he could have gotten had he sold the house. He must now reduce his cost by half. Hence, he is deemed to have paid only $25,000 for the house. Since he received $50,000 from the nonprofit, he is deemed to have made a gain of $25,000 on the deal and he must pay taxes on it. Bargain sales can be very cruel to donors because they can lead to taxes on gains never received and to a reduced deductible amount. In this case, Raymond reports a gain of $25,000 even though he sold the property for the amount he paid for it and $50,000 less than its true market value. He would have been better off selling the property, paying the tax, and taking a deduction for the contribution.

A bargain sale may also lead to loss of a deduction because a bargain sale is subject first to the regular rules of gifts and sales and then to the specific rules governing bargain sales. To illustrate, suppose Simon bought stocks a month ago for $4,000. The stocks rise to $10,000 in two months. The sale of these stocks, held for six months, under any circumstance would lead to an ordinary income tax on the $6,000 of gain. Suppose Simon decides to donate the stocks. He cannot deduct $10,000. Knowing this, he takes a check from the nonprofit for $4,000 to cover his cost and then gives them the stocks. Will he be able to deduct the $6,000 difference as a gift? No. The reasoning is that his cost was $4,000 for which he got a check from the nonprofit. The stocks, held for six months, are ordinary income property deductible at cost. The cost is $4,000, but he was paid that amount from the nonprofit so there is nothing to deduct. He has lost $10,000 worth of stocks.

A bargain sale is indicated and should be considered when the potential donor needs cash, when the asset is of value to the nonprofit and for some reason (that is, an extremely specialized piece of equipment) the donor cannot dispose of or sell the asset readily, and where the tax benefit from donating at fair market value exceeds the 10 percent of net income limit that a corporation is allowed to deduct. A firm operating at close to zero profits needs cash more than it needs a charitable deduction. Therefore, the fact that a bargain sale may reduce its charitable deduction may be less important than its ability to get cash and dispose of the asset. Similarly, a firm that has been experiencing losses for years and carrying them forward may have more than enough deductions that it can use. The charitable deduction may have little value to such a firm.

Value Illusions and Stock Bargains

It is true that value is in the eye of the beholder. If it is higher in the eyes of the organization than it is in the eyes of the donor, it is an illusion. The donor is restricted in the value that can be placed on a property to the lower of cost or market. An ordinary income property is one for which the proceeds from the sale are taxed as ordinary income, such as wages and salary, and not as a capital gain or loss. Examples of ordinary income property that may be given are (1) items from the inventory of a retailer or dealer, (2) a product in the hands of its producer, such as a piece of art in the hands of the artist or a machine in the hands of its manufacturer, (3) a piece of equipment or machinery used in a trade or business, such as a truck in the hands of a company that uses it in its business, (4) property held for investment purposes but for less than twelve months, such as stocks in the hands of an investor held for less than twelve months, and (5) some properties subject to depreciation recapture, such as a real estate, using a method of rapid depreciation. The donor is restricted in all of these properties to their costs and so the deduction to the donor might be less than the market value to the organization. Do not be surprised in these instances if the donor is reluctant to give the property. Often, as when there has been a loss, the donor is better off selling the property for a donation.

This is so because the properties enumerated in 1–4 are valued at cost even if they have appreciated in market price. The bargain comes with capital gains properties—properties in which the proceeds from their sale would be taxed as capital gains. Examples are: (1) properties held for investment purposes but for a period of greater than twelve months—which is one of the reasons appreciated stocks make excellent gifts to seek, and (2) coal and timber by special treatment of the tax law. Generally, capital gain property may be deducted at fair market value. So the donor's deduction is based on a higher figure than costs. The greater the appreciation, the better.

If the donor is in a high tax bracket and the appreciation is considerable, the deduction may compensate for the cost so that the actual cost to the donor is near zero—but does not yield a profit. This makes the giving of appreciate stocks very attractive especially since the donor foregoes the cost of selling that stock, paying the capital gains tax and making the donation. Note, however, if the donor has not held the stock long enough to qualify as capital gains, or if the stock has a loss because the market price is lower than the cost, none of this works and would produce a loss to the donor and the gift would not be made.

The price that is used to determine deductible value depends upon the date of transfer and the removal or meeting of all contingencies. If the stock certificate was put into the mail without any contingency and properly signed, the relevant date is the date of mailing. If the stock was delivered, it is the date of delivery. If the transfer had to be recorded, it is the date that was done.

If the stock is not a publicly-traded stock, then ascertaining its price must be done by a professional appraiser. A non-public stock, that would be valued at $10,000 would be valued lower if the donor is a minority shareholder rather than the majority. The reason is that the minority shareholder has virtually no control and the marketability of that stock is lower than that of the majority shareholder. But these non-public stocks present another problem: if the non-profit becomes a majority or significant minority holder it acquires management and liability problems. For these reasons, the best strategy is to sell the stock.

The Upshot: Appreciated property, including stocks, are common and wonderful gifts worth seeking. They do transfer certain risks from the donor to the organization and the latter must have a strategy for dealing with these. That is a duty of the board of trustees.

Summary, Responsibility, and Preview

This chapter has dealt with the mechanics, properties, legality, and empirical studies on charitable giving. It should help managers in their pursuit of financial gifts. But the manager has certain responsibilities in this pursuit. Among these is to describe as accurately as possible what the donation will be used for, to be respectful of restrictions, and to be clear to the potential donor the feasibility of keeping that restriction and suggesting an alternative course or language. Other responsibilities include acknowledging the receipt on a timely basis—indicating the amount, use, name of organization and its address with telephone and email, an indication if anything was received by the donor, its value and the extent to which it may be deductible, if known. Managers must also make Form 990s available to the donor and the public when requested. Most of all, avoid deceiving the donor.

Bibliography

Andreoni, James and Abigail Payne, "Charitable Giving," *Handbook of Public Economics*, 5th ed., Alan J. Auerbach, Raj Chetty, Martin Feldstein, Emmanuel Saez (eds.) (Amsterdam: North Holland) particularly pp 2–51 (2013).

Baumol W J., "Enlightened Self-Interest and Corporate Philanthropy," *Foundations, Private Giving and Public Policy: Report and Recommendations of the Commission on Foundations and Private Philanthropies*. (Chicago: University of Chicago Press), pp. 22–75 (1971).

Bekkers, Rene and Pamela Wiepking, "A Literature Review of Empirical Studies of Philanthropy: Eight Mechanisms that Drive Charitable Giving," *Nonprofit and Voluntary Sector Quarterly*, Vol. 40 #5, October 2011, pp. 924–973.

Croson, R., F. Handy, and J. Shang. Keeping up with the Joneses: The relationship of perceived descriptive social norms, social information, and charitable giving. *Nonprofit Management and Leadership*, 19: 467–489 10.1002/nml.232 (2009).

Harris, Erica E., Christine Petrovits, and Michelle H. Yetman. "The Effect of Nonprofit Governance on Donations: Evidence from the Revised Form 990." *The Accounting Review* (2014). http://dx.doi.org/10.2308/accr-50874.

Harris, James F. and Anne Klepper. "Corporate Philanthropic Public Service Activities," *Research Papers: Commission on Philanthropy and Public Needs, Vol. 3* (Washington, D.C.: U.S. Treasury, 1977), pp. 1741–1788.

Lichtenstein,Donald R., Minette E. Drumwright, Bridgette M. Braig. "The Effect of Corporate Social Responsibility on Customer Donations to Corporate-Supported Nonprofits." *Journal of Marketing*, October 2004, Vol. 68, No. 4, pp. 16–32.

Sargeant, Adrian and Stephen Lee, "Donor Trust and Relationship Commitment in the U.K. Charity Sector: The Impact on Behavior," *Nonprofit Voluntary Sector Quarterly*, June 2004, Vol. 33, #2, pp. 185–202.

Sargeant, Adrian, John B. Ford and Jane Hudson, "Charity Brand Personality: The Relationship with Giving Behavior," *Nonprofit Voluntary Sector Quarterly*, September 2008, Vol. 37 # 3, pp. 468–491.

Van Slyke, David M. and Arthur C. Brooks, "Why Do People Give? New Empirical Evidence," *The American Review of Public Administration*, September 2005, vol. 35, 3: pp. 199–222.

White, Katherine and John Peloza, "Self-Benefit Versus Other-Benefit Marketing Appeals: Their Effectiveness in Generating Charitable Support," *Journal of Marketing*: July 2009, Vol. 73, No. 4, pp. 109–124.

Winterich, Karen, Vikas Mittal, and Karl Aquino, "When Does Recognition Increase Charitable Behavior? Toward a Moral Identity-Based Model." *Journal of Marketing*: May 2013, Vol. 77, No. 3, pp. 121–134.

Chapter 9 – Financing the Burden through Business Earnings

Lessening the burden of government is often principally or exclusively financed by charging prices—business income related to the good or service they are providing. Schuyler County Human Services Development Corporation in Schuyler, New York, is an incorporated nonprofit entity which is created to lessen the burden of government. It entered into debt, on its own accord, to build a facility which it rents only to nonprofit entities and to government agencies (related income from the purpose for which the corporation was created) . The rent and the fees it charges pay off all of the expenses and debt service. There is no government guarantee or payment other than the rent. It has lowered the government's costs for space across the various agencies. That income related business income and is not taxable (a) because it is related in general, (b) because it is rental income in particular. Rental income is considered passive and therefore not taxed as long as it is derived from a mission-related activity or derived from the payments from nonprofits.

The objective of this chapter is to explain— the crafting involved in financing the lessening the burden of government through business income and through sparing the government of debt.. But, first, an organization has to be able to meet its own needs before it can rescue the government and we start there.

Business Activity as a Source of Money

An organization needs money even if it uses volunteers. That money comes from: (a) fees and other prices charged by the organization to those who use or benefit from the conduct of the mission; (b) gifts and contributions from the public—citizens, other organizations and firms; (c) debt that has to be repaid from the mission earnings; (d) government contracts, grants, or other financial support ultimately coming from taxes; (e) investment earnings; (f) earnings from other sources that may be unrelated to the mission responsibility of the organization. This latter group is called unrelated business income and is discussed separately because of its implications and the rules restraining the organization from unfairly enriching itself by veering off from what it was created to do.

Obviously, the greater the organization's dependence on government resources in any form including (d) above, the smaller the amount of net burden

DOI 10.1515/9781501505799-010

of which the government is relieved. Hence, part of the organizational design is to maximize all other sources and to bring (d) to zero. As we shall see, a strategy for this is for the government to lease an asset (for example, a building) from a nonprofit for the sole use of the government Such lease payments, fees, or prices related to the mission of the organization whether paid by the government, citizens, users, or member or beneficiaries of the mission assigned to the nonprofit is called related business income. Its advantages are: (a) there is no statutory limit on how large related business income might be or the profits that it might yield; (b) there is no income tax or other taxes on this income which increases the amount the organization may retain for operations, reserves, repairs, and replacement, and therefore increases its sustainability provided that it was designed properly and with competent management, and (c) this income is unrestricted—meaning that the management can use it with their full discretion in the best interest of the organization in lessening the burden of government, and not simply as specified by a donor. Whether or not an income stream gets this tax preference depends upon specific facts and circumstances.

The following quote taken from the New York Not-For-Profit Corporation Law § 1411 has issues beyond legal, ethical, or political because although it is not stated, any income from this source would be taxable as unrelated business income, partly but not solely, because it is unrelated to the mission to which the organization is assigned in its charter.

> A local development corporation, incorporated or reincorporated under this section, which purchases or leases real property from a county, city, town or village, shall not, without the written approval of the county, city, town or village, use such real property for any purpose except the purposes set forth in the certificate of incorporation or reincorporation of said local development corporation. In the event such real property is used in violation of the restrictions of this paragraph, the attorney-general may bring an action or special proceeding to enjoin the unauthorized use.

Dealing with this issue requires an understanding of what constitutes business income for nonprofit tax-exempt organizations, for those formed and operated by government as well as those formed and operated by citizens, and how structurally these may be managed.

What Is Business Income?

By way of definition, the revenues that are discussed in this chapter are all business income as defined by the Internal Revenue Service. As shown in Chapter 1, nonprofits in general and those lessening the burden in particular are dependent on earning their own way—business income. The more they earn, the less their dependence on government and on gifts and contributions. Hence, the diversity and stability of this source is important to financing the sustainability of the organization and its ability to perform.

Business income is any income that is derived from a sale, rental, royalties, dividends, interest or capital gains (even though these two are derived from investments), and some fees. Gaming and gambling (blackjack, keno, bingo, lottery, dice, raffles, slot machines, and door prizes) are also forms of business income. Nonprofits, unlike firms, are required to classify all such income in one of two categories: related or unrelated. Related income (program service related or program related) is income that comes from a transaction that is part of the mission of the organization. Unrelated does not. We shall discuss the implications of this distinction in Chapter 10. Here we focus on the entrepreneurial issues—creating the business income stream. What should the manager ask? What is the entrepreneurial motive or opportunity? This means that we focus on sales in this chapter, but will discuss the others in following chapters.

Any transaction to which a price can be charged is a potential producer of business income. The word "business" refers to the transaction and not necessarily to an institution or a cluster of transactions which also produces business income. So revenues from selling cookies and milk in a school are business income of the school. With nonprofits, it is essential to focus on the transaction because transactions can be treated very differently and have different impacts on the nonprofit.

All business income by a nonprofit must be classified and reported as either related or unrelated to its mission. These treatments follow strict guidelines by the IRS and may have tax consequences and affect the calculation of what constitutes public support within the 501(c)(3) entity as described in Chapter 4. This chapter looks at the tax consequences with respect to all types of business income: sales, royalties, dividends, capital gains, rentals, and dividends. It begins with understanding the sources and importance of unrelated business income, and how these fit into the corporate structure of the nonprofit for effectiveness. By definition, any business income that is not unrelated is, by deduction, related so the focus is on what is unrelated business income?

Definition of Related and Unrelated Nonprofit Businesses

A related business is one that fits integrally as part of the mission of the organization—program-related income. That is, the income it generates is directly a result of the organization's conducting its stated community or public welfare mission. Appropriately, the income from this kind of business is not taxed, and it is also categorized as public support for 509(a)(2) organizations.

An unrelated business is one that is not integrally related to the mission of the organization. Its principal purpose is to generate income. A net income (profits) generated from an unrelated business is taxed. Income from an unrelated business is classified as support in 509(a)(1) organizations.

An unrelated business is a trade or business regularly conducted by a nonprofit for the purpose of making a profit. The unrelated business makes little or no substantive or programmatic contribution to the exempt mission of the organization. Its primary contribution is money. A program-related business, on the other hand, is directly and integrally related to the programmatic and substantive goals of the nonprofit. Program-related business would be carried on even if it were not profitable. Unrelated business is pursued because it expects to be profitable. Interest earned on loans by a nonprofit that has lending as its mission is related business income.

There are three keys to determining whether an activity is an unrelated business:

First, it is a trade or a business conducted to generate a profit. There must be a clear profit motive. It is the intent, not the size of the profit that matters.

Sometimes a nonprofit might find itself trying to convince the IRS that an activity is for profit. This allows the organization to use the losses to offset gains in other unrelated businesses and therefore reduce the taxes due. In assessing whether an activity is for profit, the IRS may resort to a nine-prong test:

1. The manner in which the activity is carried on should be businesslike, with the maintenance of complete records, advertising, setting prices rationally, and so on.
2. There should be some expertise in the enterprise and knowledge of what makes the enterprise successful.
3. There should be enough time and effort spent to make the activity profitable.
4. There should be some expectation that the assets will increase in value.
5. The prospect of profits are enhanced if the taxpayer had related experience, whether profitable or unprofitable.
6. An abnormal string of early loss for the enterprise may indicate a lack of a profit motive.
7. Whether there are changes in the method of operation to improve profitability.
8. An occasional profit of some significant amount may indicate a profit motive; that is, if it shows a profit in three of the past five years, including the current year.

9. Whether the taxpayer has considerable other income such that this source may be deemed as purely a tax-avoidance activity.

In looking at profitability by individuals or from the perspective of compensation, the IRS may become suspicious if the existence of considerable elements of personal pleasure implies that pleasure is the motive—not profit-making.

Second, an unrelated business is a regular activity, not a one-time or occasional event, where the event normally will occur with greater frequency. It is regular if business is conducted by the nonprofit with the same frequency as would a for-profit firm. A one-time bake sale is not an unrelated business.

What does *regularity* mean? An example will help: Regularity is measured by the norm for that activity reflecting frequency and duration. Regularity does not mean every day. It means the frequency and duration that is customary among for-profit firms in the same trade or business. Therefore, the IRS has counted the number of real estate sales a university made in twenty-five years to determine whether its real estate sales were regular.

Third, an unrelated business is not substantially related to the tax-exempt mission of the nonprofit. It may raise money, but is not programmatically integral or related to the tax-exempt mission.

Some examples will help clarify this point: A halfway house organized to provide room, board, therapy, and counseling for persons discharged from alcoholic treatment centers also operates a furniture shop to provide full-time employment for its residents. The profits are applied to the operating costs of the halfway house. The income from this venture is not unrelated trade or business income.

An exempt organization organized and operated for the prevention of cruelty to animals receives income from providing pet boarding and grooming services for the general public. This is an income from an unrelated trade or business. But a prison that imports prisoners from other states is not only a 501(c)(3) because it is substituting for government, but the profits from this activity are related business income (Revenue Letter 9629002).

An exempt organization whose purpose is to provide for the welfare of young people rents rooms primarily to people under age twenty-five. This income is not considered unrelated business income, since the source of the in come flow is substantially related to the purpose constituting the basis for the organization's exemption.

A hospital with exempt status operates a gift shop patronized by patients, visitors making purchases for patients, and employees and medical staff. It also operates a parking lot for patients and visitors only. Both of these activities are substantially related to the hospital's exempt purpose and do not constitute unrelated trades or businesses.

These examples offered by the IRS illustrate the differences between a program-related business and an unrelated business. The former is an extension of or part of the tax-exempt function of the organization. The latter is not.

The same activity can be either a related or unrelated business depending on how it is handled. A service run exclusively for members of an organization or completely provided voluntarily by them is a related business. But the same services provided by the same nonprofit for the public or by paid employees could be an unrelated business.

A service such as a laundry or store operated exclusively for the membership of a tax-exempt organization is not an unrelated business. The rental income to a nonprofit created by a local government to provide public facilities, including a police station, is not unrelated business income (Revenue Letter 9046039).

Services only for the convenience of members, for example, dorms for students, are related businesses. Services by members or volunteers, the sale of donated property, trade shows that are educational, and the rental or sale of mailing labels to other nonprofits are also related businesses. The rental of a mailing list for commercial purposes has been an unrelated business, but a recent Tax Court decision, Disabled American Veterans v. Commissioner, said, at least in this case, it was to be treated as a royalty, which is not taxed. This was reversed on appeal by the IRS.

Excess Profits: A Distinction Between Related and Unrelated Income

An IRS regulation announced in the Internal Revenue Bulletin (No. 1986-7) is instructive. The case is that of a large metropolitan hospital that provides services such as data processing, food service, and purchasing services to other hospitals. The IRS rules that the earnings would be related income if all of three conditions hold: (1) the hospitals purchasing the service have a maximum capacity for inpatients of 100 persons; (2) the service, if performed by the recipient hospital, would have been a normal service for it; (3) the fee in excess of actual cost is not more than one-and-one-half times the average rates of interest on public debt obligations issued by the Federal Hospital Insurance Trust Fund.

If all these conditions do not hold, then the earnings are unrelated business income and taxed. This case not only shows the thin line between related and unrelated business income, but also shows that although an absolute dollar level of profits is not stipulated, any profit above a normal rate of return is likely to be considered unrelated business income. It implies a profit motive.

Integration of Business Operations Into a Conglomerate Structure

How do unrelated business operations fit into the corporate structure of a non-profit? Why is this section relevant? It is relevant because it is a common way for a nonprofit, whether created by government or citizens, to shield itself from taxation, certain liabilities, to enable collaboration, and to address the need for separate management. Some nonprofits find that it is an organizational and management advantage to set up a reasonably complex organizational struc-ture. This could inolve the following:

1. The principal organization set up auxiliary entities.
2. The princial organization divides these into those that are for-profit and those that are not.
3. It also sets up within its own body similar units. Thus, it can operate these units within its corporate body or externally as separately incorporated en-tites in which it is the sole owner or member.
4. Income derived from the for-profit entities are taxed as income tax to those individual bodies.
5. Transfers (dividends) from each of them to the principal or parent body is received by the latter tax free to it.
6. It can determine the boars of each of the units whether in its corporate body or outside of it.
7. If the for-profit entity is created outside of it, the principal or parent organi-zation can invite and accept the investment of others who ar seeking gains from that external for-profit entity.
8. But they cannot use that investment to control the nonprofits that are a part of that structure.
9. The parent is free to sell off the subsidiary if it chooses to to do so..

The Organization of an Unrelated Business

In the for-profit world, businesses are organized as corporations, sole proprie-torships, or partnerships. Joint ventures may be undertaken between two or more organizations on a specific project. A trust could also be created to hold and exercise the rights of ownership of those who own a business organization.

Except for sole proprietorships, these organizations are adaptable to an unrelated business owned and operated by a nonprofit.

A common way of organizing an unrelated business is as a corporation. A corporation, unlike a partnership or a sole proprietorship, is an independent legal and tax entity. Liabilities for failure and error of the corporation do not extend to its owner, as with partnerships and sole proprietorships. Corporations have centralized management and do not have to share management decisions with all owners, as with general partnerships. Unlike proprietorships, a corporation can raise capital by issuing and selling shares of stocks in itself. A partnership may do so by selling partnership interests, but such interests rarely have as wide a market as a public corporation's stocks. Unlike a general partnership, a corporation does not have to be dissolved in the case of withdrawal of an owner. It has a perpetual life of its own, and ownership can be easily transferred from one person to another. A corporation is easier and safer than other forms of business organizations. What is most important, even if the nonprofit organized its business as a partnership, it would be taxed as a corporation.

A nonprofit may choose to be a minority, majority, or even sole owner of a for-profit corporation. Its minority ownership may be significantly small or significantly large, but a critical concept of ownership is control. A nonprofit is said to be the controlling owner of a for-profit corporation if it owns at least 50 percent of its voting stocks and 50 percent of all other stocks. How a nonprofit is treated for tax purposes depends not on whether it is a minority or a majority stockholder, but on whether it is the controlling organization. In the case of nonstock corporations, which nonprofits are, control means controlling 80 percent or more of the board of directors or trustees.

How the unrelated business is treated depends on the form of business organization. If it is a corporation or partnership, it will face the same tax rate as other corporations. It will also be subject to a minimum tax. In a recent ruling, the IRS required a nonprofit to create a separate for-profit subsidiary or lose its exemption. Accordingly, how the nonprofit is treated may also depend on how the business is organized.

Origins of Unrelated Businesses

The entry into unrelated business is rarely a deliberate attempt to compete with for-profit firms. Sometimes it is purely defensive to protect one's space or market; for example, buying the real estate in the neighborhood of one's facilities for future expansion. Sometimes it is to capture some of the financial benefits from one's large and risky investments and to maintain property rights and control; for example, universities' licensing the products of research. It may also be the result of trying to cover large fixed and overhead costs.

Evidently, (1) there is a thin line between a related and unrelated business, and the difference is not in the name but in the relevance, frequency, and motive, and (2) unrelated business ventures can arise from an attempt to extend and serve the mission, although the legal or tax judgment is that the relevance is not strong enough to be considered integrally related. An unrelated business can arise from a tax-exempt organization using its position, process, goodwill, or reputation to make money in a way that is not directly related to its tax-exempt mission.

The IRS gives the example of exploiting a mission: An exempt scientific organization enjoys an excellent reputation in the field of biological research. It exploits this reputation regularly by selling endorsements of various items of laboratory equipment to manufacturers. The endorsement of laboratory equipment does not contribute importantly to the accomplishment of any purpose for which exemption is granted to the organization. Accordingly, the income from the sale of endorsements is gross income from an unrelated business.

An unrelated business can arise from wisely trying to cover costs while carrying out a mission. This is evidenced by the opportunity nonprofits have to make dual use of plant and equipment. The same plant or equipment that it uses for conducting its tax-exempt mission can also be used to produce unrelated business income rather than sit idle, generating costs but no revenues. The university stadium may be used for professional football. When this is done, the nonprofit must separate the two types of income and expenses for reporting purposes. The use of university facilities for professional sports is commonplace. The revenues from these leases help cover fixed costs.

Unrelated Business for Cost-Sharing Purposes

Still another example common to nonprofits is the use of their publications to generate income. This can be done by selling advertising space. The income from the advertising can be unrelated income, but the ads help advertisers speak to an audience. In a historic case, the U.S. Supreme Court in United States v. American College of Physicians:

> There is no merit to the Government's argument that Congress and the Treasury intended to establish a blanket rule requiring the taxation of income from all commercial advertising by tax-exempt professional journals without a specific analysis of the circumstances.

There is no support for such a rule in the regulations or in the legislative history of the Internal Revenue Code.

Furthermore, the publication's income and costs are divided into portions, so that if the readership portion (its tax-exempt purpose) is operating at a loss, all additional costs above that loss level may be deducted from the advertising portion (its unrelated business) as long as such a deduction does not result in the unrelated business showing a loss for tax purposes. In short, the cost of serving the readership may provide a tax deduction to the unrelated business. We shall take a deeper look at advertising in the next section.

There are several variations to this example. The basic rule is that if an unrelated business exploits the activities of a related business, the losses from the latter may be deducted from the former if such a deduction does not lead the unrelated business to report a loss. In short, the IRS is willing to reduce the taxes of the unrelated business to the extent that such reduction has a legitimate economic basis.

Accordingly, the tax-exempt mission is subsidized by the unrelated business, and the tax liability of the latter is reduced by the losses of the former.

Tax Treatment of Different Types of Business Income

In this section, we discuss various types of income and arrangements and what exposes them to unrelated business income tax. Why is this section important? Because if one checks the activities of the nonprofits such as the National Park Foundation or the Chesapeake Foundation, or similar ones created to lessen the burden of government, these activities will show up. How must they be considered? It covers various types of income because it is impossible to know which might be applicable to a specific organization at a specific time. Some such as those discussed as passive income below, are very common.

Passive Income

Royalties, rents, interests, dividends, and annuities, all passive income, are generally not considered unrelated business income and therefore are not taxed as long as the nonprofit maintains a passive role. The promotion of credit cards carrying an organization's name will convert a royalty (a passive income) into a sale that is taxable. The first caution in avoiding the tax is to avoid an active role.

Dividends are not taxed unless they are received from property subject to debt. This means that a rich source of income for nonprofits is dividends from controlled corporations or profit-making subsidiaries. Certain guidelines may help in setting up these subsidiaries so that the dividends from them will not be taxable to the nonprofit. These guidelines are as follows:

1. Although the parent (nonprofit organization) may appoint the board of the subsidiary for-profit corporation, the majority of the members of the board of directors, the employees, and the officers of the for-profit must not be related to or be agents of the nonprofit organization.
2. The parent organization must not participate in the daily activities of the for-profit firm.
3. Any business transaction between the subsidiary and the parent nonprofit organization must conform to strict business principles similar to those governing two organizations that are independent of each other. Transactions must be at arm's length.
4. The subsidiary must be organized for the purpose of conducting a legitimate business that is truly unrelated to the business of the nonprofit organization. Its purpose must be to make a profit through a trade or business unrelated to the mission of the nonprofit parent.

Under the above conditions, expressed in General Counsel Memorandum 39326, the dividends received by the nonprofit from its for-profit subsidiary are received tax free. The for-profit subsidiary, however, is subject to all taxes of normal corporations.

Interest earnings, royalties, and rents are taxable to the nonprofit if they are payments from an organization that the nonprofit controls, whether the organization is itself tax-exempt or a for-profit firm. These revenues, like dividends, are also taxable if they are derived from a debt-financed property.

Capital gains from selling property are not subject to tax as unrelated business income unless the property was part of an inventory, acquired by debt, or is sold as an ordinary practice in a trade or business. This again puts a nonprofit corporation in a position superior to most owners of property, including stocks.

The use of property that is contiguous to other property owned by a tax-exempt organization even for an unrelated business purpose may escape being treated as unrelated business if there is a clear intent to use that property within the subsequent ten years for a tax-exempt purpose. The IRS must be convinced of this intent every five years.

Some types of activities receive favorable treatment. Income from bingo is not taxed if for-profit firms within the local jurisdiction are barred from holding bingo games to make a profit. If they are permitted, then the nonprofit must pay a tax. The idea is to avoid placing the for-profit firm at a disadvantage.

Speaking of bingo, the city of Spokane, Washington, taxed a local chapter of the American Red Cross for income derived from bingo, pull-tab, and punch board games. The unrelated business income tax was overruled by the Ninth Circuit Court of Appeals in U.S. v. City of Spokane, arguing that the Red Cross, a congressionally chartered nonprofit, was exempt because it was an instrumentality of the Federal government.

Income derived by agricultural groups from growing and selling crops contiguously to a retirement home is specifically excluded as unrelated business income if the income provides less than 75 percent of the cost of running the retirement home. Income earned by religious organizations with a Federal license is excluded if that income is used for charitable purposes and the prices charged are neither significantly higher nor lower than commercial prices. Research conducted for the U.S. government, its instrumentalities or agencies, or any other level of domestic government, is not considered an unrelated business. Furthermore, fundamental research is not an unrelated business, and organizations such as hospitals and educational institutions are not subject to unrelated business tax on the income derived from research, whether fundamental or applied.

Tours

The basic tests for determining whether a tour leads to unrelated business income are (1) its time commitment to an educational or religious purpose, (2) the legitimate content of the courses conducted on the tour, (3) the degree to which the tour is unlike commercial packages, and (4) the degree to which the course is connected to and is a clear part of the exempt purpose of the organization.

An organization that conducts travel study tours as its primary activity was granted exemption for carrying on an educational mission. Its courses were taught by certified teachers and were conducted for five to six hours a day, library materials were available, exams were given, and the state board of education allowed credits for the courses taken.

An organization conducting weekend retreats is also given tax exemption for advancing religion. The participants meet on an hourly basis for seminars, lectures, prayer sessions, and meditation. No recreational activities are scheduled but individuals are free to engage in these activities on their own time.

The Cecil Bowman Queler Institute is exempt for the purpose of conducting geographic education. Teachers who are experts on the geographic area being visited conduct the tour. Only those who enroll in the courses can participate in the tour. During the tour, the students devote five or six hours per day to organized study, preparation of reports, lectures, instructions, and recitation. Library and related readings and video materials are available during the tour. Examinations are given and the state board of education awards credits for the course. A hypothetical example such as this, according to the IRS, is not likely to lead to unrelated business income.

Property Subject to Debt

Certain properties owned by a nonprofit may be subject to acquisition indebtedness. All earnings derived from such properties are considered unrelated income and subject to tax. Acquisition debt is any debt incurred (1) to acquire or improve a property, (2) in anticipation of acquisition or improvement, or (3) because of the acquisition or improvement. For example, if a nonprofit incurred a debt to acquire or improve a property, that is an acquisition debt. If after acquiring a property that might be free of debt, the nonprofit enters into debt directly linked to its decision to purchase the property, that is also acquisition indebtedness. In all these cases, the property is said to be debt financed.

Again, the consequence of acquisition indebtedness is that income derived from the property in interest, rent, royalty, dividends, or capital appreciation is, with some exceptions, unrelated business income and taxed. It does not matter whether the income is recurrent or nonrecurrent. If during the taxable year the property is subject to debt, all income that it yields during that year is unrelated business income.

There are some modifications to this seemingly harsh rule. One very important one is that property obtained upon death (bequest and devise) is not considered subject to debt for ten years after its acquisition if (1) the donor held the property for at least five years, (2) the debt is at least five years old, and (3) the nonprofit did not agree to be responsible for the debt.

Another exception to the general rule of debt-financed property occurs when the entire property (at least 85 percent) is used for a tax-exempt purpose by the organization itself or by an organization that it controls. In addition, there is a ten-year grace period with mortgages unless the nonprofit, having received real estate from a donor, assumes the mortgage payment. If it does, it is taxed under the debt-financed rule.

Finally, rents from personal property, earnings from thrift shops, and property used in research are not considered debt-financed property and, therefore, are not subject to tax as unrelated business income. Concern should center on rents and proceeds from the sale of real estate, income and proceeds from the ownership and sale of securities, and proceeds from the sale of personal property (as opposed to rents from such property).

Rental Income

Income from renting real estate shows how easy it is for a nonprofit to operate an unrelated business even when it does not intend to do so. It should also alert nonprofit managers to the questions that should be raised before accepting real estate as a gift. Here are some complexities, a simplified view is given at the end of the chapter.

As stated earlier, generally income from the rental of real estate is not unrelated income. However, if the rental is from a property subject to acquisition indebtedness, then all rental income derived from the property could be unrelated business income after ten years and immediately if the nonprofit assumes the debt.

If the rental income is from a related organization carrying out its exempt mission, it is not treated as debt financed even if the property is acquired by debt. Yet the income can be taxed if the organization is controlled by the nonprofit because, in general, all rents from a controlled organization are taxed regardless of whether the organization that pays it is tax exempt or whether it is subject to debt.

Rental from real estate is also subject to unrelated business income tax if the use of the space is coupled with a service, such as room service in a hotel. Furthermore, if the rental income is combined with a rental fee for the use of personal property, such as equipment, the entire income would be subject to tax if the personal property (equipment and machinery) part of the rental exceeds 50 percent of the total. If the personal property part is less than 10 percent of the total, the entire rental is exempt. If it is 10 percent, then only this personal property portion is taxed.

If the rental is from an organization that is controlled by the nonprofit, the rental income is unrelated business income regardless of whether the organization that pays is a for-profit or a nonprofit.

If the space is used for both tax-exempt and for-profit activities, the amount of the rental must be allocated between the two uses and taxes paid on the part that is for-profit in origin.

If the rentals are from a tax-exempt–related organization and are used for research or for a thrift shop, it is not treated as debt-financed and not subject to unrelated business tax under the debt-finance rules. However, it could be considered unrelated business income if the organization paying is controlled by the nonprofit landlord.

If the parent organization uses a debt-financed property (in which case it does not pay rent to itself) exclusively for research or a thrift shop, income derived from the use of that property is not necessarily unrelated business income.

If the property was obtained through a bequest or devise and was held by the donor for at least five years, and the debt is at least five years old and the nonprofit does not agree to assume it, then it is not immediately treated as unrelated business income. There is a ten-year grace period.

Rent becomes unrelated business income if it is tied to profits. It can be a fixed percentage of sales or receipts, but not of the profits of the occupant.

There are infinite combinations of these confounding circumstances. Some of the key questions that must be raised are as follows: Is the property debt financed? Is it to be leased along with personal property and, if so, what will be the percentage of the total rental that could be deemed to be derived from the real estate portion of the package? Are the tenants controlled by the nonprofit? Is the rent related to the profits of the tenants? For what purpose is the space being used? How much of the total space is being rented? All of these questions have been answered in this section.

Gaming

Treatment of this type of income also begins with state rules. Illinois (230 ILCS 15/2) (from Ch. 85, par. 2302) Section 2, authorizes any municipality or combination of them to give a license to a nonprofit for raising funds through poker and raffles, and to so do the following:

> The licensing system shall provide for limitations upon (1) the aggregate retail value of all prizes or merchandise awarded by a licensee in a single raffle, (2) the maximum retail value of each prize awarded by a licensee in a single raffle, (3) the maximum price which may be charged for each raffle chance issued or sold and (4) the maximum number of days during which chances may be issued or sold. The licensing system may include a fee for each license in an amount to be determined by the local governing body.

The permitted category of nonprofits includes 501(c)(3)s that serve a public purpose and in which public is defined as a indefinite number. But it then specifically uses the concept of "lessening the burden of government" when referring to granting permission to fraternal organizations. Thus, it describes the type of fraternal organization (one without indefinite membership) and when that permission is allowed:

Fraternal: An organization of persons having a common interest, the primary interest of which is to both promote the welfare of its members and to provide assistance to the general public in such a way as to lessen the burdens of government by caring for those that otherwise would be cared for by the government.

From an IRS perspective, any nonprofit, including a charity, an association, social club, or a veterans group, that conducts gaming as a primary undertaking is likely to be deprived tax exemption and, likewise, those that fail to keep proper records. These records should include prizes paid, cash receipts, disbursement journals, accounts payable journals, general ledgers, detailed source documents, and copies of any federal tax returns filed. These records must be kept for at least three years.

How a specific form of gaming is treated for tax purposes depends upon the type of game, whether it is conducted by volunteers, allowed by state law, and treated as an exception. Serious gaming can be a cumbersome activity for the records that must be kept. This is just on the Federal level. Gaming income has to be disclosed on the Form 990.

Bingo is exempt if it is allowed by state law and only if nonprofits may conduct gaming in that state and according to its rules. In general, and from the IRS's perspective, gaming that is conducted purely by volunteers is exempt. However, an "excess" amount of food or beverages may be considered compensation. And tips may be considered compensation. A person receiving any of these compensations is not considered a volunteer, so the volunteer exemption will not apply. No wonder that some gaming sites post signs prohibiting tipping. It also explains why tips are collected in a vessel: because the operator also needs to report the tips an employee gets for his or her income tax purposes. Once tips exceed $20, the person is required to inform the operator.

Qualified public entertainment may also be an exception. Public entertainment refers to fairs and expositions. Here the gaming must be in conjunction with a regional, national, state, or local fair or exposition. It must also be conducted according to and by permission of state law allowing only the nonprofit to carry on the gaming at that event. The only organizations that qualify are 501(c)(3)s, labor and agricultural associations, and civic leagues and associations, 501(c)(4)s and (c)(5)s, respectively, that conduct agricultural or educational fairs as one of their substantial exempt missions. Under these conditions, parimutuel betting may also escape treatment as unrelated trade or business.

But there is the North Dakota exception. Only the state of North Dakota qualifies for exemptions of games of chance. Only that state enjoys the exemption from non-bingo gaming.

Besides paying taxes (if due) and filing forms, the organization assumes certain other responsibilities when it indulges in gaming. These include paying withholding taxes for winners (whether or not the organization collects it). The organization is also required to make sure that no part of the proceeds is used for personal inurement. The trustees are expressly required to oversee the games as part of their duties.

Two types of taxes can result from a wager. The *wager tax* is an excise tax imposed on the gross amount of the wager received or the total potential. In pull-tabs, for example, it would be applied to the total number of tabs times the dollar value of each.

Bingo is exempt from this tax, but lotteries, pull-tabs, and raffles are not. In general, exempt organizations (charities and associations) do not pay this tax on activities not exempt unless there is some personal benefit that inures. This personal inurement does not have to be direct. Therefore, if a social club conducts one of these nonexempt activities and places the gains in the general fund, this will be considered personal inurement because doing so would reduce the cost of operating the club and therefore reduce the cost of dues and other assessments to the members. Reasoned from the opposite direction, it would increase the amount of benefits such clubs can offer members with no offsetting increase in cost to each of them.

A second tax is the *occupational tax* (stamp tax). This tax is applied to each person or entity that receives wagers. This is paid as an annual fee. The tax is applied on an entity or agent of that entity that accepts the wagers. A paid bartender in a social club would be such an agent.

Both of these taxes are significantly increased when the games are not authorized by state law (being run illegally) or operated in a way that is contrary to state law. An example of the latter is using a paid person when the state law requires that only a volunteer or member be used to accept wagers.

One way to construct a gaming activity used by some organizations is to incorporate a separate taxable corporation. It conducts the games, does the required work, plus pays the taxes. These so-called "feeder organizations" are not tax exempt. However, the money they pass on to their parents can be received tax-free. The caution here is that the parent may nevertheless carry the responsibility to ensure tax and reporting by the feeder.

While this section focuses on the unrelated business income tax and the federal level concerns, managers need know the following:
1. The type of gaming—they may be treated differently
2. When winning must be reported
3. When taxes of winners must be withheld
4. When and if the total wager for the day or event must be reported

5. When employees must report tips
6. How to keep records, report, and pay taxes if someone wins on behalf of the organization
7. If employment taxes must be withheld for employees
8. Which of several forms must be filed
9. When daily (and event) records must be kept
10. When licenses may be required and local or state fees are charged
11. Whether the conduct of that event is subject to state and local property and sales taxes

More specific information can be gotten from IRS Publication 3079 "Tax-Exempt Organizations and Raffle Prizes."

Dues

Any payment that exceeds a certain threshold that is required for an individual or entity to become an associate member of an association, particularly a business or a civic association, will be considered unrelated business income if the principal purpose for forming the associate membership class was to produce income.

The motive for creating the class is deduced from the facts and circumstances, including the minutes of the organization. Central to the determination is whether the creation of the class was motivated to enable the organization to fulfill its mission. Therefore, it is possible that in a profession where there is a recognized ladder of progression, a class of membership could be created if that allows the organization to better fulfill its mission.

Other factors that lead to an interpretation that the membership class is unrelated to the mission are the size of the differential in the fees, kinds of core services, participation in governance, and core organizational offerings between full and associate members. An associate membership that purely gives access, as opposed to benefits and participation in core programs related to the mission of the organization, will quite likely lead to a conclusion that it is unrelated business income and taxable. Such "dues" are nothing more than prices charged to outsiders to gain incidental access to a single service or limited services (for example, for admission to showings).

Portfolio and Endowment Income

Certain types of income flow into an endowment or a nonprofit's investment portfolio free of unrelated business income taxes. These are incomes from rent, royalties, annuities, interest, dividends, and capital gains unless these are from controlled groups or from properties acquired by debt, as discussed earlier. In short, it is possible to run a tax-free endowment. The tainting of any one source of income in such an endowment by its being unrelated business income could subject the entire endowment to unrelated business income tax.

Certain investment-related transactions appear to have elements of unrelated business income but are not treated as such. Income derived from lending a security by the nonprofit to an investor is not treated as unrelated. This includes the interest, fees, and dividends on the security loaned, or the earnings on any security the investor may have put up as collateral. Further, the return of these collateral securities by the nonprofit to the investor is not treated as the settlement of a debt in which the security was loaned. Neither is the lapse of an option or the exercise of an option by the nonprofit treated as unrelated.

In these transactions, the nonprofit needs to be careful to have an arm's length arrangement and to avoid dealing with a disqualified person.Moreover, the lending of the security must be subject to a written contract. This contract must include a promise that the security returned to the nonprofit be identical to the one loaned, that risks of loss or gain by the nonprofit are not changed by the loan, that the nonprofit will receive all payments to which it is entitled, that the nonprofit will receive collateral not less in value than the amount loaned, that the value of the collateral be determined daily and adjusted upwards if necessary the following day, and that the nonprofit be able to terminate the loan with five days' notice.

Magazine and Advertising Income

To understand the unrelated business income tax as it relates to magazines and advertising, it is important to see a magazine as composed of three tasks: advertising, articles, and circulation. In setting up a magazine, there should be a competent cost accounting system that recognizes these functions because they affect the potential tax. Each function has costs and revenues. When all three are put together, we have a periodical called a magazine. The periodical's costs and revenues are, obviously, the sum of these parts.

The concept of unrelated business income as it relates to the periodical presumes that the articles are written for the members or the clients of the nonprofit and are therefore related to its mission. Accordingly, it concludes that if there is unrelated business income it is due to the net income from the sale of advertisements or that the subscription price is well in excess of what is needed to support the mission (the articles), or a combination of these.

The unrelated business income of a periodical can be divided into two categories: (1) that related to advertising, and (2) that related to the entire periodical largely because the circulation income exceeds the readership costs; that is, the earnings of the periodical are in excess of the amount needed to carry out the organization's mission.

Advertising

1. If the direct advertising costs exceed the gross advertising income, the advertising loss can be used to reduce any other unrelated business income the nonprofit may have.
2. If gross advertising income exceeds direct advertising costs, the balance can be used to cover the costs of readership as long as it does not produce a loss. This is done by deducting the cost of the readership portion of the magazine (articles) from the gross income of advertising.

Entire Periodical

1. If the circulation income (all income other than advertising; that is, income from sale, distribution, and production) is equal to or greater than the readership costs, the unrelated business income is the gross income from advertising minus the direct cost of advertising. Put another way, the advertising income is not necessary to the carrying out of the mission.
2. If readership costs exceed the circulation income, the unrelated business income is the total income of the periodical (advertising plus circulation income) over the total cost of the periodical.

The reader should see that the rules have a certain consistency. The second rule under Entire Periodical implies that the advertising income is generating the excess and because total periodical cost is being subtracted and that contains readership costs, advertising income is subsidizing the readership income, just as under the first rule under Advertising.

What is gross circulation income? Mainly, it is the price of subscribing to the magazine. For a commercial magazine, this is not a problem. For a nonprofit, the subscription price depends, in part, on whether nonmembers pay a higher price for the magazine than do members. If this is the case, and at least 20 percent of the subscribers are nonmembers, the price they pay is considered to be the subscription price. If 20 percent or more members pay a lower membership dues and this is because they do not get the magazine, the difference in dues is considered to be the subscription price. Otherwise, the subscription price is obtained by taking the total membership dues and multiplying that by the cost of the magazine divided by the total cost of conducting the organization's exempt mission (including the magazine). The idea is to get a subscription price that is equivalent to what a magazine sold by a for-profit publisher would charge.

Corporate Advertising or Sponsorship

Acknowledging a corporate sponsor will not be called unrelated business income if there is no language or action to induce the audience to buy the product or service of the sponsor. Inducement can occur by mentioning price or by making qualitative comparisons with other products. An exclusive contract with the corporate sponsor so that no other sponsorship may be included in the event or in the production of a printed matter will cause the transaction to be classified as an unrelated business. Any statement of endorsement will have the same effect. So will pegging the amount the organization is paid to the exposure or potential of it, such as how many people may attend, see, or hear it, will have similar results.

Prominently displaying the sponsor's logo or name and describing the sponsor's activity in a non-comparative manner and in a manner not to promote will not be a problem; neither will giving some special considerations to the sponsor, such as free tickets to the event being sponsored, preferential tickets, or even a thank-you reception. It is within bounds to negotiate where, how, and what language will be used in the acknowledgment. An organization may do well to stick to language such as "supplying this service for so many years," or "supplying an extensive array of such services," or "dedicated to doing their best," as opposed to "being the best."

Mortgages: Income Subject to Debt

It is easier to deal with this topic by raising a set of questions and giving some preferred answers—assuming that the objective is to avoid unrelated business income tax by conforming to existing rules. Because a mortgage (and a lien) are debt instruments, a property acquired through the signing of a mortgage, or that has a lien placed on it, can yield unrelated business income in its sale or in the income it generates.

1. Is at least 85 percent of the property to be used by the organization for its exempt purpose? Yes.
2. Is at least 85 percent of the property to be used by an organization related to the mortgagee? Yes.
3. Is the mortgaged property one obtained by bequest and did the donor have the property and the mortgage for five years or more before dying? Yes.
4. Is the property adjoining to or the next closest possible parcel to the one occupied by the organization for its exempt use and is the property to be converted to exempt use in ten years (or, if a church, fifteen years without regards to the contiguity of the property)? Yes.
5. Is the property to be used as a medical clinic? Yes.
6. Is the property to be leased to a disqualified person or the person who sold the property? No.
7. Is the mortgage gotten from a disqualified person? No.
8. Is the organization one that has gotten a specific authorization or qualification to purchase, restore, or repair homes without being subject to mortgage-related tax? Yes.
9. Is the income or sale of the property being taxed as unrelated for some other reason than the existence of a mortgage and therefore will not be taxed again? Yes.
10. Is the use to which the property acquired by debt one that is exempt? Yes.

A related organization, for the purposes of debt acquisition, has a specific definition. Two organizations are related for mortgage purposes if 50 percent of the members in one are also members of the other. This is analogous to the so-called brother-sister relationship among firms. In addition, organizations are related if they are associated with a common state, Federal, or international organization, or if one controls the other, or one organization is a holding company and the other is part of that system.

It is not necessary to assume a mortgage to have it cause unrelated business income. All that is necessary is that property has a mortgage—no matter who holds the mortgage and whether it is converted, changed, or refinanced. It is the existence of the mortgage that matters. Further, a property that is exempt because it is used for an exempt purpose becomes taxable once its use is changed. It is the use, not the property itself, which matters. Therefore, question 10 above is key.

Income from Mailing Lists, Logos, and Affinity Cards

Usually there is no problem if an organization leases its mailing list or the use of its name or logos only to exempt organizations, or if it leases to a commercial enterprise at a fixed and fair market fee without getting involved beyond that point. A problem arises when there is any attempt to control the use of the mailing list or logo (for any reason whatsoever) or when there is a participation in the profits (that is, percentage of profits paid to the nonprofit), or when the nonprofit becomes involved in promoting the use of the product or service (for example, a credit card), for which the for-profit corporation leased the list, logo, or name. A problem can arise even if the nonprofit works through its own subsidiary.

Active Participation and Agency Income

Active participation in a transaction unrelated to the mission of the organization will probably trigger the unrelated business income no matter how subtle the activity. But will this tax be triggered if some other entity, even a for-profit contractor, is used as an intermediary or representative of the nonprofit? Here the question rests on whether the intermediary, a subsidiary, or an independent contractor, is serving as an agent for the nonprofit.

The facts of each case as viewed by the IRS and the courts are determinative. In Mississippi State University Alumni, Inc. v. Commissioner, Technical Memo 1997–397, the IRS argued unsuccessfully that putting applications on a table and the carrying of a newspaper article about a credit card using the university's logo were services to the issuer. It argued that allowing the bank issuer to use the mailing list of the university along with the logo on the credit card amounted to a service. It even argued that a service was provided by the university when one of its employees reviewed the endorsement letters prepared and distributed by the bank. Disagreeing with the IRS, the court argued that these were too insignificant to convert a royalty to taxable income.

One of the most arduously fought cases is Sierra Club, Inc. v. Commissioner. The club, a 501(c)(6), owns a mailing list that it sells to one of its subsidiaries at a fixed and fair market rate. The subsidiary markets the list to firms as it sees fit. The club exercises control over the dates and contents of the message for which the list is to be used. One use of the list was by a bank issuing credit cards. The club was paid a fixed percentage of the total amount charged on the card. The IRS argued that these payments to the club were not royalties exempt from tax because the club merely used the subsidiary as an agent. But the club argued that they were merely exercising quality control and that it was a "passive" participant. They were not doing the marketing or renting and did not exercise managerial control over the vendors. The courts agreed.

In State Police Association of Massachusetts v. Commissioner we see the opposite results. The association contracted with an outside vendor to solicit advertising for its journal that was distributed free by the association at its annual event. Advertising fees were paid directly to the association and it paid the vendors a fixed percentage. The president of the association wrote letters to potential advertisers encouraging them to buy spots in the journal. Both the IRS and the courts concluded that the income was taxable because the outside vendor was just an agent of the association.

In American Academy of Family Physicians v. United States, the academy sold its mailing list to a for-profit subsidiary at a fair market price. This subsidiary marketed an insurance program. The insurance premiums were paid directly to the insurance company (not the subsidiary or the academy). The insurance company paid the academy a fixed percentage of the insurance reserve. The court concluded that this fixed payment was not unrelated business income. The academy's participation in the program was not a trade or business and their payments were not for services rendered.

The IRS will challenge an arrangement in which the nonprofit attempts to be "passive" by using an intermediary if that intermediary can be considered an agent or under the control of the nonprofit. A for-profit subsidiary is considered to be under the control of a nonprofit when the nonprofit holds at least 50 percent of the voting shares of the for-profit company. With the 1997 law (Taxpayer Relief Act of 1997), this ownership is attributed to any subsidiary owned by the subsidiary that the nonprofit owns. Control is also implied when the suggestions discussed under the dividend portion of Passive Income, a section earlier in this chapter, are not observed.

That the courts or the IRS may conclude that a transaction is not unrelated business income merely means that the nonprofit does not pay an income tax on the transaction. It does not exempt the subsidiary (whether nonprofit or for-profit) or independent vendor. Consequently, many transactions of this type are set up so that the payment from an independent vendor to the nonprofit is in the form of royalties or interest, rather than in the form of dividends. Dividends cannot be deducted by the for-profit, but interest and royalties can. And interest and royalties are also received tax free by the nonprofit in a clean transaction in which they are passive. Consequently, the parent avoids taxes and the subsidiary reduces its taxes by paying royalties and interest rather than dividends. See our discussion next for more on for-profit subsidiaries.

Income from For-Profit Subsidiaries

If a Section 509(a)(3) as a nonprofit subsidiary earns unrelated business income they are taxed. What if the subsidiary is a for-profit corporation? How is this setup treated Under past laws. A nonprofit could form a for-profit subsidiary and own 79 percent of its voting stocks, the remainder of the voting stocks being owned by some friendly party or parties. The subsidiary could then own 100 percent of a for-profit firm that would pay interest, royalties, and rents to the nonprofit organization. These income flows would be received tax-free because the nonprofit owned less than 80 percent of the first-tier subsidiary (so by law it was not considered to be in control of that subsidiary). Because none of the latter's ownership of the second-tier subsidiary was attributed to the parent, the parent was not considered to be in control of this second-tier subsidiary either.

Under current law this is no longer possible. The nonprofit is considered to be in control of the first-tier subsidiary once it owns 50 percent of the voting stock of the first-tier subsidiary. Furthermore, a part of the stock of the second-tier subsidiary owned by the first is attributed to the nonprofit. This means if the first-tier completely controls the second-tier subsidiary, the nonprofit is considered to be in control of both once it controls 50 percent or more of the voting stock of the first tier.

Note that this rule omits reference to dividends. Dividends from a for-profit corporation to its parent and only stockholder are not taxable regardless of whether the parent is a for-profit or nonprofit corporation. Further, dividends are not deductible by the paying corporation, but interest, royalties, and rents are deductible by the paying corporation. Therefore, the incentive of the non-profit was to win both ways: to have its subsidiary pay interest, royalties, and rents to it, which the subsidiary would then deduct from its income tax. These payments would then be received by the parent nonprofit tax-free under the unrelated business income tax rule.

The new law still allows the payments of royalties, interest, and rents to be deducted by the for-profit subsidiary, but these are now taxable to the nonprofit, since they control the subsidiary. Note when control is absent, these flows would remain tax-free unless made taxable under some other condition, such as being debt acquired.

Income from Holding Companies of Multiple Parents

Title holding companies, as described in earlier in this bookare tax-exempt as long as they stick to their mission—acquiring and holding title to real estate, collecting income, and passing it on to the parents. If for instance, a 501(c)(25) (a title-holding corporation or trust for multiple parent corporations) should vary from this, it loses its exemption. Technically, therefore, there is no unrelated business income arising from activities unrelated to their mission. Since the 501(c)(25)s are expected to be active and are controlled by their parents, these activities would hardly give rise to unrelated business income.

But what about property acquired by borrowing? The rules allow that these properties would not yield unrelated business income for certain types of nonprofits—particularly educational institutions. For all other institutions, their liability for this type of unrelated business income will relate to their pro rata share of ownership of the holding company.

Key Points on Entrepreneurial Income in Nonprofits

1. Any tax-exempt organization, even one dedicated to lessening the burden of government may make a profit.
2. There is no absolute dollar limit on that profit.
3. The profit must be used to advance the organization's mission which includes services such as infrastructure, equipment, salaries used substantially for mission purposes, and in general the lessening of the specific burden of government for which it was created or given to the government.
4. No part of the earnings can be used for personal or private inurement and conflicts of interest should be avoided.
5. The organization cannot be deemed to have profit-making or a commercial activity as its principal purpose is a public purpose (in this case the lessening of the burden of government) must be the principal motive.
6. The related business profits are not taxed and are a source of unrestricted funds. The fees earned from conducting its mission are not taxed.
7. Generally passive income is not taxed and is also a source of unrestricted funds. This causes an exclusion for most investment income except that which is subject to debt.
8. Profits from unrelated activities are subject to the corporate income tax at rates firms pay. This is true whether the entity was created by government or private citizens, or whether or not it remains part of government.
9. Even if a profit is derived from mission-related activities, it cannot impede the mission, that is, exclude natural clients for that specific mission activity. For example, so high that it makes it impossible for low income tenants to live in a low-income housing project even if that "charitable" project is to lessen the burden of government. It does not matter.

10. No, it is not sufficient that the profits are used for the mission, it also must be evident that profit-making was not the principal purpose of the business activity. Sources of evidence include method of marketing, price determination, and extent of utilization of volunteers, and whether the activity (for example, parking) was for the convenience of staff and clients.
11. In a structured arrangement, the tax is placed on the taxpaying unit that made it.

Summary and Preview

A very large percentage of nonprofits, created to lessen the burden of government must earn their way through business income. Many, if not most, charge for their services. This chapter provides guidance and a framework for the entrepreneurial revenues needed to finance an organization to relieve the burden of government. It focuses on a variety of such income streams since all may be available to the organization but also because it is impossible to decide at this juncture which burden an organization may choose to lessen and therefore which income stream may be most relevant to it when.

Chapter 10 – Financing the Burden through Debt

The nonprofit has three principal sources of cash: cash from operations, cash from financing activities, and cash from investments. For most entities, debt (cash from financing) is an important source of financing sustainably because it is the principal source of financing long-term projects and capital investments and because the organization cannot produce enough cash from its operations or from its investments to undertake large expenditures; for example, purchasing a building or even buying vehicles or starting up new programs that are not pre-funded. Congregations take out mortgages (debt) to acquire their houses of worship. Government enters into debt to pay for roads, airports, and other capital projects. Often collaborations involve the taking out of debt simply because of their size, need for the organization not to drain its treasury or deprive its other responsibilities, and to get a project moving forward. Understanding debt is central to understanding organizational survival and sustainability.

This chapter is based on the proposition that in order to undertake any of the themes in this book, the nonprofit organization must have the capacity to borrow because expenditure requirements likely will exceed what it can obtain through its own operations or through its own investments—including its endowment. How is this capacity established?

The Need for a Charter and Other Documentary Powers

The organization typically cannot enter into a debt arrangement with a financial institution or with the public at large through the financial markets or even an astute individual lender unless all of these are met: (a) a charter gives it that power, (b) bylaws that provide for a way to enact that power, (c) a resolution of the board to enter into the specific debt arrangement, and (d) a letter of good standing from the state. It is the board that represents the organization, the bylaws that create and instruct the board, the charter that gives the bylaws and board that power, and the state certificate of good standing that says the organization still exists, and is in violation of no state law that threatens its existence. All serious lenders of money or extenders of credit will require either a direct presentation of these documents and a statement warranting and representing that they remain as presented at the time of the loan or during its terms. The lender requires these not only to be sure of the legitimacy of the transactions but because the lender is making the loan to the organization, which cannot speak or write for itself, not to the individuals signing the loan. With these doc-

DOI 10.1515/9781501505799-011

uments, those who sign them could die or be removed from the organization and the organization will still be in debt to the lender.

Terms of Debt

Debt may be short- or long-term. *A short-term debt* simply means that it has to be paid back within a year or so. This type of debt has little to do with sustainability and more to do with survival. It has to do with the rise of an unexpected need for cash, often to cover some operating need or taking advantage of an unexpected opportunity. Short-term debt comes in two forms. In one form, one gets a lump sum and pays it back by the end of a specific term, usually within a year. In another form, it comes as a line of credit, such as an equity line or credit card. This latter is useful in making perfunctory transactions: paying the airlines, the hotel, the taxi driver, the restaurant, and the merchant. It is virtually impossible for an organization to function without this level of debt.

Two other types of short-term loan that facilitate the organization operating are trade credits and advances. Trade credit occurs when the organization purchases supplies and has thirty days to pay. If it pays within those thirty days, it pays no finance charge and may even get a discount. This is free trade credit. But if it pays after that, there is a finance charge. One of the ways of getting a short-term loan is through an advance payment on a contract or grant. Sometimes it is possible to arrange these before the contract or program period. Other times it is done when money is needed. Consider an advance as a retainer. It is also a debt.

Long-term debt is one that extends a year and more—as much as 30 years. This type of debt has more to do with sustainability and advancement than with survival. It is a capital debt because its principal use is not to cover current operations, but to acquire a long-lasting asset such as furniture, automobiles, leasing arrangements, or mortgages. It is almost impossible for an organization to grow into the future without this type of debt.

These types of debt have different requirements. The long-term debt usually would require a periodic delivery of information often satisfied with the annual Form 990, a resolution of the board authorizing it, a higher level of creditworthiness (explained next), and an estimate of the quantity and quality of commitment-free revenues to the organization for at least the life of the debt. Long-term debt are also generally *secured* debt meaning that the organization has some assets that the lender can attach or acquire should the organization not be able to pay the debt.

Creditworthiness of the Organization

The ability of the organization to be an acceptable borrower to a lender and the rate of interest that will be charged will depend upon a number of factors. They include the following:

1. That the organization has the power to enter into debt as specifically stated in its charter.
2. That there is a resolution of the board authorizing that specific transaction for purposes as in Chapter 6.
3. The quality and quantity of expected revenues of the organization over the life of the debt.
4. The extent to which the organization has other assets exceeding the amount of the debt that is not already attached or encumbered so that it is virtually untouchable by the proposed lender without permission from those who have encumbered it.
5. The extent to which the quantity and quality of revenues are free of commitments and exceed the debt or the interest to be paid.
6. The quality of its board and management .
7. The organization's most recent operating, financial, and debt history.
8. Any legal or other contingent liabilities that are outstanding and that the organization will have to meet—requiring cash.
9. The purpose for which the debt is being requested.
10. The ability of the organization to obtain a guarantor or other co-signer for the loan and the creditworthiness of that person.

A Secured Loan

Most long-term loans are secured. A loan to purchase a car is secured by the car, to purchase a building is secured by the building. In the end, all loans are secured or unsecured (meaning no asset is attached as security if the debt is not paid) by the quantity, quality, and degree of encumbrance on that income. For the nonprofit, a government contract or commitment, or some forms of contribution, make excellent securities for a loan; for example, a permanent insurance policy given to it or an annuity given to it can be used .

A particular problem in using contributions to secure debt is the concept of donor restrictions. (When the donor places a restriction on the donation, it is eligible to be used only in accordance with that restriction and may be used to secure a debt only if the debt is connected to that restriction, the donor or successor approves.

A secured loan may reduce the interest payments but increase other costs. The lender may require an assessment before closing the loan; an annual or periodic inspection to ensure that the asset is being maintained; an insurance policy to protect against fire and other damages. The lender may also require maintenance of the visual presentation of the property and its compliance with zoning codes. These expenses will fall on the nonprofit borrower. Furthermore, any asset that is used to secure a loan encumbers that asset. For example, the property that is used to secure a loan encumbers it—meaning that a lien is placed on it which gives the lender a right to demand that the property not be used in certain ways, not be used to support another loan, or not be sold.

Non-Deductibility and Taxability of Interest

Nonprofits that are tax exempt get no tax benefit from the interest they pay on mortgages. But they could be taxed on the interest earned on property they own that are subject to debt. This includes rental property if more than 85 percent of the space is rented to a for-profit entity.

Debt as Credit Facility

A credit facility is simply an arrangement the nonprofit makes with a financial institution that when it needs cash it will be available without the extra hassle of applying, waiting, or additional proof. The simplest form of such a facility is the credit card. It takes a quick application, is subject to a limit and terms of agreement, and once one has it (often within 10 days of application), it can be used when and anywhere it is accepted. Moreover, one pays interest only on the amount outstanding, makes a minimum payment on a known date every month, may replenish the amount available by the amount of payment one makes on that date or any time thereafter, and may bring the interest payment to zero by paying off the full amount as chosen. It is debt—a revolving loan.

A credit facility may also be a letter of credit. This is often not available to smaller nonprofits. A letter of credit is given by a financial institution that assures the nonprofit that it has access through the bank to a specific amount for a specific time period. This amount may well exceed the balance the nonprofit has in the bank, but some balance will normally be required. Letters of credit facilitate large, difficult, and often foreign transactions because the other party uses the letter as assurance from the bank that payment will be made even if it has to do so.

Covenants, Default, Bankruptcy

Every loan, even a credit card, is subject to a letter of agreement between the borrower and the lender. This letter, called an *indenture*, covers a variety of things. The interest rate, the length of the loan, how billing and payments will be done, whether the loan is subject to a variable or a fixed rate, how disputes will be handled, what constitutes default and how that will be handled.

In general, default is the breaking of any of the terms of the covenant (any stipulation in the indenture). This goes beyond not being able to make payment on time. Covenants may include operating and reporting requirements. Did the board lose a member, was the executive fired, was there a deficit in one year, was there a loss of property, was property sold, was there a negative audit, did the government take action against the nonprofit including removing or putting its tax exempt status in abeyance? Was there a consequential lawsuit? Any of these and more can cause a default. A default allows the lender to renegotiate the loan, call for accelerated payments, or just close it down. Furthermore, there may be a cross-default clause. This simply means that the organization is in default with the lender if it is in default with any other lender. This allows lenders to protect themselves.

Default is not bankruptcy and default does not necessarily lead to bankruptcy. Default is an early warning to the lender to protect itself against the possibility of bankruptcy or the inability of the organization to perform or to protect itself. Unlike firms, the occurrence of a default does not give the lender the power to force the organization to declare bankruptcy and does not give the lender the right to the organization's assets.

Strategies for Treating a Loan Due

When a loan is due, the management of the organization has several options. It can redeem the debt—meaning closing it off by paying the remaining principal and interest. It can renegotiate the debt maturity—meaning extending its term. If it does not have the cash to pay off the debt, it can refinance the loan—meaning borrowing perhaps at a lower rate to pay off the creditors. It can negotiate with the lender to take less. It may seek help from a private foundation or other nonprofits, some supported by government funds for financing assistance to others. In short, bankruptcy is not the first step.

Loan agreements may also provide for early payments with or without penalty. Some loans (for example, bonds discussed in the next section) also provide for them to be called—meaning that the organization has the right to retire the bond after the passage of an agreed time with or without penalty, but with payment of all outstanding interest.

Borrowing from the Securities Market

The nonprofit may be empowered by the State to issue bonds and other debt securities on the market; and they may be further empowered by the Securities and Exchange Commission to sell those securities across state lines without the formality of registering them, as firms must. The principal way of doing this is through the issuing of revenue bonds. Generally, a nonprofit has to be quite sizeable (museums, firms, hospitals, universities, authorities) to be allowed this privilege or even to be able to afford it.

A revenue bond is a long-term debt obligation issued by a jurisdiction or by a nonprofit designated with the authority to do so. A revenue bond is an unsecured bond in that there are no assets to secure it other than the income stream from the activity it finances. Most revenues bonds do not have the security of the state—that is, the state makes no guarantee that it will make good to the creditors in case the nonprofit or the authority is unable to pay. At best it may say that the state will consider calling the legislature to see what they decide. This is not considered a guarantee. By not guaranteeing the bond, the state does not carry it as a liability and it does not affect the state debt limit even when the state may issue the bond on behalf of a group of nonprofits and even when the project relieves the burden of the state.

This makes a lot of sense. First, the investors in these bonds assess not the government but the project in which they are investing to determine if the bond fits their portfolio and they are subject to the same discounting as a corporate bond. Moreover, all states and jurisdictions have debt limits and if these bonds (usually hundreds of thousands of dollars) were to count against that limit, the government could not fund other necessary projects, including schools, even if they were funded by general obligation bonds—those with the full faith and credit of the government, which means its taxing and revenue powers, because the credit rating would decline.

Revenue bonds are self-liquidating—meaning that when they are issued, they fund a project with an income stream that will amortize (make the monthly payments) of interest and principal plus any fees so that the project fully covers the debt and related services.

Borrowing from Nonfinancial Sources

Financial institutions and the capital markets are not the only sources of borrowing for a nonprofit. Private foundations make loans to nonprofits, so do some state agencies and many are financed through revenue bonds and use the proceeds to make loans or grants to nonprofits. Loans may also be obtained from nonprofit fund pools that may also provide technical assistance in accessing capital. A relatively easy source of loans is the organization's own endowment .(Loans can also be gotten from insurance policies that have cash value if they were not restricted by the donor It's "easy" to borrow from these sources because it foregoes many of the qualifying considerations discussed above especially under creditworthiness.

Preparing to Borrow

The following steps may help an organization ready itself to make a debt move:
1. Obtain a resolution by the board authorizing it to borrow.
2. Have its financial statements, tax statements, and filings in order.
3. Obtain, if necessary, a letter of good standing from the state of incorporation. This is a certificate from the state indicating that it has filed annual reports and tax returns as required.
4. Determine whether there are outstanding encumbrances to its going into debt. An outstanding debt may prohibit further bother without the authorization of the creditor.
5. Ascertain whether it will have the cash flow to make debt payments.
6. Determine the length of time for which it needs the loan and match it with its ability to pay.
7. Decide whether it has collateral for the loan and the extent to which it may wish to encumber that collateral. Collateral may be accounts receivable, future grants or contract revenues already committed, or contributions.
8. Determine whether the loan would lead to opportunities for self-dealing and devise a preventative strategy.
9. Understand, before closing the loan, the conditions under which the loan is being made. These conditions may state what the organization must do to get the money and what it must continue to do while the loan is enforced. This may involve holding cash in the bank, it may require the board to make annual restrictions on specific monies, and it may even prohibit the organization from making significant increases in salaries. Please note that breaking a condition in the contract amounts to defaulting on the loan.

10. Learn what the penalties are.
11. Be prepared to do the annual reporting that may be required.
12. Consider getting a financial advisor, if the loan requires the issuing of a bond or is sizable.
13. Be prepared to be truthful with the lenders and in applications. Lenders will require the management of the organization to make certain warranties and representations. It is a crime to misrepresent the facts and this may be punishable both by jail time and penalties.
14. Be prepared for conditions precedent. These are conditions that the lender may require before the conversation or exercise of the loan may move forward (see item 9 above).

Debt Limits and the Nonprofit

Nonprofit organizations, unless specified in their bylaws, have only an implicit debt limit decided by their creditors. This debt limit may vary from transaction to transaction; for example, the debt limit on a credit card is different from the limit on mortgages. In general, the debt limit is calculated by some percentage of expected income over a specific period of time by the amount of debt already outstanding and that which is to be added. This ratio is frequently multiplied by a factor which gives the lender an estimate of what it desires to lend.

This is different from the way the federal government's debt limit works. This is an absolute number negotiable between the executive and legislative branches. States and localities have constitutionally set debt limits often set as a percentage of the average revenue (as it is defined to include) over a set period of time. Changes in that debt limit often require a state constitutional change, increasing the tax base of the state and the revenue it generates, or increasing revenues and then waiting to for the debt capacity to accommodate the required borrowing or foregoing the project. There is another alternative, create a 501(c)(3) and operate as in the next section.

Subsidized Infrastructure Debt Available to Nonprofits

Below is a short summary of three types of long-term infrastructure debt which nonprofits may directly or indirectly have access to in order to build infrastructure themselves or to finance their contributions to a public private partnership (3Ps):

1. *Grant Application Revenue Vehicle*: Provides loans secured by a contractual expectation of a flow of funds; e.g., payment by the government for a contract performance. A principal advantage is that it accelerates project starting and reduces costs due to delaying of project. Availability and use of these debt facilities is determined by project qualification. Therefore, a nonprofit could qualify for this type of loan depending upon the project, and this could be its contribution to a partnership with a firm. In general, these credit facilities are indicated when the project does not have an independent stream of income on which to depend and therefore relies on a payment from an expected and pre-scheduled federal grant transfer. Instead of waiting for that transfer to take place, the entity borrows the money.

2. *Build America Bonds*: These are taxable loans to state and local governments or their subdivisions including public authority but the cost of issuing that loan is subsidized by a federal government of up to 35 percent of the issuing costs. Research https://www.treasury.gov/initiatives/recovery/Documents/BABs%20Report.pdfs shows that this subsidy makes these loans less expensive to issue than tax-exempt municipal bonds. Certain 501(c)(3)s such as hospitals and universities are also eligible for these loans to build their mission-related infrastructure.

3. *Qualified Private Purpose Revenue Bonds*: These bonds may be issued by 501(c)(3)s with access to the capital markets. These bonds may or may not be secured by the state or local government and usually they are not inclined to do so because it counts against their debt limit if they do. Debt service for these bonds comes from the earnings of the project. They are subsidized to the extent that the interest on these debt are lowered by the amount of taxes foregone by the exemption of their interests. This type of bond is described below.

4. *Section 63–20 Bonds*: A revenue bond issued by the 501(c)(3) but for the benefit and use of the state or local government. Discussed immediately below.

Long-Term Debt tor Infrastructure Used by the Nonprofit

In this section, we describe tax-exempt debt that the IRS allows nonprofits, specifically 501(c)(3)s, to issue whether the organization is privately or governmentally created. It is referred to as qualified private use debt in which the creditors pay no taxes on the interest earned. This provides the nonprofit a lower than market rate of interest. These are the conditions that must be met for the interest on the bonds to be tax-exempt:

1. The organization issuing the bond has to be certified as a 501(c)(3) by the IRS (see Chapters 2, 3 and 4).
2. The proceeds of the loan have to be used for a property owned by the 501(c)(3)—called the ownership test.
3. The use of the property has to be by a 501(c)(3), even if it is not the issuer.
4. All of the above have to endure the length of the loan.
5. The amount cannot exceed a limit stated at the time by the IRS.
6. There can be no personal inurement.

The IRS provides a number of ways in which some failures to comply may be cured. For example, point 4 does not mean that the nonprofit cannot, for economic reasons, sell the property to a for-profit; but it does have to then pay off the loan within 90 days of that sale. Similarly, point 3 does not mean that there can be no private users, but does create a concern for nonprofit collaboration with for-profit firms either as renters or as co-users of a space. In general, no more than 15 percent of that space or the income from that space can be for the firm if the loan continues to be tax exempt. The debt described above is issued by government created nonprofits (for example, public universities) and private nonprofits as well but for their use in the public interest (for example, building a new wing to a museum).

Long-Term Debt Issued by Nonprofits on Behalf of the Government for Public Purpose Infrastructure Called 63-20 Debt

Revenue Ruling 63-20 provides for the government or private citizens to create a nonprofit to issue debt on behalf of the government. The government may create what is called a *constituted authority*—a nonprofit entity controlled by the government. This relieves the government in that the debt does not count against the debt limit of the government although it may count against its credit rating since the government is considered the ultimate borrower and responsible for the lease payments to service the debt when it is the user of the facility which the debt financed. Using this procedure also enables the government to shift development, maintenance, and managements risks and responsibilities away from itself to the authority or to the private developer—meaning a three-entity, cross-sector collaboration with the nonprofit at the center.

An alternative to the constituted authority is a nonprofit created by government or citizens and incorporated under the state laws. This nonprofit would look like any other nonprofit described in Chapters 1, 2, 3 and 6, although it does not need to receive a specific 501(c)(3) exemption. But its purpose would be to issue debt on behalf of or for the benefit of the government. This nonprofit is not a government entity but it operates on behalf of the government; and therefore the government has a beneficial interest in it. For this entity to issue tax-exempt bonds and to be itself tax exempt, the following must be true:

1. The project must be of significant public benefit, such as infrastructure.
2. The government must have a beneficial interest, which means that it is the 95 percent user of the project or that it names 85 percent of the board which it may remove as it sees fit.
3. The security for the loan comes from the toll or rent from the project. Even if the government is the sole user, it pays rent to cover the debt and other costs.
4. The government must have the unfettered right to the project at any time and after the debt is paid off.
5. The refinancing of the debt will not extend its initial maturity date.
6. No part of the debt proceeds can be used for working capital—all must be used to acquire the infrastructure and the equipment and other personal assets it needs. Any excess is used to redeem the debt.
7. There can be no personal inurement.

How Does This Work in Practice?

The Federal, state, local, county, or township government or one of its agencies (housing, transportation, environment, or defense, or any other) creates a nonprofit corporation that basically meets the terms of a 501(c)(3) It is therefore capable of doing four things: (a) issuing debt, (b) acquiring assets, (c) entering into contracts, and (d) it has the other powers as stipulated in Chapter 2 because it is a corporation as discussed in that chapter with a board of directors. The directors are the ones who authorize by their signatures each of the agreements below to enable the 63-20 financing, design, development, operation, and maintenance of the infrastructure.

A franchise or development agreement: One that defines the project, its geographical borders, the assignment of responsibilities and liabilities—all those considerations encompassed in the planning and construction of the project. This agreement may be signed by the government and the nonprofit or with the private developer and then transferred to the nonprofit. In either case, the franchise winds up with the nonprofit as the franchisee.

A development or management agreement: This is the agreement between the nonprofit and the project developer. In it, the nonprofit through an agency it forms or with which it contracts, oversees the development of the project and assumes, along with the developer, project development and management risks which it may share it with the firm it hires as an intermediary between it and the developer.

An operating or maintenance agreement: This an agreement between the nonprofit and a private firm to operate the facility, collect fees, and to maintain the facility. This is a management contract and subject to the same IRS rules between any nonprofit and a private firm.

A bond indenture: This is an agreement between the nonprofit issuer and the debtholders. It contains a full description of the projects, the income stream to build and to support it, the role of the government and the nonprofit, the terms of the bonds, the covenants or restrictions on the project and on the nonprofit.

The impact is obvious. It reduces the burden of the debt of the government because it is the nonprofit, not the government that issues the bonds. But it also reduces the development, development oversight, and project administration from the government and the liabilities associated with each of these phases. The government having ascertained a need, arranges for that need to be met and may provide in each of these contracts the terms of disclosure, public participation, and public hearings. The government may even provide for public representation, in the person of elected officials or citizens appointed by the government, on the board of the nonprofit. While ownership title for the facility is owned by the nonprofit, the government maintains a beneficiary interest as described above. This strategy is available for any time of facility—housing, hospitals, roads or other transportation facilities. Furthermore, within the context of this book, this arrangement provides for cross-sectoral collaboration among the government, the nonprofit, and the for-profit firms that do the construction and may also do the management servicing. And issuing a bond on behalf of the government means the government must approve both the issue and the project.

Issuing of Debt (Bonds) by an Authority

Authorities may issue three kinds of long-term debt. They are listed and described below in the order in which they may have the greatest and most direct impact on lessening the burden of government.

Debt on behalf of the jurisdiction: This debt is issued for the benefit of a jurisdiction. The legislature of jurisdiction must have voted in favor of it and the executive must have approved it. This debt may be guaranteed by the jurisdiction. The debt proceeds are not for the use of the authority but the jurisdiction and therefore debt services may come from any combination of taxes and fees. States such as Oklahoma (Title 60, Section 176) require passage by the State Legislature and the signature of the Governor if the state is the beneficiary and 2/3 of the legislature if the beneficiary is a county or a municipality. States may vary in these numbers, but they all require at least a vote by the governing body of the government for whom the debt is being issued. This is Federal law.

Debt on behalf of the Authority: This debt is issued for the benefit of the authority itself. This debt is serviced by the fees and earnings of the authority and not by taxes.

Conduit Debt: This debt is issued usually for the benefit of a firm or firms—a private party. These parties pay the debt service and the obligation is theirs. Such a debt may be issued to further the mission of an authority; for example, to help finance the location of a firm or to help finance an infrastructure item by reducing the cost to the firm.

This is how the power of the authority to issue bonds is written in the cases of the Chesapeake Authority in Chesapeake Virginia:

> The Authority is hereby authorized to issue bonds from time to time in its discretion for the purpose of paying all or any part of the cost of any Authority facility or for the purpose of paying or refunding, at or prior to the maturity thereof, any bonds previously issued by it or by the Commonwealth or any other agency or political subdivision thereof originally issued for a purpose not inconsistent with the purposes of this act. The Authority may issue such types of bonds as it may determine including, without limitation, bonds payable as to principal and interest from any one or more of the following: (i) its revenues generally; (ii) the income and revenues of a particular Authority facility; (iii) the income and revenues of certain designated Authority facilities, including the revenues from the sale or lease of such Authority facilities, whether they are financed in whole or in part from the proceeds of such bonds; (iv) the proceeds of the sale or lease of any one or more Authority facilities, whether or not they are financed from the proceeds of such bonds; (v) funds realized from the enforcement of security interests or other liens securing such bonds; (vi) proceeds from the sale of bonds of the Authority; (vii) payments due under letters of credit, policies of bond insurance, bond purchase agreements or other credit enhancements securing payment of principal of and interest on bonds of the Authority; (viii) any reserve or sinking funds created to secure such payment; or (ix) other available funds of the Authority; provided, that bonds issued to finance the construction or acquisition of any Authority facility that is not an operating facility shall not be payable from revenues of the Authority generally or from any revenues derived from operating facilities.

> Any such bonds may be additionally secured by a pledge of any grant or contribution from the City, the Commonwealth or any political subdivision, agency or instrumentality thereof, any federal agency or any unit, private corporation, co-partnership, association or individual, or a pledge of any income or revenues of the Authority, or a mortgage of or a

deed of trust or other lien on or a security interest in any particular Authority facility or other property of the Authority.

This is a description of the bond concepts in the above:

1. These are revenue bonds (other nonprofits may also issue), not general obligation bonds. General obligations can only be issued by a jurisdiction or one of their subdivisions, and the latter only by express permission of the jurisdiction. A general obligation bond carries the promise that the issuer will back the bond with its full faith and credit; translated, this means its taxing powers. These bonds cannot be issued without the vote of the citizens. The bonds that are referred to in the above are revenue bonds. These are secured by the income stream of the project and any other enhancement or promise the authority might get; but not by taxes, which the authority cannot impose. These bonds are technically not backed by the government unless it says so. A promise to consider payment is not a promise to pay and a promise to pay or a commitment to do so places the contingent liability on the jurisdiction and counts against its credit limits. Therefore, jurisdictions are careful not to go beyond a promise to consider. Revenue bonds do not need the vote of citizens, but they need the vote of the legislative branch of the issuing jurisdiction and the signature of the executive branch of the jurisdiction. The 501(c)(3)s may issue revenue bonds based upon a resolution of their board of trustees.

2. The security for these bonds is the income stream from the project they finance or any other earned income the authority might have. However, if that earned income is unrelated to the mission of the authority and not otherwise exempt (usually because it is from rent, capital gains, royalties, or investments) of the authority, it is taxed.

3. The state or any other jurisdiction is under no obligation to secure these bonds unless they elect to do so.

4. The infrastructure is not owned by the authority so it cannot pledge it, but other properties it might well own such as other lands, buildings, equipment, receivables, and the income stream to back any loan may be pledged. That income stream may be the revenues from operating the infrastructure or any other revenues as permitted.

5. The role of letter of credit, sinking fund and bond insurance; instead of getting the jurisdiction to back the bond, often the same effect can be obtained, if not better, by having an unrelated third party back the bond. With a letter of credit, a bank or similar financial institution simply promises that, if the borrower cannot pay, it will. Obviously, there is a fee for this service and the authority has to be creditworthy. In addition, it usually has to

be a long-time depositor at the bank. Bond insurance works similarly in that the bond is insured by the issuer. The sinking fund is simply a requirement that the issuer must made periodic payments to a third party to cover the amount that given a present value of a future amount would be sufficient to make good on the principal and interest that would be due on maturity. These are among the techniques that are used to reduce the risk of not being able to make interest and principal payments when due. The effect is to reduce the interest rate the bond issuer has to pay.

Debt Through Tax Increment Financing

Tax increment financing works like this: The state demarcates a geographic area with specific boundaries for development. It creates and incorporates a non-profit tax exempt organization as an instrumentality of the municipality, specifically, an authority to plan, oversee, manage, finance, and achieve that development. The authority is managed by a board of directors comprised primarily of municipal officials and persons from the area to be developed. Among the duties of the governing board is to determine if the plan is in the public interest, feasible, desirable, and if the method of financing is acceptable.

The authority has the power of a corporation and of government as specifically enumerated and given by the specific law that creates it, but exercises eminent domain through the municipality. The municipality may issue revenue bonds or general obligation bonds to finance the authority (commonly called a *special district authority*). When the authority revenue bonds are issued, the municipality is under no obligation or liability for the bond and may elect whether it wants to use its full faith and credit (taxing powers) to back the bond. Otherwise, the obligation it has is to (a) do assessment of the property in the beginning period and some designated period, (b) impose a tax on the increase in value, and (c) remit the receipt to the authority.

With those funds, the authority meets its capital and debt expenses, its reserve requirements, and its operating requirements. Any excess is then remitted by the authority to the taxing governmental agency. This process is called tax-increment financing because the tax to pay the debt service is imposed on the increase in property tax due to the development of the area.

The municipality may elect whether it wants to make additional contributions to the authority.

The law also provides that if the educational tax for the district reduces the amount that the authority would have received, the municipality would remit the difference to assure that the obligations of the authority can be paid.

The entire development from the inception to planning and financing are subject to public hearings and a number of mandatory reports. If for some reason the special district is dissolved, its assets go to the government that created it and on behalf of which it worked. See Michigan (http://www.legislature.mi.gov/documents/mcl/pdf/mcl-act-450-of-1980.pdf) especially sections 12 and 15.

Long-Term Lease Arrangements of Property

Both 501(c)(3)s and authorities are eligible to enter into long-term leasing arrangements. Aside from the well-established sale-leaseback arrangements—where the nonprofit would sell a facility and then lease it back, is the rapidly rising use of another strategy. Therefore, of particular interest because of its rising popularity amidst controversy, is the lease-leaseback arrangement. In this case a private corporation leases a piece of property; say, on the campus of a university for a small amount ($1 per year) and finances the construction of a building, which it then leases back to the university. The rental covers the pay-off the builder-financer. It is a long-term debt obligation of the nonprofit. It reduces the burden of government because it lowers the upfront cost of the facility, the beneficial interest in it always remains in the nonprofit or authority acting to further a public interest.

Summary and Preview

This brief chapter makes the point that debt is a financing strategy almost unavoidable by any organization designed to lessen the burden of government. It therefore walks the reader through various conditions of debt and preparations for entering into debt, the determination of debt ratings and of the interest cost, and various designs of debt, especially for infrastructure projects—from buildings to ports. This debt may be as simple as a credit card or as complex as the issuing of tax-exempt bonds inn the bond market.

Bibliography

Allison, Barney, Nossam, LLP, "The Use of 63-20 Nonprofit Corporations in Infrastructure Facility Development," (http://www.Nossaman.com/showarticle.aspx?Show=854).
Federal Highway Administration, U.S. Department of Transportation (www.fhwa.dot.gov/ipd/p3/defined/dbfo_6320.aspx).

Chapter 11 – Establishing Cash Flows for Sustainability

For the most part, creating a nonprofit to lessen the burden of government comes with a recognition that Americans, while generous to nonprofits in general, are not particularly generous in donations to reduce the burden of government—this is evidenced by the fact that donations to reduce the size of the debt are constantly by my own calculations (of total national debt divided by the donation for reducing the debt) between 1–2 percent of the debt per year for the past 15 years. This would not go far.

Moreover, donors are more attracted to a cause than to a need of government. But a nonprofit has, at its disposal, various instruments that it can employ. In addition, lessening the burden of government incentivizes a type of giving called "in-kind" from the government agency itself. For example, the giving of space and the rendering of service are not normally deductible, so the citizen's incentive to give them is lessened. However, the agency will often provide space and services; for example, the police and park service around the Vietnam War Memorial. These considerations drive the need for this and the previous chapter.

The City Parks Foundation of New York City is a 501(c)(3). It revitalizes and encourages various levels of recreation in parks throughout the city under the jurisdiction of the New York City Parks and Recreation Division. It does so primarily by raising funds, but it gets gifts in-kind from New York City upon which it required that these donations, for its own accounting, to be valued in dollars annually. Some of its gift come in the form of arrangements to be discussed in the next chapter. Some are restricted to a particular use; others are not. But the organization needs to employ certain tools such as annuities and endowments. This is also true of organizations in Chapter 1 directed by Congress to raise funds from private sources. This chapter is about those tools.

This chapter continues to address the need for an organization to finance itself without resource dependence on the government except for performance contracts, such as leases, if it is to fully relieve the burden of government. In addition to earning income from the services it sells or its investments, it could receive gifts and contributions as described in Chapter 10; but to sustain itself financially over a period of time it needs to assure a flow of income into the future. One way of doing this is through: (a) its earnings from project performance, (b) its earnings from investment including investment in endowments, and (c) promises from contributors which are secured. This chapter deals with the last two, the first having been discussed already. The basic question is: How

DOI 10.1515/9781501505799-012

does an organization secure a future cash flow through its contribution and investment programs and thereby (a) reduce the risk that the burden will be abandoned by the organization, (b) reduce the risk that the donor will cancel the promise? All of this is accomplished through the use of certain specified instruments and arrangements to be described in this chapter. They are applicable when the organization relieving the burden of government is a 501(c)(3) and the collection, accumulation, and use is for that purpose. For example, to cover the fees and costs of treating the indigent, or paying the tuition of a needy student in a public college registered as a 501(c)(3)—most of them are. Finally, all these instruments are treated as if they were private foundations.

Why is this chapter relevant? Because it is not unusual that when donors make large gifts to nonprofits they do so through these instruments. They do not give cash out of pocket and they make the gift with the intent of supporting the organization over a long period of time.

At times when a jurisdiction creates a nonprofit it would also create a trust for it to get it started that would be a source of cash over time. Sometimes a jurisdiction would create a nonprofit that is a trust rather than a corporation because it is concerned with the accumulation, management, and distribution to claimants, rather than running a specific program. Furthermore, once the 501(c)(3) is off on its own, it needs to create a contribution and investment program so that it is assured some continuous future cash flow. This long-term accumulation-investment-withdrawal program for self-financing is often called an *endowment*. An endowment needs to be structured and financed, and this is the central concern of this chapter. Most endowments discussed are basically trusts. Therefore, the elements described in this chapter are part of the design of a sustainable nonprofit to relieve the burden of government. How does the design provide for financial sustainability? The bottom line: It is the fiduciary responsibility of the management of the nonprofit even though created by government, and any created by government or citizens, to be self-sufficient and supporting long after the initial start.

The Trust

A trust may be created by a government as a tax-exempt nonprofit to receive, protect and invest and to make periodic payments over a period of time all in accordance with the terms of the deed of trust. This fund may and often is the result of some settlement; and, therefore, is called by the professionals a *structured settlement*. A trust may also be set up by a nonprofit or its donor to pay off its debt and to assure its creditors and therefore they lend to the organization at a lower rate of interest (called a *sinking fund*). A trust may also be set up to in-sure a flow of funds to protect a public treasure such as a park or a monument which may have limited capacity to earn its keep. A trust is versatile and it is an independent legal and tax entity with its own designated management exer-cised by a trustee or a board of trustees.

A trust may also be set up by a nonprofit created by citizens for some similar specialized purposes. Whether created or engaged by citizens or by government, a trust is similar to a corporation except: (a) it does not have a mission to do something concrete other than to collect, manage, and distribute funds; and (b) it is not presumed to have a perpetual life, but a set term in years or contingent upon the occurrence of an event. Sustainability is about meeting the set life span of the trust.

Every trust is set up according to the laws in the state in which it is estab-lished, very much like a corporation except that it uses a deed of trust rather than a charter. The deed must contain among other things: (1) the number of trustees and their powers including the powers and duties to hire a custodian to hold the trust assets, managers, auditors, consultants, and lawyers, and to de-termine their compensation; (2) the duty of the trustees to write and enforce an investment policy if that is not already set by the government; (3) to make and to determine the timing, amount, distribution, and destinations of funds; and (4) the duty to an orderly dissolution of the trust.

Endowments: Perpetuating a Gift

Unlike a trust, an *endowment*, also a tax-exempt nonprofit, is normally, alt-hough not absolutely necessarily so, set up with some purpose of perpetuity. The term "quasi-endowment" (or *exhaustible endowments*) designates those that are not planned as perpetuities. These include building and construction funds. Furthermore, while trusts usually are created by a one-time payment, endowments offer considerably greater flexibility because of the number and types of accounts and trusts it may contain, the types of assets it is capable of handling, and because the endowment is not set in a tight deed as is a trust. An endowment can be created as a corporation or subsidiary such as a 509(a)(3). In terms of this book, an endowment is most frequently an internal financial facili-tator.

Use of Endowments

An endowment serves several important purposes. One purpose is to provide a pool of funds to which the organization can turn in an emergency. As such, it gives some financial stability and quick-response capability to the organization.

A closely related use occurs when the endowment is used to cover shortfalls between the expenditures and revenues of the organization. Continuous invasion of an endowment for this purpose, however, is not encouraged, this problem should be solved by better financial management. These types of "endowments" are usually set up as board-designated restricted funds. Sometimes the trustees will approve an interfund transfer from an endowment to operating funds or set up an income stabilization fund to offset operating deficits, the fund is financed by transfers from general operations.

Endowments provide a source of funds that the organization may use to finance activities that are important to it but for which it cannot readily obtain support from outside sources. Many organizations use endowments to finance activities that are innovative, experimental, and developmental. When used this way, the endowment serves to push the organization forward. It helps the organization carry out its mission without having to meet the constraints and demands of an outside funding agency.

- An endowment might be used to separate out and finance specific charitable missions.
- Endowments are sometimes required by funding sources to ensure the organization's financial stability and to reduce its decline.
- Endowments provide for accumulating funds to finance long-term and major activities or acquisitions by the organization. In this vein are building funds, scholarships, and so on.

All these ideal uses of endowments can be defeated, however, if (1) the endowment is unintentionally exhausted, and (2) restrictions are violated. Let's deal with these in turn. In practice, there is something called an exhaustible or expendable endowment. These are really restricted funds that may be treated as though they were endowments. So sometimes the term *quasi-endowment* is used. A true endowment is a perpetuity even though for some purposes, such as life annuities, it may be defined in terms of life expectancy.

A quasi-endowment connotes that the principal—not just the earnings—of the fund may be spent. This implies that the fund could be exhausted or totally expended. Even in these cases, however, unless the conditions specified in the gifts call for total exhaustion, management is wise to treat these funds as true endowments—perpetuities.

Structure of Endowment

An endowment should be organized around four functions or responsibility centers: (1) revenue-raising, (2) investment management, (3) disbursement, and (4) guardian or stewardship. Note that the investment advisor and custodian report to the committee of the trustees of the organization, even though they may do this through the CEO. They, like auditors, are accountable directly to the trustees.

The investment advisors make investment recommendations and invest the funds. In large endowments, there may be several advisors competing with the funds assigned them. Advisors may specialize—oil, stock, bonds, real estate, and so on. The custodian's job is to hold the funds or securities. Custodians are often banks.

The revenue function is what fundraising does. It feeds the endowment portfolio with seed money and a continuous flow of fresh funds. Natural lapse of time means that these funds rarely go directly to the investment advisor. In the interim, they should be managed as short-term cash. From there the funds pass to the discretion of the investment advisor who, given the limits placed on that discretion by the trustees, proceeds to invest.

The trustees review this performance and make decisions annually about whether to retain an advisor or change the amount under his or her guidance. They also decide how much to disburse from the endowment. Many endowments operate by simple, fixed rules set by the board of trustees. For example, it may disburse only a fixed percentage of the total endowment or a fixed percentage of its growth. Its growth may be calculated for the most recent year or for the most recent couple of years. For example, the board of trustees may decide that every year they will calculate the amount of earnings (dividends and appreciation) in the portfolio for the most recent five years and disburse only 5 percent of that amount.

One advantage of using a moving average (using the last five years) is that it smooths out variations. If the organization used only the most recent year, if it is a good year, the disbursement will be high; if it is a very poor year, the disbursement will be very low. The objective should always be to (1) develop a simple rule, and (2) enable the endowment principal or corpus to be preserved and grow so as to finance future needs.

Donor-Designated Funds as an Endowment

Though generally associated with commercial brokerages, donor-designated funds are sometimes included as part of the endowment strategy of large and sophisticated nonprofits; so it is discussed here. Moreover, there are citizen (brokerage) created nonprofits to supply, for a fee, an endowment and tax advantaged option to donors. These are not intended to reduce the burden of government, but they constitute part of the financial awareness of the managers of those organizations formed to reduce the burden of government.

Accordingly, whether through a brokerage-formed nonprofit or a nonprofit doing it with others, a supporting organization 509(a)(3), may exist solely to provide financial support to the 501(c)(3) formed by government or by citizens. These supporting organizations do not need to qualify for exemptions but get their exempt status from the organization(s) they support. Donor-advised funds fall into this category.

The donor-advised fund receives funds donated irrevocably by persons and entities and usually engages an investment advisor to guide and to carry out its investments; it distributes its assets to 501(c)(3)s generally in response to the requests of its sponsoring organization. Since the sponsoring organization is a charity (even though it may have been created by a financial institution such as a mutual fund family), distributions can be made to it or as it directs to other organizations qualifying as 501(c)(3)s. A sponsoring organization, a 501(c)(3), can create one of these funds for its own benefit or can create one jointly with others for their group benefit.

The donor's contact is with the sponsoring organization, both in terms of making the donation and in directing where it should go. Neither the sponsoring organizations nor the donor-advised-fund is obligated to follow these instructions, which are treated as recommendations although they are usually followed after due diligence to cover the qualification and eligibility of the beneficiary organization and the guidelines set by the sponsoring organization or the donor-advised fund. Treating them as recommendations implies that the donor has not retained control--which would disallow the deduction. The donor gets an immediate income tax deduction for the gift to the directed fund and also gets the associated gift and estate tax benefits.

The contribution can be in cash, securities, or any other asset. This is an alternative to the creation of a private foundation, with lower administrative costs, but also with the possibility that the initial gift and any amount given thereafter may grow. It may also be seen as an alternative to a community foundation, which, in turn, is an alternative to private foundations. One advantage of a donor-designated fund to the community foundation is that the charitable beneficiary can be in any part of the country. Community foundations have the local area as their first priority, although some may fund projects outside that area to the extent that they have an impact on the area; for example, the funding of an evaluation project or demonstration project elsewhere as long as the results are relevant to similar situations in the local community. A 501(c)(3) may access a donation made to a donor-designated mutual fund no matter where the nonprofit is or where the donor resides.

Funding an Endowment

Funding an endowment is merely putting money or other property in it. An endowment can therefore be funded singularly or in combination with outright gifts and contributions, annuities, life insurance, and lifetime or testamentary gifts. This section explains all but the outright gifts of cash and property, as they were the subjects of the last chapter. These gifts can be made during the lifetime of an individual or as a bequest through a properly drawn will. A gift through a will does have certain risks and it is for this reason that the recipient nonprofit needs to be alert. These risks include whether or not the person making the gift is qualified to do so by age, mental status, or ownership of the asset—given that many assets are jointly owned or owned with a right of survivorship (meaning that upon death the ownership goes to another party as determined in state law), whether the gift is made as a residual (after every other gift and obligation is accounted for), or whether it is a specific gift and therefore a specific amount and so on.

Specific Long-Term Assets In an Endowment: Trusts

An endowment may be funded by any of the assets described in the last chapter or by those in this one. This chapter deals with assets that require patience because the nonprofit does not receive the full benefits until some passage of time, perhaps the lifetime of a specified person or persons, a passage of decades. But they are so very, very valuable.

The Charitable Remainder Trust

A charitable remainder trust permits the donor to make a contribution, get an immediate tax deduction on that contribution, and still get an annual income from the gift, or to provide for self, spouse, children, or some other beneficiary that is not a charity for a period up to twenty years or for the remainder of their lives. The beneficiary cannot be unborn and obviously not dead. Some or all of this income may be free from taxes. At the termination of the designated period, the remainder that is left in the trust will go to the 501(c)(3) whether created by citizens or the government that is the remainderman—a legal term meaning that organization that was designated to receive what is there at the termination of the trust's term.

Although these trusts are used throughout a spectrum of asset size classes, the very largest of these gets a disproportionate share. The reader may hypothesize why this is the case, but it may well be due to the simple fact of scale; the larger the size of the organization, the easier it is for it to attract large deferred gifts, to invest the effort into getting such gifts and to maintain a portfolio over time with a higher risk-reward ratio often meaning long-term equities and direct business investment. They may be able to afford greater patience waiting for the large payout at the end. This is purely hypothetical but too interesting to ignore.

Meeting Different Donor Objectives with the Remainder Trust

A donor can choose a fixed amount in dollars or percentage of the initial donation called the res or corpus to be received at least once a year and amounting to at least five percent of that initial amount. These payments can be received over a period of years or until some event occurs as specified by the donor. But no funds can be added after the initial donation. Because of this obligation to make fixed payments, annuity funds tend to be invested in stable securities.

Alternatively, the donor may choose to receive a variable amount that changes with the performance of the assets in the trust. These, called *unitrusts*, also allow the donor to add to the funds and stipulate what date the fund would be valued for payments. They also tend to be invested more in stocks and investments that vary, but with a growth trajectory. Hence, the donor participates both in the growth and decline of the value of the fund. To insure the life of the fund, unitrusts tend to restrict all payments to a percentage of capital gains—preserving the res or corpus plus some growth into prolonging the cash flow from the fund for the donor but also the amount the nonprofit will receive when that payment, according to the contract, ends.

Donors do not have to be super rich to be involved in these trusts. They can pool or have the organization pool their donations with others into a *pooled income trust*. In this case, the payments received by those non-charities entitled to a percentage of the earnings of the trust are based on their proportionate share of the pooled trust. So a donor whose contribution makes up 10 percent of the pooled income trust will get 10 percent of the earnings it distributes.

Charitable Lead Trusts

These trusts reverse the direction of cash flow. Now the donor and non-charity beneficiaries wait for the termination of the trust based on the terms set by the donor, while the 501(c)(3) created by the citizens or government receives annual payouts. The payments can be variable or fixed as described earlier.

Why would the donor make this deal? Because the donor does not need the cash flow, but is interested in accumulating the deductions that these trusts earn into increasing the charitable deduction in his or her estate and thereby reducing the estate tax liability. The donor accumulates deductions by not taking the tax deduction up front or periodically as the payments are made. But accumulates them until the termination.

Table 11.1 compares and summarizes some of the basic features of the trusts we have discussed. All can be *inter vivos* (created during life) or *testamentary* (at death). There are other features they have in common. Each provides for a gift to the nonprofit that is deductible by the donor. Some provide for an annuity to the donor or beneficiaries while the remainder goes to the nonprofit. This remainder, depending on the financial and investment management of the gift, can be substantially larger than the initial gift. This is because only a portion of the income in many cases will go to the donor. The remainder accumulates and grows with the investment experience of the fund, and the gift itself may appreciate several times in value by the time it is turned over to the nonprofit.

Table 11.1. Comparison of Advantages and Disadvantages of Trusts by Type

	Type of Trust	Advantages	Disadvantages
Income Flow to donor, Remainder to Charity	Pooled Income	Small gifts can be placed in a pool for more efficient investment management	Income must flow for life of one or more individuals; not for term; Income is usually fully taxed
	Remainder unitrust	Income flows for life of one or more non-charity recipients or for a specified term; some or all of the income may be untaxed; income keeps pace with growth of value	Because income is percentage of value, year to year income declines if value declines
	Remainder annuity	Same as above except income is a fixed percentage of initial value; income is protected against decline in value	Income does not keep pace with growth

	Type of Trust	Advantages	Disadvantages
Income Flow to charity, Remainder to Donor	Guaranteed (Gift or Charitable annuity)	Income is assured	Assets of nonprofit exposed to need to pay donors guaranteed income
	Charitable lead unitrust	Flow of income to nonprofit keeps pace with growth of trust	Exposes recipient to tax liability if annual deduction chosen
	Charitable lead annuity	Flow of income to charity not jeopardized by slow growth	Same as above

Specific Long-Term Assets for Endowments: Life Insurance Policies

Through life insurance policies, it is possible for persons of modest means to make gifts of hundreds of thousands of dollars. Anyone can give well above his or her means. When the person departs, the policy matures and death benefits received by the nonprofit are many times larger than premiums paid by the donor.

Insurance allows the donor to stretch out a gift. This is the case when the donor makes a gift of a policy that requires periodic premium payments. In this way, the organization gets a regular and long-lasting commitment for an annual donation—the premiums—and it maintains contact to facilitate additional giving.

If the policy is one that accumulates savings, called cash value, the organization also gets a valuable pool of funds that it can use within years, even though the donor is very much alive. Moreover, regular premium payments shift the burden of fundraising to the insurance company, which sends the donor notices when the premium is due. It replaces the telephone call and letter from the nonprofit asking for annual donations.

Death and the Collection of the Gift

An insurance policy may be used to make a joint gift. Frequently, a husband and wife may want to make a joint gift to a nonprofit. If each bought an insurance policy separately, it would be more expensive than if they bought it jointly.

In a joint policy, sometimes called last to die, both persons should agree to take it out and to give the policy to the nonprofit. This strategy has some peculiarities that call for caution. One is that joint policies often pay only after the last of the two persons has died, hence its nicknames "last-to-die" and "survivor" policy. Some policies pay only a portion of the face value after the first has died; the balance is paid at the death of the second person.

Even though the death of the first spouse could yield no immediate benefit to the nonprofit, this does not make such a strategy useless. The nonprofit will get some or all of the proceeds eventually; both parties will die. In the meantime, the cash value (if it is provided in the contract) and collateral value of the policy are always available as long as the organization owns the policy.

Alternatively, a policy could be bought on the life of each person separately and the proceeds will be obtained by the nonprofit on each person's death, rather than upon the eventual death of both. These policies are more expensive than joint policies.

Ownership

An insurance policy that is owned by the donor, even if it is being held by the nonprofit, is subject to the control of the donor. The owner can cancel the policy or permit it to lapse so that it no longer exists. Nothing bars an owner from dropping the name of the nonprofit as beneficiary. If any of these happens, the nonprofit will not collect, even though it may have the policy in its possession. Furthermore, if the policy is owned by the donor, he or she may borrow on it. Should that be done and the loan not be repaid prior to the death of the donor, the proceeds that will go to the nonprofit will be the face value minus the amount of indebtedness. In short, the nonprofit could end up with less than the face value if there is outstanding indebtedness.

The outcome could be worse if the owner used the policy as collateral for a loan. In that case, depending on state law, the creditor of the donor may have first claim. Not only will the amount obtained by the nonprofit be less than the face value, but the nonprofit could get nothing at all if the owner, in the process of getting the loan, made a permanent assignment of the policy to the creditor. A permanent assignment cannot be reversed; the creditor owns the policy as long as the credit is outstanding and even then, until it is formally released.

An insurance policy that is owned by the donor may be included in his or her estate even though it is in the physical possession of the nonprofit. This could mean that some or all the proceeds may be subject to estate (not income) tax, and some or all the proceeds could be subject to the claims of the creditors of the donor and to claims of the donor's spouse should the latter choose to take action against the will. Insurance proceeds, while exempt from income tax, are not automatically exempt from estate tax. The donor must have either (1) named the nonprofit or any other qualified charity as a beneficiary of the policy, or (2) designated them as donees of the proceeds as it goes through the estate.

These difficulties as the proceeds go through the estate may not be resolved in favor of the nonprofit, even if it could prove that it paid the premiums. Ironically, one possible interpretation of paying the premiums is that the nonprofit in its charitable benevolence made a nondeductible gift to the insured. The point simply is that the nonprofit should own, not merely hold, the policy. It does this by being sure that its name appears on the policy not only as beneficiary but also as owner.

Ownership and possession of the policy give the nonprofit another benefit. The nonprofit does not have to wait for the donor to die; for, as owner, the nonprofit may assign the policy, use it as collateral for loans, or borrow the cash value of the policy. The nonprofit will also be able to avoid the creditors of the donor and legal fights over the instructions in the will. The policy will be nonprobate property, meaning that it will escape the legal hassle, delays, costs, and claims that are likely in the settlement of an estate. Ownership options and outcomes are reviewed in this chapter.

Form of Gift

The donor does not have to purchase insurance or use a paid-up policy in order to make a gift. It is possible to make a gift of insurance in the form of the face value in excess of $50,000 in a qualified employee insurance contract, as discussed in Chapter 13. Such a gift is not likely to bring any deduction to the donor, but the excess premium is not taxable as income. The employer who pays the excess may deduct it if it is customary for the firm to give in this fashion. Many corporations are offering a similar option to their officers and directors, who choose which charity they wish to be beneficiaries.

Life Insurance Risks by Ownership Option
Risks to which the nonprofit is exposed under various ownership options:
- **Option 1.** The donor owns the policy and names the nonprofit as a beneficiary on the policy. The donor may change beneficiary unless the nonprofit is named an irrevocable beneficiary. In either case, the risks are the use of the cash value by the donor, and cessation of payments by donor without

knowledge of nonprofit but with non-ownership precluding the nonprofit from picking up payments. This strategy avoids probate and lump-sum proceeds go directly to the nonprofit tax-free.

- **Option 2.** The donor owns the policy and makes his or her estate the beneficiary. The nonprofit can collect only if donors will so specify. As part of the estate, an additional risk is that the proceeds become exposed to creditors of both the decedent and the estate itself and may be used not only to satisfy such debt but also to pay taxes of the estate and to satisfy other beneficiaries, such as spouse and dependent children. Probate and settlement of estate may prolong receiving gift.
- **Option 3.** The nonprofit owns the policy. Upon death of the donor, the proceeds go directly to the nonprofit without probate and without exposure to creditors of the decedent or the estate. IRS Private Ruling 9110016 reminds us to check state law to be sure that insurable interest, defined as at risk of economic loss if person dies, is satisfied. If not, a Federal donation may be denied.

Key to all options: To reduce default of nonpayment of premiums, have the donor make an annual gift of at least the premium amount directly to the nonprofit, which uses it to pay the premium.

A gift of insurance can be made in the form of an outright gift of the contract itself; or the policy could be placed in a trust. The trust should be irrevocable, permitting an immediate tax deduction for the gift and immediate ownership by the nonprofit. The deduction of premiums can be lost, however, if the trust is not properly set up, because an insurance policy in a trust is a future interest, since the gift cannot be obtained until the person dies. To qualify the premium payments for immediate tax deduction, the trust agreement should contain a promise to make the premium available to the nonprofit at the time premiums are paid. The nonprofit need not take the money; it must simply have the option to do so.

If the insurance policy is in a trust, there is a second concern; the policy could be considered to have been acquired by debt and, as discussed earlier, lead to unrelated business income tax. To avoid this, the trust agreement should not permit a person who is a noncharitable beneficiary to have an interest in the income of the trust that exceeds the person's lifetime. That is, all such interests should cease upon the person's death so that the remainder goes to the charitable beneficiary rather than being bequeathed by the person to some other beneficiary.

A gift of insurance may also be made through a will at the time of death. The will might provide for the formation of a trust or for outright gift of the insurance proceeds to the nonprofit. One disadvantage of giving at the time of death is that the proceeds must be included in the donor's estate, albeit that a 100 percent tax deduction is available for charitable donation. It precludes, however, any annual deduction for premiums paid.

As part of the estate, the insurance proceeds are also exposed to the claims of the creditors of the deceased, and if the gift is made by a trust that becomes irrevocable at the time of death, the charity is less protected, since there is some passage of time, generally after the Federal taxes are paid, before the trust becomes a charitable trust and subject to the rules covering private foundations. These rules protect the corpus of a trust for charitable purposes.

Comparison of Contract of Use

Life insurance, through its death benefits, magnifies a gift many times. This is leverage. All policies except term provide for a cash value, which is the money that accumulates with interest. This money can be borrowed, used as collateral, used to pay premiums, or even used to purchase additional insurance on the donor with the same company. If a loan is taken to purchase an income producing asset, then that income would be taxed as unrelated since the property was acquired through debt (Mose and Garrison Siskin Memorial Foundation v. U.S., 55 AFTR 2d 95-1024).

The dollars that accumulate grow according to the interest being paid and the length of time it is permitted to remain undistributed. The amount borrowed never has to be repaid and neither does the interest on the loan, which is generally well below market rate and fixed in the contract at the time the insurance is bought. Any principal and interest owed at the time of death are subtracted from the face value.

Table 11.2 summarizes four types of policies based on their generic nature. Term policies are the cheapest and single-premium policies are the most expensive; but the amount of leverage is just the reverse. That is, if the donor should die immediately or within a few years after the creation of the gift, the death benefit per dollar of premium paid is highest with a term policy and lowest with a single-premium; hence, the term gets you a lot more insurance dollars per dollar invested. However, term policies have no loan value and require the longest period of donor commitment, since the premiums must be paid every year until either the policy ends or the donor dies.

Universal life is the most flexible. Flexibility is not an issue with single premiums because the policy is fully paid up at the inception. Generally, there is no flexibility with whole-life or term policies, although some companies will sell term policies in which you may, in the future, elect a different premium or a face value. On the other extreme is the single premium. It is the most expensive, but it requires the least amount of donor commitment—only long enough to write the check. It also creates the biggest nest egg that can be used by the nonprofit.

Because insurance companies are imaginative in how they configure a policy, Table 11.2 should be considered a guide to the fundamentals. When working with a potential donor, illustrations of specific and actual policies should be used. The companies will gladly supply them.

A whole-life policy called a split-dollar policy has become a popular policy for the wealthy to use in making a contribution. Such a policy splits the interest into a cash value amount and the proceeds available at death. One of these goes to the charity and the other to the nonprofit beneficiary.

Table 11.2. Insurance Policies by Characteristics

Type	Cost	Leverage[a]	Loan[b]	Flexibility	Length of Commitment Required
Term	1	4	1	2	4
Universal	2	3	2	4	2
Whole Life	3	2	3	3	3
Single Premium	4	1	4	1	1

Key: 1 lowest, 4 highest
[a] Death benefits relative to premium costs
[b] Cash value

Safety

Insurance policies are reasonably safe even when the company is shaky. Insurance companies are required to carry reserves to cover their potential claims, and most insurance companies also engage in reinsurance. This is a process through which companies try not to keep too many high-risk policies on their books. By prior agreement, through reinsurance they sell some of these high-risk policies to other companies. Moreover, in most states, the insurance companies guarantee payments through an insurance pool, thus protecting the citizens of that state against the bankruptcy of any company selling in that state. Insurance companies are rated in several ways, including their ability to settle claims, and they must make their ratings known.

Gifts of Iras, Gift Annuities, and Other Such Contracts

Congress provided for retirees to make a direct contribution of required minimum distributions to a 501(c)(3). This is attractive, presuming that they do not need the money, because that amount is not taxable. It is an *exclusion*. There is also, of course, that any commercial annuity can be given and the organization can elect the time period over which it can receive the cash once the contract matures—usually by the occasion of death or the period of time stipulated in the contract.

In the giving or receiving of annuities, care must be taken that the potential donor actually owns the annuity. Most pension annuities have a period that must lapse before the accounts are vested and fully owned by the future annuitant. Until that time has elapsed, the person does not own the balance in the account and is not legally able to donate it, even though the account may be in his or her name. The surviving spouse may also have a legal claim on the annuity.

In the case of gift annuities, the donor gives the nonprofit a large amount of money or property with the understanding that the nonprofit will guarantee a specific annual payment to the donor or to some other person for life or for the joint lives of two or more persons. Gift annuities are not issued for a term less than life. The nonprofit takes the property and then turns to an insurance company and buys an annuity that will generate the income required to meet the guaranteed payments to the donor. The risk of payment is shifted from the nonprofit to an insurance company. In some states, gift annuities are regulated and therefore state law should be consulted. For federal tax purposes a gift annuity must either be in the form of a trust or an insurance contract and to avoid unrelated business income tax. The General Counsel Memorandum 39826 suggests:

1. The annuity should be the only thing—called consideration—the donor receives in exchange for the gift.
2. It must be less than 90 percent of the value of the donation.
3. Payment must be scheduled over the life of one or two individuals alive (not unborn) at the time the gift was made.
4. The issuing of annuities must not be a substantial part of the activities of the recipient organization.
5. The contract must not guarantee a minimum payment or maximum payments that vary with changing values of the original gift.

The Power of a Will

All of the contributions in this and in the previous chapter can be made either *inter vivos* (during lifetime) or *testamentary* (at time of death). In the latter, state probate laws govern. There are certain risks, which is the reason why many nonprofits like to be involved with the donor in crafting a will statement. The risks start with whether or not the will is properly crafted, whether it is challenged, whether the property is the person's to give, whether the will sets conditions and these are not met, whether or not there are other creditors with superior standing, including the undertaker, hospital, and state, and so on. Yet a will is essential for making a charitable contribution because this cannot be a choice of the executor or executrix of the estate.

Table 11.3 summarizes the risks of not getting anything when a nonprofit depends upon transfer of properties at the time of death even though there may be a will. These risks vary by the way the nonprofit is named by the donor. The weakest position is to be included among the residue, because the residue is what's left over after all other gifts and liabilities are paid. This may be zero or a very large number. At the other extreme, if one is the owner through survivorship, the property gets passed automatically and is not determined by the will at all.

Table 11.3. Relative Risk of Bequests Through a Will

Rank	Status of Nonprofit in Estate Settlement
1	Ownership, lifetime or by survivorship: automatic ownership
2	Irrevocable beneficiary: cannot be removed
3	Beneficiary: can be removed without warning
4	Specific bequest: gets only a specific amount or property if available
5	Residue: gets what's left over

Note: Number 1 is the strongest position, and 5 is the weakest.

Gifts occurring at death are more favorably treated than gifts made during one's lifetime. The latter are subject to deductible limits as described in Chapter Seven, but there are no limits to how much one may give to a charity at time of death—once all legal claims are satisfied. No wonder that bequests are usually the largest single gifts and this chapter is so important to nonprofit managers—knowing the terms of the deal.

Summary and Preview

This chapter has been about the financial instruments that can be used to set the ground for sustainability of an organization. All of these instruments can be a source of future cash flow to support the earnings power of the project and the organization and can allow an organization that is expressly set up to relieve the burden of government to be charitable in doing so by collecting and using these funds for the charitable aspects of exigencies of their operations.

Bibliography

Fontenrose, Robert and Susan Kassell. Department of the Treasury (2011) Report to Congress on Supporting Organizations and Donor Advised Funds.

Chapter 12 – Corruption and Control: Protecting the Assets for Lessening the Burden of Government

Corruption and the inefficient management of costs, including cost overruns, are organization killers. They reduce the ability of the organization to successfully transfer a burden of government, destroy the confidence that collaborators and others have in the organization, and left unattended will render the organization either a corrupt entity as in Chapter 1 or a financially challenged one. In either case, this spells failure in the mission of relieving of the burden of government. It would be much too easy to recommend that nonprofits lessening the burden of government adopt a control system used by government such as delineated in the OMB Circular A – 123. This chapter takes the reader beyond even abroad for insights.

Part of the challenge in the design and in the engagement of any nonprofit intended to assume an important burden of the government is to embed in it effective protections and defenses against corruption, of cost and expenditure manipulation, and of managerial alertness to both. It has been argued that a major inducement to corruption is managerial action, inaction, or lack of response. As a result, the government or other collaborators will require evidence that such protections are built into the structure and operation of the organization. They go beyond monitoring and reporting diversions in the Form 990 and the audit function of the trustees, and focus on the protective and preventative design of the organization and how it is required to operate so as to reduce the risk of corruption and of cost manipulation. Without these, the transfer of a burden of the government places the government, its decision-makers, the organization, and the public at risk of being victims and the organization is, in these terms, a bad candidate to which to transfer a burden of the government.

Corruption

What is corruption, how does it occur, and what are the opportunities for its occurrence? How does the nonprofit defend itself by taking preventive actions and what may these be? What are the concerns and questions that should guide the manager in creating an internal control system that mitigates the risk of corruption? What should that system look like?

DOI 10.1515/9781501505799-013

This chapter approaches the above question in parts. It begins with a discussion of corruption, its sources, and what gives opportunities for it. Then it transitions to different types of strategies for mitigating financial corruption, leaving the human corruption problem of abuse and discrimination for a separate discussion. Then it focuses on management and its duties. To avoid repetition, the reader is referred to the enumeration of various forms of financial and transactional forms of corruption in Chapter 1—this chapter has to do with control and management to minimize and to protect against those types of corruption.

Types and Effects of Corruption in Nonprofit Organizations

Nonprofits are exposed to countless risks of corruption that are itemized in the very first chapter of this book. In most of those cases, the nonprofit is the victim of corruption from within. These include: The falsification and destruction of records (destruction of evidence), the abuse of clients—by age and infirmity, embezzlement, stealing, the abuse of mission for the benefit of management and others, and the manipulation of accounting and financial data. The motive for the corruption could be to benefit an individual, to cover for them or for management, or to cover or "benefit" the organization such as the payment of bribes (whether domestic or foreign), and the falsification of data such as the deliberate overvaluing of an art donation.

The organization can also be the tool or intermediary or the "actor" of corruptive acts so that it becomes a corruptive enterprise. This corruption also destroys trust, the organization, and lives of individuals who may be the direct or indirect victims. This type of corruption also exposes the organization, its board, and its management to criminal and civil charges under various state laws, and federal charges under the Racketeer Influenced and Corrupt Organizations Act (RICO). Under this law, individuals, corporations, associations, and enterprises are deemed to act illegally if in two or more circumstances over ten years that person is found to have acted consciously contrary to law with respect to crimes associated with interstate commerce. Nonprofits are not exempt under this law because the "enterprise" does not have to be profit-making and because the law relates to corporations and associations. The penalties include personal and organizational fines, jail time, and/or the loss of any asset or benefit derived from the transaction, even if they were derived at a loss.

Under RICO, the government has to prove: (a) that an enterprise existed, (b) that the transaction is effected through interstate commerce, (c) a conduct, and (d) a pattern of *racketeering*. Racketeering is not a single or isolated action. It is a composite of related actions that can bring about an unlawful result, not necessarily immediately but over a continued long-term period, and that the act is related to the normal course or way of doing business by the entity; for example, a nonprofit rigging its solicitation for donations across state lines and paying a corporation owned by the spouse of the CEO a percentage of the collection that is significantly higher than the norm for equivalent cases (http://www.justice.gov/usao/eousa/foia_reading_room/usam/title9/crm00109.htm).

The above example not only smells of a RICO violation, but of a second and separate corrupt act—self-dealing—to which managers are vulnerable by their own action or inaction. Self-dealing is any act that is between the organization and a disqualified person—generally described as a member of the management including trustees—or major donors, and the immediate relatives and business associates of these people. Self-dealing is subject to fines by all involved and that, unlike RICO administered by the U.S. Justice Department, is actionable by the IRS and any state or local government with such statutes.

Money laundering is another type of corrupt act that brings forth the investigative and prosecutorial powers of the Federal government. Money laundering is the process of channeling money or securities that are gained illegally through a process called layering so that it comes out as legal funds in fact or in use. The nonprofit—especially those that do business abroad—might be especially vulnerable.

Money laundering can subject the nonprofit to the penalties and electronic scrutiny authorized under the Patriot Act (Uniting and Strengthening America by Providing Appropriate Tools Required to Intercept and Obstruct Terrorism Act of 2001 or USA PATRIOT) due to any of the following circumstances: (a) the nonprofit itself is a tool through which money is transported to or from the U.S. as an act or in support of terrorism; (b) one or more employees or officers of the nonprofit use it for this purpose, or transports bulk money in violation of reporting and disclosure requirements or concealed; (c) there is a reasonable assumption that the nonprofit knows or should have known—there are obvious clues—that it might be facilitating or engaging in such bulk money transfers (defined as in excess of $10,000) and failed to report it; (d) after reporting or with strong supposition of this violation, the nonprofit informs the person that they have been reported—presumably allowing the person to evade the scrutiny of the Act or to defeat it; (e) the nonprofit deals with a foreign bank or with foreign persons or in a foreign country on the list of suspicious transactions—a list that is available; (f) the nonprofit deals with a U.S. financial institution that is a corresponding institution to such foreign entities as in (e); and (g) the use of the facilities or equipment of the organization abroad for purposes of terrorism, to support terrorism or money laundering or the production and use of counterfeit, (see http://www.gpo.gov/fdsys/pkg/PLAW-107publ56/pdf/PLAW-107publ56.pdf).

To the extent that the nonprofit is in violation of or is a participant in violations of the Patriot Act two or more times in ten years, it is also chargeable as committing a RICO infraction. The general rule for avoiding being used as a tool for money laundering is knowing and identifying your donors and reporting to the Financial Crimes Enforcement Network (FinCEN) of the U.S. Treasury Department any suspicions without, as the law stipulates, notifying the person or donor, or calling this to the attention of the bank or broker with whom the funds are deposited. One way to approach this is to make a public announcement of extremely large gifts and, if the gift comes from abroad, complying with the Form 990 requirement to disclose if the organization has a foreign bank account or signatory authority over it, and to specify the country, and to file IRS Form FinCEN Form 114 if required to do so; and to develop and implement a system of internal controls (as described later in this chapter) and the monitoring of these transactions.

The section above and Chapter 1 itemizes specific corrupt behaviors and the ways in which they are interpreted and acted upon. The issue for each organization is to discern how these may translate to specific transactions and situations in the organization for which they have responsibility. Fraud is fraud, but it manifests itself and finds opportunities in sector- and organization-specific ways. In each major sector and in each organization, the exposure might be materially idiosyncratic but nevertheless there. For example, in health care, corruption can occur through referrals to specific sources of services in which the person making the referral or a relation has some financial connection, so there is a law called the Stark Law. Corruption can also occur from systematically misrepresenting or falsifying claims or eligibility or costs. Kickbacks can occur with any one of the providers of medication, services, or referrals. With nonprofits that deal with elected officials abroad, bribes are a corrupt act, but may be different from bribing the local ambulance driver. So the next section essentially identifies the opportunities for particular classes of corruption in each organization and ascertaining how it might be conducted and plugging that hole in an organization.

Sources and Opportunities for Corruption

Internal corruption is caused by many factors including trust and employee disposition, corporate culture, and cognitive psychological factors (Burke 2009). Indeed, there are numerous perspectives requiring "an interactive, interactions and processual approach" (Ashforth, Gioia, Robinson and Trevino

(2008)). Institutional corruption may occur because of the lack of, adequacy of, turning off of, or subversion of such controls—the choice being in part distinguishable by the power position in the organizational structure of the particular actor over resources, rules, and employees. Furthermore, corrupt activity often does not involve money, or only money, directly. It may involve sharing sensitive information, hiring and compensation, taking and receiving bribes, falsification of documents and in the reporting of activities and expenses, and manipulating the administrative or contracting processes (Javor and Jancsics, 2013). Which form corruption takes positively correlates with the actor's place in the power structure of the organization, which is what determines the person's access to the resource or activity that is being wrongfully used in the corruption.

Organizational corruption might come from a single individual or a network of individuals in or connected to the outside, or from an environment or cluster in the organization that is corrupt (Kish-Gephart, Harrison, and Trevino (2010)). One view is that an individual corrupt person or persons, given the right circumstances, can eventually turn an organization into a corrupt organization. Another view is that some top managers may be corrupt or lack set standards that invite or induce lower ranking persons to be corrupt, or promote corrupt activities, or look the other way as they, in the end, benefit from it either financially or otherwise (Javo and Jancsics, 2013). This can be done by setting performance processes, standards, and rewards that invite corruption. Yet another view (drawn from the experience of countries) is that corruption is not primarily the product of bad people but of bad systems that can be fixed (Klitgaard and Baser, 1998).

A considerable motive for corruption or near-corrupt behavior is to promote (or to avoid defaming) the organization. Such is the case when accounting data are manipulated to show acceptable fund-raising ratios and organizational expenses (Keating, Parsons and Roberts, 2008; Greenlee, Fishcer, Gordon and Keating 2007) and, therefore, efficiency, ethics, and yield in fundraising or misreporting taxable income to avoid taxes (Omer and Yetman, 2007). A managerial incentive to misreport seems to be at play in nonprofit misreporting (Krishnan, Yetman and Yetman, 2006; Schmidt, 2007).

How can the system be fixed so it does not provide opportunities and incentives for corruption? Luo (2005) states that it is important in understanding organizational corruption to differentiate between what happens at different levels of the power and management structure of the organization, the organizational complexity—opaqueness, complexity, and unevenness—that encourages illicit acts, and the role of a corruption-resisting corporate, structural, and compliance system. In a study of the commitment of fraud in the nonprofit sector, Greenlee, Fischer, Gordon and Keating (2007) after studying various fraudulent events in nonprofits using data from the Certified Fraud Examiner, concluded that governing bodies needed to consider various forms of controls rather than relying on the audit of financial statements (Piaszczyk, Arthur http://www.opf.slu.cz/aak/2011/04/piaszczyk.pdf).

In the following section, we help the manager to think about internal controls with the caution that no set of rules or guidelines is effective without a strong enforcement mechanism, a finding by Gugerty (2009) in her study of nonprofits.

Managing the Risks of Corruption and Fraud

All the approaches below have the following in common: They recognize the exposure of organizations to the risk of corruption and fraud that can bring significant losses to the organization and its stakeholders, they all point to the need for internal controls to diminish that risk and assign the ultimate responsibilities for creating, monitoring, enforcing, and publicly reporting those controls, their impairment, and what management plans to do or has done about them. They recognize internal controls as procedures, processes, policies, and assignment of responsibility to diminish the chances that the organization and its stakeholders will be victimized by fraud and corruption. They emphasize different approaches toward this common objective.

These approaches require management to first identify the risk and its materiality or importance; for example, receiving or drawing checks, or receiving payments. The second step is to assemble a set of controls (a good auditor can advise) to follow a payment from the time it is received to the time and place it is deposited. These controls may be different for each transaction and each organization. The manager uses expert judgment about the risk and the appropriate control. The third step is instituting, monitoring, and updating these controls for effectiveness that does not seriously impede performance.

Controls: An Accounting Approach

The accounting approach to internal control refers to procedures and processes—the chain of action that allow a transaction to occur, to act upon it, and to report it in a timely and accurate basis according to generally accepted accounting principles (GAAP) while minimizing the risk of misuse, mistakes, or misrepresentation (intentional or not) in the information provided in the financial statements as recorded by the accountants. It recognizes that the accountant can be misled and, as a consequence, mislead those who use the accounting data. This exercise goes beyond an analysis of a financial statement. Looking at all the ratios will not necessarily reveal if there is fraud or misrepresentation or bribes; but tracing a transaction (the role of the auditor) might. Therefore, for nonprofit managers, a leading source on internal control is the Fraud Resource Center of the American Institute of Certified Public Accountants.

According to their logic, the organization needs to develop controls for the flow of revenues by type, recognizing that each type presents a different risk and opportunity set for error and corruption; for example, the flow of revenues from bingo is different from the acquisition, storage, sale, and collection process for inventory. Controls should also be developed for different types of expenses reflecting the process and steps through which (1) a liability occurs and is discharged with (2) who is making decisions, approvals, recording, and making payment and (3) from what account to whom and what supporting documents throughout the process. A different set of controls would also have to be made for gifts and contributions—from whom, with what restrictions, with what acknowledgement and how timely, and with what disposition. In addition, a set of controls are needed for loans and debt incurred and discharged—for what purpose, with what vote of the trustees, by which officer, the terms, to whom and from whom, and the relationships of the parties to each other and to the organization, whether the type of loan or debt is consistent with the powers in the charter of the organization, and the state of domestication or location. Internal controls should also be developed for the acquisition, use, and disposition of property and equipment, and for the management and investment into other long-term assets such as securities.

Controls: A Transaction Approach

We have taken the Public Company Accounting Oversight Board (PCAOB) (2013) suggestions about assessing a control system for public corporations and their accounting systems and have come up with these questions and considerations that a nonprofit manager may ask about any system of control against corruption by looking at the act or the transaction.

1. What is the nature, importance, and relevance of the transaction that the control is intended to protect? Is it enough to set up an elaborate system of control? How much control does it merit—granting that controls are not necessarily at zero cost and may cause a delay?

2. What are the chances that something wrong (a corrupt act) will occur and in what ways? How and by whom? How can controls be instituted against the most consequential acts given its frequency of exposure?

3. How frequently does the event causing the risk exposure occur? Is the event irregular, of known regularity, so frequent that not only does the control have to be used regularly, but that it could be defeated? Does it have to be monitored regularly and probably upgraded regularly—as with a password?

4. Are these transactions or events with a history of something going wrong? Bbear in mind that frequency may signal a need to repair or replace the system as much as a signal for the need to control the existing system.

5. In a multi-unit or -person access or use system, does each require a unique control or access? If so, is it necessary to integrate them? Is it necessary that they be individualized?

6. The nature of the control and the frequency with which it operates—are there windows of opportunity for doing wrong? Are these windows covered? If the control is infrequent or intermittent, do they need to be occasionally tested or changed? Is there need for redundancy?

7. The degree to which the control relies on the effectiveness of other controls or multiple parties may require some simplification regardless of the need for safety and double check. It may also require controls at every stage or station. The path of the transaction matters and vulnerability may differ at each point.

8. Controls are as good as the people who perform them—their competence, alertness, and honesty. It matters who assigns whom to what, with or without oversight.

9. How much does the control rely upon discretion and how much is built into the flow and is automated—a camera in a store, stored records of telephone calls, a computer memory?

10. In test runs does the system work? Is it over-burdensome?

Controls: A Flow Approach

This is tantamount to the "chain of custody" of evidence in law and involves identifying the various stations or persons who would handle a transaction or event and asking what the risk exposures are at each point. A sale involves the purchase of inventory, the storage and display of the inventory, custody over the place or inventory during time of traffic and during times after the store is closed. It involves inventory-taking and verification, accounting for the disposition of the inventory, the cashier who collects for the inventory, the person who collects all cash at night, the person who picks it up and takes it the bank, and the bank recording of receipt for the dedicated account. At each point, an act of corruption could occur with or without collusion. Preventing collusion using this approach means identifying the points at which corruption could occur, how the network may be self-policing or whether it be partially or totally corrupt.

Controls: Organizational Lines of Defense

To the Institute of Internal Auditors, every organization has three lines of defense against corruption and fraud. The first line is those functions that own and manage risks—principally the operational manager who, along with mid-level managers, design and implement detailed procedures that serve as controls and who supervise execution of those procedures by the employees who report to them. Therefore, at this first level there should be controls designed into systems and processes under these managers, but also adequate managerial and supervisory controls in place to ensure compliance and to highlight problems such as inadequate processes, and unexpected events. The second line of defense oversees risks, ensures the writing and adoption of procedures communicated to the operation managers, and monitors performance to mitigate risks as they arise, and then certifies compliance with the risk-management strategy adopted by the organization. The third line of defense is the internal audit—looking over the entire organization including the interaction between and network of operational managers and management to make recommendations of risk minimization including procedures, policies, contacts, processes from their starting point to their finishing point to identify and assess risks, and to make recommendations.

The above may seem elaborate for most small- or medium-sized nonprofits. For this reason, we develop another perspective that may be more applicable. It says that there are three elements in every transaction that needs control:(1)the individual(s) who are involved, (2) the institutional arrangement, and (3) the transaction itself. Hence, the strategy should be geared to each of these:

- *Individual*: These refer to policies toward persons in the transaction chain. These include clarity of task, procedures, reporting content, form, frequency and channel; proper orientation toward mission and relationship to the team; a sense of pride and commitment to the mission and organization and a lack of incentive, inducement, or temptation—opportunity for corruption.
- *Institutional Arrangement*: Reducing complexity and obstacles that provide for cover and collusion; avoiding sloppy and inefficient procedures in accounting for delays, in requiring informative and shared records kept for at least a decade, in reducing nepotism and conflict of interests, in establishing a smooth transaction chain with known points of responsibility and custody and accountability throughout the chain of the transaction, in report-

ing and in obtaining acknowledgement and responses and complaints, in periodic audits and in penalizing infractions, and in rewarding suggestions.

– *Reliance on Board Resolutions*: Corruption can be abated by requiring a second look and an official response before certain actions are taken. The policies of the board regarding contracts, financial institution arrangements, about selecting external auditors, and receiving information directly or through an appointed committee are all ways of reducing the organization's exposure to corruption assuming that the board is not corrupt or involved in self-dealing. There is the case of a well-known organization having a board with members who, with the organization, were involved in questionable land deals that benefited the specific board members.

– *The Transaction*: The transaction itself can be the opportunity or condition for corruption. A system using no cash is less vulnerable to corruption than one that does. How the transaction is designed creates opportunities for corruption.

A Comprehensive Approach to Corruption

The American Institute of Certified Public Accounts (AICPA) in Internal Control–Integrated Framework (2013) emphasizes the importance of management judgment in designing, implementing, and conducting a system of internal controls, and in assessing its effectiveness. It covers internal controls in addressing operations and in reporting objectives; it states the requirements for determining what constitutes an effective internal control system, how to set one up and how to evaluate it; and it states the role of various management personnel in carrying out such a comprehensive system and to recognize its limitations. The work of The Independent Commission Against Corruption (ICAC) in New South Wales, Australia, is also recommended to the readers of this book because of its accessibility on the Internet and because of its extensive coverage, but principally because it draws on real public sector cases, gives clues on recognition of potential corruptive acts at various operating centers, and also supplies strategies for defending against them.

ICAC has studied corruption across that government and reports that most corruption can be traced to:

1. The absence of clear policies and procedures or their enforcement
2. Inadequate employee training
3. Monitoring and auditing being insufficient or lacking
4. Unclear reporting and communication lines
5. Inadequate supervision and evaluation of employees

6. High level of discretion in decisions and actions
7. Close relationship between employees and external stakeholders
8. Absence of ethical standards
9. Organizational culture that allows rule-breaking

Based on these and an extensive collection of evidence, it put forward several pieces of advice about managing the risk of corruption. In Table 12.1, we collect some key points. The reader may appreciate some of the complexities. It is generally assumed that good supervision and a clear delegation of authority over an act or transaction, clearly defined and monitored, would reduce the risk and temptation of corruption. However, the overseer or gatekeeper might be corrupt and use his or her authority to further the corruption and indeed to induce those supervised into corrupt actions, especially if they are ignorant, fearful, or unquestioning.

Table 12.1. ICAC Anti-corruption Advice

Activity Station	Act	Caution
Managing people	Delegation of authority:	Need, but it could be corrupt.
	Post-separation employment	Abuse of contact and information
	Recruitment and selection	Based not on merit but connection
	Secondary employment	Conflict of interest and devotion
	Supervision of staff	Failure to properly supervise
Managing external relationships	Commercial activities	Biased decisions, fraud, and access
	Conflicts of interest	Abuse, misplaced loyalty, disclosure
	Gifts and benefits	Improper receiving and extending
	Joint ventures	Conflict of interest, misuse of data
	Procurement	Improper procedures, pays, information
	Sponsorship	Influence, payments, favors
Managing services & products	Client relationships	Soliciting, accepting, favors, bribes
	Community affiliations	Favoritism, bribe, incorrect payments
	Regulatory functions	Soliciting favors, illegal disclosures
	Resource allocation	Allocating wrong entity, timing and amount
Managing money	Accounts management	Improper billing and posting payments
	Cash handling	Diversion and improper recording
	Credit cards	Improper charges

Activity Station	Act	Caution
	Grants and program funding	Improper management and allocation
	Payroll	Destruction of integrity and misuse of
	Ticket vending	Manipulation
Managing information	Confidential information	Leaking and using
	Electronic transactions	Use for illegal, improper transactions
	IT systems	Access to and use of data
Managing assets	Disposal of goods and property	improper valuing, recording, disposal
	Intellectual property	Personal or commercial use
	Management of resources	Diversion, misuse, destruction, theft
	Use of resources	Misused for self or other interests

Prepared by author from report of Independent Commission Against Corruption (New South Wales) https://www.icac.nsw.gov.au/preventing-corruption/knowing-your-risks/

The corruption of the gatekeeper is often a very serious problem in nonprofits as it is in any hierarchical system or in organizations that require a belief system that binds or gives one person in a decision-making or power position with privileges including undue privacy. The thought here is that acts of various indiscretion of one human being in power over another gives a subordinate person the power to gather information on a superior and use it against him or her. These are not only illegal acts in themselves, but they are capable of corrupting the system. Think for a second of a supervisor who seeks sexual favors from subordinates and a peer who hides it. What are the possible extensions of this into further corruption? Many acts of in-house corruption are merely extensions of personal behavior, some external to the organization and some internal. No tabular presentation gets it all, but they do give a thinking manager a focus and launching point. Perhaps this entire report should be serious reading. It gives examples of corruption and strategies to mitigate them.

Once corruption has been uncovered or revealed, however, the management has certain duties. The remainder of this chapter discusses various dimensions of these after-occurrence duties. It begins with the protection of information, sources, and records up the chain of custody. An essential part of the investigation and discovery is typically an audit, pointing to the specific category of financial transaction—leaving the aspects of corruption against human beings for later. Finally, what should management not fail to do as gatekeepers?

The Discovery of Corruption

Before proceeding to whistleblowers, it is important to note that the revelation of corruption comes from a variety of sources. These include complaints from suppliers, clients, relatives of clients, victims, unrelated observers, routine audits, maintenance and security people who observe unusual or suspicious behaviors, past employees, the exercise of due diligence by trustees, donors, partners, regular audits and audits by government contractors or collaborators. Sometimes the government audit exposes the corrupt act well before any clue of corruption is revealed. The inspector general, for example, audits to be sure of compliance with rules and regulations set by the government and to assure that the government's involvement is proper, efficient and productive, and that the record keeping is proper and records are maintained for the requisite period of time. Yet, it frequently discovers corruption or the doors to it.

The Protection of Sources and Records

Nonprofits are required to have a policy to hear and protect whistleblowers and to protect records. These are records not only having to do with the whistleblower, but with transactions provided in an accessible manner. When collaborating with government, this manner may be stipulated in the agreement. Whistleblowers are viewed as a prime source of information about corruption within the organization. The law is very open on what those policies should be, recognizing that one size does not fit all. Below are some considerations in crafting first a whistleblower policy and then document protection policy.

Whistleblower

Nonprofits are required to have guidelines and policies for the treatment of whistleblowers and require their subsidiaries and affiliates to do the same. It seems that in forming such policies, it is incumbent on management to consider:
1. The protection of those who are presumed innocent until proven otherwise
2. The possible injury to the reputation of the organization (not easily recoverable if the allegation is wrong)
3. The possible injury to the internal morale as associates and others come to believe that they can be unjustly accused or are being watched, or that their discovery will be ignored making them possible victims

4. The possible disincentive to report wrongdoing because it is felt that nothing will happen or that one can bring upon him or herself retribution from superiors, colleagues, and the governance structure itself
5. The possible need for assurance that one's allegation or insight is not being ignored, minimized, or cynically treated
6. The possible need for assurance that there is a reasonable time after which a formal acknowledgement of the complaint is made and a time line of action followed
7. The establishment and publicizing of a reasonable channel and order of attention that would be given allegations or complaints
8. The validation that there be confidentiality of all parties including those who may choose to be witnesses or adjudicate the matter, and especially if they voice an opinion about who did or did not participate
9. The establishment of a schedule of possible penalties for malicious allegations
10. The allowance of paid or unpaid leave while an allegation is being pursued
11. The need for a policy on when an allegation should be referred to authorities
12. The need for a formal means of communication about the closing of the case or its continuation
13. The need for a policing mechanism to protect records in an organized and traceable way.

No one answer fits all, but at least these factors should not be ignored.

Protection of Records

Some documents have legally required periods for their retention. This is true of IRS documents and the supporting documents to IRS filings. State laws may have similar retention periods. Other documents may be determined by the state statutes of limitations. Others documents, such as personnel files, should be retained at least as long as the person is employed and for some time thereafter. Medical documents are subject to their own rules. In the case of settlements, a settlement document may specify the terms of retention. Protection of records may also fall under the rules against the destruction of evidence.

In addition to retention of documents, the organization's policy may also have to include who makes the decision about retention and destruction, the method of destruction, who takes custody during the period of retention, and access to documents and the conditions or place of retention.

The Internal Audit and Required Disclosures

The internal audit tests the needs for internal control, recommends their improvements, and why. The internal audit function is an independent function of the organization authorized by the board of directors, that enforces, reports, and controls to ensure that internal controls are effective in producing honesty, accuracy, timeliness, accountability, and transparency in financial reporting and are in adherence to all the reporting requirements of the organization whether imposed by local, state, or Federal laws or by the terms of grants, donations, or contracts. In large nonprofits, the internal audit function has the advantage of being part of the organization and therefore has accessibility to observe and collect information on the activities and transactions subject to or that should be subject to internal controls and how to repair them. The internal audit itself may be subject to external audit to be sure that it is sufficiently resourced, competent, and has communication with the board. But the internal audit also reduces the risk of corruption and the opportunities for it to occur.

So does disclosure. The 990 Form identifies transactions that the organization has undertaken during the course of the year, so that the management and auditors can quickly spot areas in which corruption might have or could occur and the importance to the organization. It displays:

- *Breakdown of Revenues*: Amounts by sources including donations, investments, and business income so that unusual movements in these numbers might warrant explanation or curiosity.
- *Breakdown of Expenses*: Amounts by use such as administration, program, lobbying, and property acquisition so that unusual movements in these numbers might warrant investigation or explanation.
- *Mergers, Divestitures, and Acquisitions Large Investments*: conflicts of interest, graft, fraud, money laundering
- *Disposition of Assets*: The sale or disposition of assets after a certain threshold must be reported.
- *Compensation of Key Persons*: Misuse of funds by management for self-dealing may be exposed
- *Governance*: Self-dealing, collusion, channeling of contracts may be exposed.
- *Diversion of Resources and Corruption*: Form 990 requires that these be reported. Caution: some transactions may not be corruption but the use of resources in ways not consistent with the mission or intent.
- *Foreign*: Existence of foreign accounts and transactions and deposits used for money laundering or theft may be exposed.

There are other disclosures that are required by the Federal government other than the Form 990 that go directly to corruption and the misuse of the assets or clients of the organization. The Patriot Act requires disclosures to protect against the support of terrorism, money laundering, racketeering, and other financial crimes. There are also annual disclosures required by the Foreign Account Tax Compliance Act (FATCA) (2010) that organizations that hold accounts totaling $10,000 or more, or that offer tax shelters must make to the Federal government. Similarly, if the nonprofit issues bonds, it has to make disclosures about itself and its financing available through its prospectus. There are also industry-specific disclosures required by Federal and state governments. For example, schools must report enrollment and attendance, completion, and learning performance. Hospitals must report on births, deaths, inpatient and outpatient enrollment, and payment coverage. Child care centers must report on suspected incidents of abuse. It therefore behooves managers to be aware of the disclosures that are required by their states and their industries. These disclosures are good tools in the management of corruption—assuming that the internal control system works to make the information available and reliable.

Insurance Against Corruption

The financial cost of corruption can be reduced by insurance bonds to cover losses, bonds to cover failure to perform (surety bonds), and insurance to reduce the loss due to liability. Insurance, in addition, provides information. First, most insurance and bond companies would assess the organization's general situation and perhaps give valuable intelligence about where, how, and from what positions in the organization the nonprofit may be vulnerable, to what type of corruption or diversion of its assets, and what steps may be taken as a condition of the provision of insurance or of the premiums charged. Second, the insurance company may require periodic reporting or inspection, which is also a line of defense. Third, in the event of an instance of corruption, the payments from the insurance company would reduce if not eliminate the loss suffered, including legal costs.

The Manager as Gatekeeper

It is not enough to blame management or to expect management to create and enforce anti-corruption procedures. Management also needs guidance against its own actions and omissions. Here are some instances that emanate in part from the basic rule that there can be no use of the assets of the organization for personal inurement (benefits) or diversion from its contract promise. What may be typical pitfalls for the management? They include:

1. Failure to communicate applicable rules
2. Failure to evaluate, refresh, clarify and re-establish rules
3. Failure to give relevant examples and reasons for rules
4. Failure to enforce rules and procedures
5. Failure to establish route for reporting actual or reasonable suspicion about rule-breaking
6. Failure to take investigative action or to report to higher ups or authority about rule-breaking on a timely basis
7. Failure to protect those who reveal information and to reward factual and consequential reporting
8. Failure to protect the integrity of the process; that is, to compromise or to condone compromising of the system
9. Failure to advise or seek advice about specific situations
10. Failure to appreciate that even when management is not the perpetrator it could be a facilitator whether co-collaterally, intentionally or unintentionally
11. Failure to recognize that management could be the perpetrator or itself harbor corruption
12. Failure to advise external actors (suppliers and clients) of ways they can protect themselves against internal corruption and encourage their reporting of suspicious action against them by the organization or its agents
13. Failure to make the organization, rules, transactions, and expectations as transparent as possible
14. Failure to set up multiple internal systems of recording and approving transactions when that does not compromise privacy or privileged information or time of completion
15. Failure to handle invoicing, payments, receipts, and internal communication, and negotiating improperly or being a source of leaks
16. Failure to abide by promises to donors, employees, contacts or upper ups
17. Failure to establish secure systems or channels of custody
18. Failure to protect privacy
19. Failure to abide by external rules—reporting on activities, child abuse, limits on occupancy, area and facility requirements, and zoning
20. Failure to recognize that corruption is not only the act, but creating the opportunity for exploitation, commitment, perpetuation and protection

Embedding the Control of Expenditures, Costs, and the Early Detection of Risks Potential Problems

To design an organization to reduce the burden of government is equivalent to transferring certain costs to the organization. How these costs will be treated is significant to the successful operation and management of the organization and its survivability. Instituting a system through which variations in these costs from their planned trajectory can be spotted early enough so that corrections or adjustments can be made may significantly reduce the risk of failure. Collaboration is a method of sharing costs but only when that arrangement (which begins with identifying the costs and method of cost-sharing) is pre-arranged. When the government is the collaborator, it may refuse to pay certain costs. If the collaborator is a firm, the nonprofit may be prohibited from covering or shielding the firm's costs or losses. For all intents and purposes, cost is important first as a concept rather than a measurement.

Classification and Treatment of Certain Costs

This section focuses on certain specific cost concepts that are particularly germane.

Organizing Costs

There are costs associated with creating and designing the organization as a corporation. These costs are usually small, relative to others. They include legal fees, fees for incorporation, registration fees, and those fees required to receive the bylaws and other documentation. They also include fees for preparing and applying for tax exemption. Various portions of these fees go the Federal, state, and local governments and, of course, most go to the lawyers and accountants. They are generally not chargeable to any entity other than the organization itself and its founders.

Capital Costs

Capital costs are those that cover the acquisition of assets that have a useful life of more than a year. These costs can be so large that they are the principal motivator of the strategy to shift the burden of government to a nonprofit, with the principal source of the revenues to cover it being revenues from user fees generated by the project itself. Examples of capital costs are the cost of machines and equipment, as well as costs of the infrastructure itself, such as buildings, land, highways, and so on. Capital costs are fixed costs since they normally require a fixed payment over a period of time to cover their acquisition. These payments may be in the form of debt service or long-term lease payments. The acquisition of the asset may be through debt, transfer of parsimony (the state transferring an asset to the organization temporarily or permanently such as the transfer of the Panama Canal), gifts and contributions, or any combination of these. A common motivation for transferring a burden to the government is to transfer the capital cost and its associated operating costs and replacement costs.

Operating and Replacement Costs

Operating costs are those that occur regularly—even by the second—to keep the capital assets and the organization functioning. Most operating costs are variable. That is to say, they vary by use and are not fixed as are the capital costs. Replacement cost is the estimate of what it will cost to replace over time various capital costs. Replacement costs are usually best estimates because each capital item has a different life expectancy, various periods of major repairs, obsolescence, innovation, rates of inflation, and so on. But replacement costs are important because they help to set pricing so that fees and other assessments will be sufficient for the sustainability of the project. For a project to be sustainable, its capital assets have to be replenished, refurbished, and replaced. This cost can be met through endowments especially set aside for this purpose, restrictions made by the trustees to set aside a portion of the fees, and special events.

Direct and Indirect (Overhead) Costs

Direct costs are the costs directly due to the carrying out of a burden. When there are several activities, each one may have a direct cost. That is the amount of cost that can be eliminated if that activity is terminated. Indirect costs are those that would continue, perhaps smaller, even if the project ended but the organization continued; for example, the management and accounting costs. The government is extremely particular about why and how it recognizes indirect costs. As the government auditor who assigned a significantly higher overhead rate explained, the government cannot afford to have you fail with its projects simply because you cannot pay the bill for operating this building and also take care of the organization's needs.

But the government does have strict rules about what it would pay and how it is to be calculated. One rule of thumb for calculating the overhead rate (sometimes called the overhead burden) is 1 minus the percentage direct cost over total costs:

$$1 - \text{direct cost/total cost}$$

Another rule of thumb is to calculate the overhead as a multiple of direct labor costs. When the organization is a single-product producer (that is, the only thing it does is what is necessary to relieve the burden of government), then it may treat all costs as direct. The overhead rate is determined by the government as in OMB Circular A–122 ("Cost Principles for Non-Profit Organizations") and may resort to a sophisticated system called activity-based costing in which several overhead pools (for example, telephone, maintenance, publications) are set up and regressions are run to see how the movement in one program causes that pool to change and the regression coefficient becomes a proxy for the rate. What the designer of the nonprofit and manager needs to know is that when dealing with the government as a collaborator (and firms do require the same), some form of determining overhead charge is mandatory and that form is what the government says it is willing to take. It will not take a rate that places it at a disadvantage to what any other organization is being charged by the organization (see Federal Register 45 (132), July 8, 1980, A6025).

Fixed and Variable Costs

In designing the organization, the ratio of variable to fixed costs matters. The greater the variable costs, the greater the flexibility, but the lower the operating leverage. This means that expansion can occur with already existing fixed factors, such as capacity. But this is not always as neat as it seems because having excess capacity comes at a cost of carrying and holding it and at a risk that, when it is time to be used, it has to be updated or replaced because it no longer fits the need. Furthermore, the greater the fixed costs, the hard it is for the organization to be innovative with new money, even if it is unrestricted, because a greater portion of it has to go to cover the fixed costs to the extent that those costs are not otherwise covered. The discretion in the design is limited by the underlying nature of the assets that the burden requires, the technology, and the skill of putting these together. There is always a trade-off: The more leverage, the less flexibility, and vice-versa.

Common and Joint Costs

The organization may be designed to have a functional specialty that it can sell to one (or more) sections of government or one (or more) governments. This may not bring efficiency of scale, but it provides for cost sharing. Here is a variation: By the time we do A we have incurred a substantial part of the cost of producing B. Why not do B and add to our output, especially if the additional cost for completing B (its marginal cost) is small and can generate additional revenues (marginal revenue) equal to or greater than the additional cost? Doing both is only slightly more costly than doing one. As a matter of fact, the revenues from B might cover its additional cost plus the common costs it shares with A.

Consequently, two products or programs are said to have a common cost when they share an identical cost factor so that the production of one of the programs means incurring part if not most of the costs of producing the other. The same thing is true with joint costs. However, with joint costs, unlike common costs, the ratio of the output of the two products remains the same. To illustrate, the production of beef and hide are joint costs because they have the same cost factors (the production of cattle) and they occur roughly in the same ratio: so many pounds of beef and so much hide in an animal.

The important aspect shared by common and joint costs is that they provide ways of fulfilling and financing the charitable mission of the nonprofit and the cost sharing of projects. The selling of advertising space in the nonprofit's publication is an example. The advertising (business) and the articles (nonbusiness) activities share common costs: printing, editorial, circulation, material, and space costs.

These costs are important in accounting and in budgeting. We must determine what portion of the common costs is to be allocated among the activities before we can calculate the total cost for each. Obviously, if A and B share a common cost, we need to decide how much of that cost is to be covered by A and how much by B. The more of the common cost we allocate to A, the more costly we make it. We may choose to allocate most of the common costs to A if A can be sold and generate revenues to help pay for B.

So it is desirable that an organizational design allows and encourages joint costs and common costs: cost sharing is advantageous to the organization and to government by lowering cost, sharing from experiences, and having the ability to reduce the burden of more than one government agency or department simultaneously. The delivery system in reducing a burden of government may be divided into various responsibility centers for purposes of accountability, cost control, efficiency, and for grouping activities that serve different customers, even if they are within the government, and to maintain communication and interaction among them or a complete wall when that is necessary.

A Tool of Cost Control, Avoidance of Cost Overruns, and Detection of the Risk of Inefficiency or Fraud

Some combined system of performance and cost variance will help to improve the performance and accountability of the organization to its supporters, its collaborators, and its managers. It should then be alert all to a potential problem, generate an interest in a solution to avoid the problem, and reduce the openings for corrupt behavior or cost overruns. Accordingly, this system (Bryce 1986, 1992, and 2000) is offered: It assumes an organization that has taken over several burdens of government (each a responsibility center), and in each there are multiple identifiable programs. This complexity is not essential but it is used to show the wide applicability of the procedure. Table 12.2 shows a list of over 100 programs according to the responsibility centers under which they fall.

Table 12.2. Format for Flagging Potential Budgetary Problems

Responsibility Center-01			Responsibility Center-02			Responsibility Center-03			Responsibility Center-04		
Program Code	Status	Flag	Program Code	Status	Flag	Program Code	Status	Flag	Program Code	Status	Flag
0100			0200			0300			0400		
0101			0201			0301			0401		
0102			0202			0302			0402		
0103			0203			0303	2/4/ 80/70		0403		
0104			0204			0304			0404		
0105			0205			0305			0405		
0106			0206	3/4/ 99/50		0306			0406		
0107			0207			0307			0407		
0108			0208			0308	1/2/ 110/60		0408	3/5/ 80/60	
0109			0209			0309			0409		
0110	3/4/ 10/90		0210			0310			0410		
0111			0211			0311			0411		
0112			0212			0312			0412		

Each program has a control number to identify it. The first two digits identify the responsibility center and the other digits identify the specific program within the center; hence 0110 is a program in the responsibility center designated 01. The number 10 identifies the program. In this display, we show each responsibility center as having 12 programs. It is not necessary for purposes of financial flagging to deal with specific program names.

The program code is followed by a code such as 2/4/80/70. The first number represents the current year of the program; 2 would mean that the program is in its second year, the year for which the present budget is being submitted. The second number indicates the expected life of the program; 4 means that the program is planned for four years. The third number is the percentage of the total allocation that will be consumed by the end of the year for which the budget is being submitted; 80 means that by the end of this year, 80 percent of the budget allotment would have been used up. The fourth number indicates the program manager's assessment of the amount of work that will have been done by the end of the budget year; 70 percent means that by the end of this present budget year only 30 percent of the promised activities will be left to be done.

This technique provides several advantages. First, the financial manager can focus on the possibilities of cost overruns on each program within the organization because the pertinent information is given in simple form. Second, it gives the individual program manager, the manager of the responsibility center in which the program falls, and management of the organization an early warning of trouble. Third, it forces the program manager to assess how much has been accomplished and how much is still left to be done and, consequently, to be accountable as to how the remaining task will get done.

Now, it is not unusual to find program managers who would try to escape this responsibility by saying that "it is hard to measure how much is left to be done." Such a plea of impotence is often no more than a sign of incompetence. The fact is that you cannot manage a multiyear program under budget constraints if you cannot see the end of the project and cannot ascertain where you are, where you are going, and roughly what it will take to get there. The judgment does not have to be 100 percent accurate. It has to be reasonable. The users of such information should keep in mind that an objective of all control systems is to be able to flag and avoid potential problems. Control systems do not give answers as much as they flag situations where managerial attention ought to be focused and questions raised.

In addition to reducing the probability of cost overruns, this system also alerts managers to projects that are lagging behind the funding schedule. Some contracts are written in such a way that they terminate at a specific period and must be renegotiated at the risk that they will not be extended. Unspent funds may be lost. So a program that shows 3/4/10/90 is as much a potential problem as one that shows 3/4/99/50. The first has to find a way to justifiably use 90 percent of the funding in one year when only 10 percent of the job is left to be done. This is not a problem only if the last 10 percent can justifiably use the remaining funds. The latter program has to do 50 percent of the work with one percent of the funds.

A display such as 1/2/110/60 would raise serious questions about cutting losses. This is a two-year program that at the end of its first year has overspent its budget by 10 percent and still has 40 percent of the expected work to be completed. A program of 3/5/80/60 is a five-year program that already in its third year and shows signs of a potential need for more funding. This process of seeking additional funding can be started well before the project enters into serious cost overruns.

Summary and Preview

The nonprofit has a duty of care and a responsibility to stewardship of the assets committed to its custody. These assets can be diverted into corrupt uses, waste by inefficient use, suboptimal production, cost-over runs, and public purpose badly served if, in the engagement or design of the organization, certain defenses were not embedded. Furthermore, collaborators could also be placed at risk and the assets they contributed to the cause are also at similar risk. This chapter, therefore, has been about preventive tools that can be built into the design and operation of the nonprofit to reduce these risks. All of them have common characteristics: they are preventive and proactive (Sims 2009) and they require alert and astute management. They are not automatic triggers. They must be part of the operating design of the organization and part of the managerial ritual.

Bibliography

Greenlee, Janet, Mary Fischer, Teresa Gordon and Elizabeth Keating, "An Investigation of Fraud in Nonprofit Organizations: Occurrences and Deterrents," *Nonprofit Voluntary Sector Quarterly*, Vol.36, No.4 (2007), pp. 676–694.

Gugerty, Mary Kay, "Signaling Virtue: Voluntary Accountability Programs among Nonprofit Organizations," *Policy Sciences*, Vol. 42, Issue 3 (2009), pp. 243–273.

Hung, Li-Hwa, "Prevention and Identification of Organizational Corruption," *Organization and Management*, Issue 1 (139) (2010), pp. 153–169.

Burke, Ronald J., Edward C. Tomlison and Cary L. Cooper. *Crime and Corruption in Organizations : Why It Occurs and What to Do about It* (Surrey, UK, Gower Publishers, 2010).

Ashforth, Blake E., Dennis A. Gioia, Sandra L. Robinson, and Linda K. Trevino, "Re-Viewing Organizational Corruption," *Academy of Management Review*, July 2008, Vol. 33, Issue #3, pp. 670–684.

Luo, Yadong, *Management and Organization Review*, Vol. 1, Issue 1 (2005), pp. 119–154.

Kiltgaard, Robert and Heather Baser, *Working together to Fight Corruption: State, Society and the Private Sector in Partnership* (Santa Monica, CA: The Rand Corporation, 1998 reprint).

The Role of Power in Organizational Corruption, Istvan Javor and David Jancsics, *Administration & Society*, December 2013.

Kish-Gephart, J. J., Harrison, D. A., and Treviño, L. K. "Bad apples, bad cases, and bad barrels: Meta-analytic evidence about sources of unethical decisions at work," *Journal of Applied Psychology*, 95, 1–31 (2010).

Dirks, Kurt T., Ferrin, Donald L. "Trust in leadership: Meta-analytic findings and implications for research and practice," *Journal of Applied Psychology*, Vol 87(4), Aug 2002, 611–628. 10.1037/0021-9010.87.4.61.

The Institute of Internal Auditors, *The Three Lines of Defense in Effective Risk Management and Control* (January 2013) (https://na.theiia.org/standards-guidance/Public%20Documents/ PP%20The%20Three%20Lines%20of%20Defense%20in%20Effective%20Risk%20 Management%20and%20Control.pdf).

Iyer, Venkataraman M. and Ann L. Watkins. "Adoption of Sarbanes-Oxley Measures by Non-profit Organizations: An Empirical Study." *Accounting Horizons*: September 2008, Vol. 22, No. 3, pp. 255–277 (http://dx.doi.org/10.2308/acch.2008.22.3.255).

Keating, Elizabeth K., Linda M. Parsons, and Andrea Alston Roberts. "Misreporting Fundrais-ing: How Do Nonprofit Organizations Account for Telemarketing Campaigns?" *The Accounting Review*, March 2008, Vol. 83, No. 2, pp. 417–446 (http://dx.doi.org/10.2308/ accr.2008.83.2.417).

Association of Certified Fraud Examiners (ACFE), *Report to the Nation on Occupational Fraud and Abuse*, 1996.

Omer, Thomas C. and Robert J. Yetman. "Tax Misreporting and Avoidance by Nonprofit Organi-zations." *The Journal of the American Taxation Association*, Spring 2007, Vol. 29, No. 1, pp. 61–86 (http://dx.doi.org/10.2308/jata.2007.29.1.61).

Krishnan, Ranjani, Michelle H. Yetman, and Robert J. Yetman. "Expense Misreporting in Non-profit Organizations." *The Accounting Review*: March 2006, Vol. 81, No. 2, pp. 399–420.

Schmidt, Andrew. "Discussion of Tax Misreporting and Avoidance by Nonprofit Organizations," *Journal of the American Taxation Association*, March 2007, Vol. 29, No. 1, pp. 87–82.

Sims, Ronald. "Toward a Better Understanding of Organizational Efforts to Rebuild Reputation Following an Ethical Standard," *Journal of Business Ethics*, December 2009, Vol. 90, pp. 453.472.

Chapter 13 – Discussion and Dialogue

The author presents a theory in the opening chapter grounded in the concepts of the economics of choice (not in the economics of externalities) to explain why expanding the the creation and utilization of nonprofits to lessen the fiscal, capacity and debt burdens of governments at all levels, leads to an equitable and efficient solution. Numerous real world examples are given, along with a dissecting of what makes them work and consequently what are the necessary planks upon which policymakers may pursue this option to dealing with the fiscal and capacity constraints on governments. The book begins with a definition of lessening the burden of government as it is in IRS rules, pronouncements and regulations, to show as the IRS does, that this allows the creation of nonprofits that are not traditionally charitable and therefore can service specific policy objectives that affect the general population and that are not defined in terms of income. Such is the case of infrastructure, the environment, the development of parks and ports. The problem, the perspective, and the principal planks for implimenting such a strategy are the concerns of this book.

This book falls in the conceptual tradition of the author's *Players in the Public Policy Process: Nonprofits as Social Capital and Agents* (Palgrave Macmillan, 2005 and 2012) which was the winner of the Charles Levine Memorial Book Award of 2006. It is a continuous codification of the utililty of the nonprofit across the spectrum of human activity but in a very disciplined theoretical and empirical (the presentation of true actual cases) manner. This particular book is born of a public policy problem: There is an urgent need for infrastructure, expenditures on the environment, local economic development, and public services such as libraries among other "big problems." At the very same time there is a public resistance to increasing government size, debt, and expenditures at all levels of government. The central question of this book: Can nonprofits created by governments or citizens to lessen the burden of governments help even if this takes us beyond the traditional concept of charity? Can they do big things? That question does not begin with this author, but as Chapter 1 points out is the very question exPrime Minister David Cameron posed in the Big Society.

This takes us beyond the traditional view of nonprofits and charity, but not an unreal journey since, as this book demonstrates, there are real siginficant examples available to test the proposition. To work, n the United States this proposition must be based on the IRS Code since it is that which defines the concept of lessening the burden of government as one for which tax exemption is available. States and localities adopt or follow the IRS procedure and criteria. They are these for qualfication:

DOI 10.1515/9781501505799-014

1. That the activity is a burden of government as evidenced by the fact that the government carries it on or plans to do so.
2. That the organization is designed and operated such that it does and can relieve that burden
3. That in doing so the general public is defined by the scope of the jurisdiction and the burden is lessened and no benefits (such as profits and special privileges) inure to individual entities or persons.

This book is based on the IRS approach because without it tax exemption is not available on the Federal level, or on the state level because the latter requires the former. Not only does the IRS version simplify matters and is necessary, but it forces the question: Why, really, is the government or are individuals creating this organization? Is it really to help poor people (the traditional meaning of charity) or is it to lessen the burden of government even for those functions that primarily serve middle and upper income people, the public in general, or commercial entities? Who is the primary beneficiary and who gets the spillovers, significant as they are? These are not political issues, they are policy ones: for which part of the general public is the policy most likely to directly affect? If there is a non-charitable group, can they pay for that service rather than have the government do so?

In virtually all of the examples used in this book, the nonprofit is self-sufficient—meaning that their lessening of the burden of government involves raising outside funds, or earning those funds and not having resource dependency on the government. In addition, the service is paid for through voluntary contributions (to which the government has no access) but which captures the value of the spillover effect; the value to the general public.

Levels of Lessening the Burden of Government

The full weight of responsibility and the full burden of the implementation of a public policy can be lifted from the government:
1. Optimally or completely by those nonprofits that take over the implementation and financing of a public policy.
2. Less than completely by those nonprofits that do financing or implementation without government assistance—the burden being lessened by the amount they do
3. Less than completely by a nonprofit that collaborates

The Richmond Public Library Foundation, in Richmond, Virginia (http://www.lva.virginia.gov/about/contact.asp?dept=foundation), raises private funds and enlists public support and volunteers to, in their words, "provide the extra margin of excellence for the public library system in the city of Richmond." Its director is the director of libraries for the City. It has one full-time employee and 19 volunteers. The Tennessee Valley Authority does everything including running its own back office to the tune of over $20,000 million dollars in annual expense that does not come out of any government budget or guarantee (http://www.snl.com/IRW/AsReported/4063363/Index).

Therefore 1 and 2 above describe the possible end points of a continuum. Size is a measure of the amount of burden reduced, but not its relative significance. The Richmond Public Library Foundation in Richmond, California (http://www.rplf.org/giving.htm) was started as a response to what they describe as "deep" budget cuts. It raises money for books, vans, and programs. It lessens a burden of government by assuming an essential public service that would otherwise have been badly served if at all.

Types of Nonprofits Lessening the Burden of Government

This book places the nonprofits lessening the burden of government into two classes: The doers and the facilitators. Using this bifurcation allows us to respect the IRS statement and advice to its agents that to lessen a burden of government, one can be a 501(c)(3) or a (c)(4) or a (c)(6)—a charity, a social welfare or civic organization, or a professional or business organization. The doers are those nonprofits that lessen the burden of government not only by raising their own funds but, importantly, by actually carrying out the policy function. They do it and fund it. The facilitators make the work of the doers easier either by raising private funds (to replace the tax dollars), doing the ground work that is necessary to reduce the cost of the operation, or coordinating all parties so that the work gets done.

Take the New Jersey Economic Development Authority. It is classified as a facilitator. It is a 501(c)(4). It provides loans and incentives, it counsels and helps to create public-private partnerships but it does not do the work. Take the National Park Foundation, it is a 501(c)(3). It raises private funds for the operation of the National Park Service. Take the Retiree Resource Corporation, it is a 501(c)(3) and, more specifically in that category, a 509(a)(2) as explained in this book. It provides support to the Tennessee Valley Authority, a U.S.-created corporation. Both are self-financing at zero tax dollars.

A principal contribution of the facilitators is that they give access to dollars the government would not otherwise have and provide services that the government could not, at least not as easily.

The Authority to Perform

Lessening the burden of government by itself or lessening the burden of government in a specific class of policy requires both a virtual license and commitment to do what, where, and for whom. In one of the early articles of the charter (the license or agreement signed by the state where the organization is chartered) is the purpose or mission of the organization. It is a contractual promise to do what that article says and is commonly known as the *mission* of the organization even though that word "mission" may not appear in the statement itself. The basic source of authority is the statutory power and permission to act with respect to a specific burden of government that must be specified or reasonably inferred given the facts and circumstances but identifying which burden, what government, and by doing what.

Capitalize Albany Corporation is in its words:

> a catalyst for economic growth....serving as the City of Albany's economic development arm. A registered 501 (c) (3) not-for-profit organization implementing programs and resources to create, retain, and attract business in the City of Albany.

> Powered by investors composed of Albany's community and business leaders, Capitalize Albany manages and coordinates all local economic development functions. The Corporation works alongside the City of Albany's Industrial Development Agency (IDA) and Capital Resource Corporation (CRC) under a professional services agreement allowing Capitalize Albany to match transformational projects with the right tools and resources.

> Two important resources for developers, the IDA and CRC assist in local development by acquiring, constructing, improving, maintaining or equipping eligible projects. Any project undertaken by either entity must advance job opportunities, health, general prosperity and the economic welfare of the people of the City of Albany. The assistance offered may include conduit bond financing, tax exemptions and abatements. To obtain assistance, applicants must satisfy eligibility requirements and demonstrate a need for assistance (http://capitalizealbany.com/about/).

Again, one does not back into it. Lessening the burden of government is an expressed purpose by declaration or inference upfront: what burden, is it a burden, of what government, and does the government acknowledge that burden either by saying it or unequivocally treating it?

The Nature of the Promise to Lessen the Burden of Government

The promise has legal force. It is a contractual promise between the organization and the people as represented by the government. It is perpetual unless mutually amended. It is clear—usually stated in about 50 words. It is verifiable, that is, the organization says it is going to do something and needs to show that it has done it and how. The granting of the charter is its acceptance by the government. Two points follow: (a) that this promise is not a planning or sales or marketing pitch. It is more than an ethical commitment. It is a legal one, and (b) it is also a permanent one. Therefore a nonprofit formed to lessen the burden of a specific government—which most are, such as the one above—are space specific. This is reinforced by the fact that their boards—the ultimate decider of change--tend to be populated by local officials, residents, and entities.

In its own words,

> The Dutchess County Local Development Corporation (DCLDC) is a Not ForProfit Corporation created by the Dutchess County government under the New York Not For-Profit Corporation Law 2010 to promote economic development and job creation in Dutchess County. The DCLDC induces companies to invest capital in projects that create jobs and increase the county's tax base, thereby improving the quality of life for Dutchess County residents....LDC was created to further economic development in Dutchess County through the issuance of bonds to facilitate the building of capital projects by not-for-profit corporations in Dutchess County with the resultant construction jobs and permanent follow on employment (http://www.dutchesscountyldc.com/documents/2015DCLDCMission StatementandPerformanceMeasurementsPolicy.pdf).

One can hardly be more space and purpose specific, but not rare.

To Exercise Authority the Nonprofit Needs Powers

To discharge its promise and commitment to lessen a burden of government, the nonprofit must have transactional powers—some are basic, others are not. In the latter group are powers that are similar to sovereign powers—the power to police, to tax, of eminent domain, to commit the government, and so on. In granting these powers to an entity which is not government, they must be limited; for example, to exercise the power to maintain peace on a college campus and give tickets for traffic violations on campus, but the obligation to defer to local government in the case of murder and the absence of any police powers unless by local agreement off campus. Nonprofits lessening the burden of government through the exercise of regulatory powers may do so through punitive sanctions on their members.

Aside from these powers, however, the nonprofit needs specifically named powers for most ordinary and necessary transactions, such as to enter into contracts, acquire and dispose of property, to spend, to be liable, to be sued and to sue, and importantly to borrow and to lend, and to raise funds through business transactions and contributions. In addition, they may need specifically named powers commensurate with the burden they are attempting to lessen. They may also have specifically named prohibitions such as to engage in politics or to encumber the government. It is the duty of the legislature or the citizens that are creating the nonprofit to be sure that the standard inventory of powers is present and sufficient, adding as needed.

The important point is that without the powers specifically enumerated in the charter, the nonprofit remains liable for them if they are exercised.

The Power to Finance and the Motive for Action

The nonprofit does not have the power of government to compel payments through taxes from citizens or from the government whose burdens it is lessening. The power to finance then depends upon the power and skill to persuade. Donors and contributors must be persuaded to give and their choices must be accommodated through the various ways and with the various tools they may use. In addition, clients must be persuaded to buy either the service or the product. Meaning that the nonprofit has to be able to market and to conduct a business. Income from business transactions may be related to the mission of the nonprofit or unrelated to it. This distinction is consequential.

Notwithstanding its ability to compel the financing of a burden, there are political, prudent, and realistic limits to a government's using its power to compel; and these are often prime reasons for engaging a nonprofit to have access to private and voluntary funding that the government cannot. It is not charity.

Governance Structure

A board of directors is required by state and Federal laws. Without a board, decisions cannot be made or powers and authority exercised. But the board has to function and this is especially true when the lessening of a burden of government is the mission. A misunderstanding prevails that the board's primary function is to give guidance to management. Without a board, there can be no management for it is the board's duty to design and to appoint managers to whom they delegate the daily operation of the nonprofit. It is the board's signature that is needed on organic and basic policy documents and its expressed approval that allows certain transactions to take place including opening of a bank or other financial accounts.

When the government creates a nonprofit to lessen its burden, it specifies how many persons will be on that board, what government offices will be represented on that board, what positions they will hold, their terms of office, how many times they must meet, and what constitutes a quorum. To obtain exemption under the terms of the IRS, an organization created by citizens would have a similar profile. In all, the board must reflect the jurisdictional profile of the burden so that a local burden calls for a local board made up of residents.

Accountability and Disclosures

This book covered public assets and responsibilities for national heritage, commerce, recreation, the environment, and local economic development, among others. Because the burden that is lessened is always one of significant public benefit and of the scope currently or presumably offered by government, the need for public accountability is undeniable and expected. This accountability begins with making the board of trustees responsible for decisions, overseeing, and reporting by the use of their voting, signatures, and commitment to loyalty, care, and responsibility for maintaining the mission purpose. They exercise their duties through a variety of vehicles including certified audits, instituting methods of internal control, requiring and receiving regular reports from the management, hiring experts, and creating specialized committees and subcommittees.

It extends to reporting what is required by Federal, state, and local governments including the Form 990, and to state agencies that are overseers as well as the state agency that is connected to the burden. It includes annual reports to the public at large that cover activities and finances during the year as well as the status of major plans. Also included are the required public hearings and open meetings, and the power of the legislature to subpoena and the attorney general to dissolve the organization for major violations or dysfunctions.

Accountability and the need to disclose also comes from partners, investors such as creditors, members, and specialized agencies and the various watchdog agencies including the press when it raises questions. Some of these organizations are directly or indirectly exposed to the freedom of information acts.

The tools for accountability and disclosures of what, to whom, and when are required and many are not only compulsory but have severe penalties on management for failure to disclose, for abuse, and for falsification.

A word of caution: The fact that these burdens are the responsibilities of nonelected boards could be exaggerated. Most public policy is implemented by appointed, not elected, officials with a considerable amount of discretion. The elected officials are the persons accountable for corrective action. When an activity is placed in a nonprofit rather than in a larger agency, its budgets and actions are evident and affect its ability to function in markets and in collaboration. The information is not enveloped in a larger agency where separating it out is a challenge and the larger agency is not a cover or protection.

The rationale for spin-off of a public activity is not so different from the rationale for spin-off of a firm: If it is so good, let it stand alone and the value it creates be evident in what the public is willing to pay for it. In the nonprofit world, that value is evident by public support in the form of contributions, fees, and the organization's business income. Often the public speaks loudly, clearly, and positively. As one study in this book finds, often people prefer to pay voluntarily than through compulsion for some goods and services and the operation allowed by the organizational design is not to disappoint and not to misinform or misrepresent.

Types and Range of Collaboration

The creation of a nonprofit to lessen the burden of government implies some level of cooperation to obtain tax exemption. The fact is that there is an entire class of nonprofits that do nothing but serve as facilitators or catalysts. Here are some that are covered in this book:

1. There are the doers who work collaboratively with a government agency, co-producers, and the public or jurisdiction to get the job done.
2. There are facilitators that may be subsidiaries, auxiliaries, or independent financers
3. There may be formal or informal collaborations.
4. Most meaningful collaboration would be by agreement or by contract.
5. Collaboration may take a structural form of a partnership or a joint venture, or a management contract or a cooperative sharing

The Conflict Between Collaboration and Control

The concept of lessening a burden of government implies some form of collaboration moderated by control. In the case of a nonprofit that remains an integral part of the government, collaboration and control go hand in hand. Where the nonprofit is created by government to be a 501(c)(3) or created by citizens, collaboration is still necessary but control is minimized to the essentials of being able to monitor and to have a say but not to direct or be determinative by command or to determine the flow of finance to support or to sustain. The power to do any of these is tantamount to the power to control. Where **A** controls **B** the latter is for all intents and purposes not separate from the former and the former remains liable or can be declared liable for the latter. In essence, then, the former retains the burden, just in a different design. One way of theoretically and partially resolving this issue, in the rare case where it cannot be resolved fully by a working agreement or protocol which is usually sufficient, is by creating a third organization, a joint venture, in which both parties are members. The upshot of this is that in the design or engagement of a nonprofit to lessen the burden of government, legislative designers need to avoid the trap of making collaboration, accountability, and oversight extend to control.

The concept of control is a two-edged sword. Some control by the government is *prima facie* evidence that the organization serves to lessen the burden of government—at least it core corpus. Control can also lead to denial of 501(c)(3) tax exemption if the structure and content of the control lead to the organization's being an instrumentality of government or an agency of government. In that case, they are not separate entities and not only cannot get 501(c)(3), (4) or (6) status, but the accounting and some legal rules would dictate that the liabilities of the organization are the liabilities of the government. Crafting these relationships as discussed in Chapter 5 must follow a delicate path.

Sources of Legitimacy

Clearly the legitimacy of the organization matters for several reasons including that it affects its ability to perform its mission and therefore lessen the burden of government. The nonprofit derives legitimacy when the government creates it by its very creation; but the government and the IRS do more not only for government-created but also for citizen-created nonprofits that gives them legitimacy to lessen the specific burden of government. Among these are:

Board: A principal way of dealing with legitimacy is in the construction of the board of directors. The board is usually drawn from residents or institutions within the jurisdictional boundaries that are served by the organization, or those who qualify for membership because of a shared interest in the case of membership organizations, and a specified number of board seats as well as board positions are reserved solely for incumbents in specified positions of the local, state, or Federal government reflecting the jurisdiction of operation.

Agreement: Agreements between the government and the nonprofit are a principal source of legitimacy and authority to the nonprofit. The simple format of an agreement of that kind is as follows:

> The government of.......or....... agency of that government has statutory authority and responsibility to perform......function and to delegate that responsibility. Under this statutory authority it delegates ......function to......a nonstock, nonprofit corporation chartered in......as its agent for performing.....function for......period of time and in.......places. The specific responsibilities of each party under this agreement are as follows and include reservation of the agency on the board of directors and specific advisory councils, accountability, reporting, coordination, and mutual responsiveness requirements: For an example, see the agreement between the U.S. Coast Guard and the American Bureau of Shipping: https://www.uscg.mil/hq/cg5/acp/docs/uscgabs.pdf); or the several agreements between the Financial Industry Regulatory Authority (FINRA), a 501(c)(6); and the Securities and Exchange Commission Agreements are constantly updated to reflect new developments and realities.

Notice that these agreements confirm that the burden is borne by the government and it has the appropriate authority and has chosen to delegate it; that it has delegated it to a competent agent (one who is incorporated and therefore has the authority to accept and to act and the competency to do so); that it establishes an unequivocal connection to that agent so that it has oversight over the performance and assets in the public's interest; that there is an option to change and to withdraw; that there is an established communication connection and reporting requirement. Notice also that these agreements do not require the government to pay the nonprofit, but provide the nonprofit the right (at least does not interfere with it) to calculate and charge fees to the users of their services.

Performance: These measures notwithstanding, legitimacy is dependent upon the efficient, ethical, and dependable performance of the nonprofit. Corruption (Chapter 12) destroys legitimacy.

Imprimateur: Unlike other nonprofits, those that lessen the burden of government are frequently referred to by government, recognized by government, carry some for of government cerftification by government, used by government—all forms of imprimateur. Governments and firms require accounting to be according to certain general acceptable principles All of these are promulgated by 501 (c)(3) or (c)(6)s. The act of requiring is a rendering of legitimacy.

Growth and Competition

Some aspect of growth attends every nonprofit even if its "public" is restricted to a small jurisdiction.

1. Growth may have to do with membership, participants, or public support drawn from that jurisdiction.
2. Growth may pertain to revenues either through fundraising or through business income—particularly income from membership fees or from fees charged for the services and goods of the organization.
3. Growth may result from geographic extensions within the territory or space defined by the burden and the charter of the organization. This space might be a neighborhood, city, county, state, region, the nation or international.
4. Growth may occur through organic expansion such as adding new programs or through accretion such as through mergers and acquisitions.

These various forms of growth are discussed in (Bryce, *Financial and Strategic Management for Nonprofit Organizations*, 2017), but there are some specific applications with respect to nonprofits created to lessen the burden of government. Most of them are restricted by the nature of the mission. A nonprofit created by a jurisdiction is restricted to that jurisdiction to serve that jurisdiction. Even national nonprofits designed to lessen the burden of government are restricted, perhaps not spatially, but in terms of the subject matter. The American Bureau of Shipping, a 501(c)(6), grows as fleets around the world grow, marine infrastructure, and as marine products and incidents of safety concern grow. The Tennessee Valley Authority grows not only because it covers a vast region that transcends the state, but power, energy, recreation, and other activities also grow. A local economic development corporation is usually restricted to its local territory, as defined, but it can do a variety of things with respect to job training, unemployment, attracting and retaining business for various parts of its territory, and thus lessen the burden of government (see Article 3 of the charter of the Hudson Development Corporation as an example, http://hudsonfirst. com/wp-content/uploads/2012/04/HDC-Articles.pdf). On the other hand:

> The Economic Development Corporation (EDC) of Kansas City, Missouri, is a 501c4 non-profit agency created to manage the efforts of six statutory redevelopment agencies, and to serve as Kansas City, Missouri's link to business and the economic development community. The EDC and our agencies work cooperatively to project a local identity and ensure a competitive, vibrant and self-sustaining economy. We also collaborate with the City of KCMO and other organizations and rely on our talented, technologically advanced, diverse workforce to achieve these goals (http://edckc.com/about-edc/).

The point is that even with these natural restrictions, lessening the burden of government offers growth opportunities and challenges. Ports compete for shipping; local development corporations compete for firms and persons; local library foundations compete for volunteers who may go to other activities and donors who may use their resources otherwise. In the case of the Economic Development Corporation of Kansas City, it grows as its constituent agencies grow. Lessening the burden of government has multiple paths for growth and competition.

Debt and Off-Balance Sheet Financing

Off-balance sheet financing refers to paying for an asset using a method that would avoid having the liabilities associated with that project, in particular the debt does not appear on the entity's balance sheet. This is a standard technique used by firms and governments for purposes that are ethical, efficient, and, if used properly, good for the public as a whole. Because this is such a controversial strategy, especially among academics, let me begin by writing that what I am about to describe comes from (a) an academic experience specializing in public finance and over 30 years of teaching corporate finance and holding two of the highest designations in the professional field, (b) an equal number of years holding securities licenses, and (c) four years of serving as a trustee (one who oversees and agrees to the structure and terms of municipal bonds and signs the indenture that allow and accompanies their issue to the public), and that many of those criticisms are simply dated. Here is the set of arguments:

1. Off-balance sheet financing is a regulated and a normal form of issuing debt and building infrastructure and can hardly be sold on the public market if they do not comply with IRS, SEC, and in the case of international financing, international financing and accounting rules.
2. Any jurisdiction that does not consider this strategy when it can is lax in its financial duty and stewardship. Why?
    a. First, it is true that if it were on the jurisdiction's balance sheet it would count against its debt limit and the jurisdiction may precisely try to avoid that. This makes sense: When a project counts against a jurisdiction's debt limit it means that it is a current or contingent liability of the jurisdiction, not only limits the amount of debt the jurisdiction can issue for any purpose, including schools, but it increases the cost of future debt and diminishes the price of the existing ones. It also places an effective lien on the incomes of taxpayers who one way or the other will pay for it.

b. Because it limits the debt of the jurisdiction it means that other projects cannot be financed unless by increasing taxes—an almost impossible thing to do without a long debate in the legislative branch, a risk of rejection of tax increase, unnecessary delay and increased inflationary costs. Other things go because a project that could have been financed otherwise and perhaps more cheaply was not.

c. Less expensive or cheaper not only because of the result of waiting, but also because a government-created entity often has a better credit rating than the government itself. At one time, the city of New York was virtually locked out of the debt market. Creating these entities helped providing services and financing for specific projects.

3. Neither the citizens nor the investor is duped or tricked. The creation and design of these entities are done by open legislative action, as is any other law, and signed by the executive. That is why the IRS and states use the word "statutory" as a requirement for claiming lessening the burden of government and why the charter of these organizations make reference to the law that permits them.

4. The bonds of these organizations do not constitute obligations of the government unless it says so. The phrasing in the charter may say that these debts do not constitute liabilities of the state.

5. The state guarantee of these bonds (revenue bonds supported by revenues from the activity or infrastructure being financed) does not, under ordinary circumstances, require government guarantee. A savvy issuer would use a letter of credit from a bank or bond insurance (perfectly acceptable enhancements) which give the same if not better guarantee in addition to giving the first lien against the income stream from the project to the creditors.

6. A revenue bond, issued by a nonprofit created to lessen the burden of government can be made to stand on its own weight—supported by the revenues from the project it finances be it a dormitory, a hospital, college, a toll bridge or highway, an airport, low-income housing, and so on. They are like a debenture of a firm—they are unsecured debt.

7. Because they are unsecured debt, nonprofits that are qualified to use these type of debt can point to a stream of income (not government) to support them unless the government elects to do so, which is often unwise. Further, they must point to that income in the indenture (the deed or contract) that they issue along with the debt. These are required by SEC law if the debt is to be sold by use of mail, telephone, brokerage, newspaper, internet, or public media to the public.

8. Because the debt must pay for itself, they are financed by the earnings of the project, which means that they are financed by user charges, which fur-

ther means that those who benefit most from the project pay for it and not the general public subsidizing them by paying for it. Hence, they lead to a more efficient and equitable choice when that choice is available.

9. Projects off-balance sheet tend to have more transparency and accountability than projects financed through instrumentalities or agencies. They stand alone, must account regularly to their creditors, must publish comprehensive reports, must file income tax returns and Form 990s, as a condition of their tax exemption (agencies or instrumentalities do not file unless they have unrelated business income to report), must provide for regular reports or responsiveness to some government agency. Voters do have less of a voice over their debt since their debt limits are usually not a liability to the voter and because the voter may influence that debt decision only through their legislature and executive—not an up or down vote.

10. Nonprofits can only issue revenue bonds. They cannot, unless specifically authorized, obligate the state or its taxpayers to guarantee or cover these bonds. In virtually every case in this book, there is a specific statement in the charter of the nonprofit (many quoted in this book) saying that the government or the taxpayers by implication holds no obligation for this debt. This is also stated to the investors in every issue of debt that that nonprofit makes. The investor knows that fact. For details, see the chart I created in Chapter 5.

Who Subsidizes Whom

A nonprofit created to lessen the burden of government might do so on any level as described above since it is by itself and on its own with a purpose for which the U.S. Treasury and IRS recognize as a reason for exemption either under 501(c)(3), (4) or (6). In various parts of this book, we point to examples. Notice a common feature, most if not all are fully self-funding (not relying on the government) and some, the facilitators, help fund a government agency. Therefore, the subsidy runs from them to the government to the general public. For most of these organizations, the concept that they are being subsidized by government is mistaken; rather, they bring and attract private funds and earned funds to the table.

Tax Exemption as Price and Incentive

The price the government pays for having its burden lessened is the noncash price of a tax exemption unless it chooses in its wisdom to transfer cash or other properties, and the latter is rarely ever given but loaned and remains an interest of the government. Tax exemption is annual into perpetuity as long as the organization remains compliant with rules set by (a) the agency from which the burden is being lessened if there is an agreement to support or to collaborate, and (b) the Internal Revenue Service, which is not the agency where the burden was lodged. The IRS simply determines, if tax exemption is warranted and under what set of rules determines what income streams of the organization are exempt. In short, what noncash price the taxpayer will pay, from what income stream of the organization, and, consequently, how much the organization would have available after the consideration of taxes. Understanding the impact of lessening the burden of government is not simply about the bureaucracy and how it operates, it is also about (a) a method of pricing that transaction, and (b) the determination of revenue retention by the organization.

Two implications follow: Because the rules require that excess revenues (that which remains after all expenses, plus reserves for future operations) be retained for the purpose of the burden (the mission), the effect of tax exemption is for the government to prepay for the future operation, sustainability, and expansion of "lessening its burden" to the extent that the mission statement of the organization permits and is limited by it crafting, the imagination, will and skill of its management. This is due not "to better management" but to wide discretion. When a burden is undertaken by a nonprofit, the management has discretion over pricing and contracting. Other choices become available. The success of any choice, however, depends upon compliance with the rules that fund them—the tax rules. There is no escaping a modicum of their constraints on policy design, implementation, and management.

A second implication is that because tax exemption is effective only if there is a healthy income stream specifically from contributions and business income related to the mission, and because these can only occur if people give and also buy the products and services related to the purpose, the IRS in its exemption gives an incentive to the organization to serve the public well, so by their buying and giving they finance the organization making the policy of lessening the burden of government financially more likely to succeed.

The Rationale for This Direction

Why the Nonprofit Option to Lessen the Burden of Government at All Levels

Below, five key points are presented and then encapsulated in a supporting theory. The nonprofit created to lessen the burden of government if properly designed with the powers and capacities in this book has these properties:

1. It is financed voluntarily—not by compulsory taxation that is disconnected to even the consciousness of its existence.
2. It is financed by investors using their own assessment of the economic worthiness of the project—not by the unwilling taxpayer.
3. It will be financed mostly or substantially, if not exclusively, by user fees; thus, those who get the direct benefits pay directly.
4. Those who benefit indirectly (spillovers) pay indirectly; e.g., the truck that pays the toll incorporates the toll in what it charges and the retailer incorporates that margin in the price it charges its customers.
5. It creates an organization focused on a core mission for the same reasons that a large firm does a spin-off and subsequently an elevation of the value created by each part.

Thus, this theory based on voluntary choice, operational efficiency and social equity as the value of the positive spillovers (externalities) are reflected in the voluntary contributions of gifts and donations of citizens and firms who are not necessarily users or payments beyond the price of use.

The theory goes as follows: Because it is based on fees for services—earned business income, rather than upon compulsory payment of taxes imposed by government, people can choose to purchase as much as they want of the service being performed by the nonprofit to lessen the burden of government. Others (mostly nonusers) may voluntarily choose to donate as much as they wish based on their ability to give, their private estimates of the utility of the organization, and what it provides in services not just to them, but to the community at large. Thus, both the market value and the externalities (gifts reflecting the value to the community, including nonusers) are reflected.

Furthermore, because the donor, as well as the user, are operating within a fixed bucket of income and therefore must make choices as to what deserves their spending, the choice of the nonprofit lessening the burden of government reflects a comparative value choice and therefore approximates an expression of preferences; and, consequently, is more efficient. When the government does it by compulsion, this efficient choice is not available. The correlation between value and payments is destroyed.

The IRS is an arbiter between the supply (the nonprofit) and demand (the user) and the donor. It monitors the nonprofit's performance. It requires and publicly reports annually on the organization and requires the organization to do the same. This information increases transparency, but it also reduces risks of loss or inaction due to asymmetry of information. The choice is informed.

Moreover, the IRS sets an efficiency threshold for its own decision of support in the form of tax exemption. The exemption is in reality a reservation price as much as a reward, but it is also an imprimatur; e.g., the government does not look at disfavor on the nonprofit lessening its burden in providing this service. Further, the IRS by its public support measure and requirements, sets a measurable minimum of public support that must be demonstrated in order to obtain this exemption, and the nonprofit has to verify it annually in its Form 990. To receive tax exemption, the nonprofit (unlike government) must demonstrate a numerical minimum. Tax exemption is not a free good to the nonprofit. To get it, it has to perform. A 30 percent tax exemption on zero income is zero. Therefore, the nonprofit, unlike government must perform to receive the benefits of its existence.

This is the logic in which this book is contained. Now, to accomplish this efficiency and all of its benefits, the nonprofit has to have both the power and the capacity to act. This book showed what these are.

Index